KT-448-146

Children and the Changing Family

Between transformation and negotiation

**Edited by An–Magritt Jensen
and Lorna McKee**

RoutledgeFalmer
Taylor & Francis Group

LONDON AND NEW YORK

STOCKPORT COLLEGE
LIBRARY

| LR 2202 L63771 | 27/5/03 |
| 100875 Iwk | 305·23 Jen |

First published 2003 by RoutledgeFalmer
11 New Fetter Lane, London EC4P 4EE

Simultaneously published in the USA and Canada
by RoutledgeFalmer
29 West 35th Street, New York, NY 10001

RoutledgeFalmer is an imprint of the Taylor and Francis Group

Selection and editorial matter © 2003 An-Magritt Jensen and Lorna McKee; individual chapters © their authors

Typeset in Bembo by GreenGate Publishing Services, Tonbridge, Kent
Printed and bound in Great Britain by Biddles Ltd, Guildford and King's Lynn

All rights reserved. No part of this book may be reprinted or reproduced or utilised in any form or by any electronic, mechanical, or other means, now known or hereafter invented, including photocopying and recording, or in any information storage or retrieval system, without permission in writing from the publishers.

British Library Cataloguing in Publication Data
A catalogue record for this book is available from the British Library

Library of Congress Cataloging in Publication Data
Children and the changing family: between transformation and negotiation/edited by An-Magritt Jensen and Lorna McKee.
        p. cm.
    Includes bibliographical references and index.
    ISBN 0-415-27773-6 – ISBN 0-415-27774-4 (pbk.)
    1. Children–Social conditions. 2. Children–Family relationships. 3. Work and family.
    4. Children of divorced parents. 5. Social change. I. Jensen, An-Magritt. II. McKee, Lorna.

    HQ767.9.C4485 2003
    305.23–dc2l

                                                                    2002068262

ISBN 0-415-27773-6 (hbk)
ISBN 0-415-27774-4 (pbk)

Contents

List of contributors

Lars-Erik Berg is Associate Professor in Sociology, University of Göteborg, Sweden. He studies social psychological aspects of family in late modern society, childhood, children, child development and identity formation, play and toys. His theoretical orientation is symbolic interactionism. This report is part of his research on divorced fathers and their children. At present Berg is researching fathers taking parental leave for small children. He has published books (in Swedish) on play, an article (in English) on divorced fathers and children (Berg 2001), and the role of toys and child identity formation and an article on play stages.

Berit Brandth is a Professor of Sociology at the Department of Sociology and Political Science at the Norwegian University of Science and Technology (NTNU) in Trondheim. Her work is in the areas of gender, work and family focuses on fathering and the parental leave system. She has also published widely in the area of rural studies, particularly on gender in agriculture.

Ian Butler is a qualified social worker with considerable practical and managerial experience. He has been Professor of Social Work at Keele University since 2000.

Lynda Clarke is Senior Lecturer in Family Demography at the London School of Hygiene and Tropical Medicine. She has analysed the demography of children's family lives for many years. Her current research interests include grandparenthood, fatherhood, teenage pregnancy and older parenthood.

Gillian Douglas has been Professor of Law at Cardiff Law School since 1998. She was a member of the Child Support Appeal Tribunal between 1993 and 1999, and was an academic member of the Civil and then Family Committees of the Judicial Studies Board from 1996 to 2001.

John Galilee is an experienced researcher who has worked on a variety of academic research projects including the Children, Family, Community and Work study. He is currently employed as a full-time researcher (and is a co-grantholder with Professor McKee and Dr Mauthner) of the 'Corporate Men In Late Middle Age' research project at the University of Aberdeen.

John R. Gillis is Professor of History at Rutgers University, USA. He is a social/cultural historian interested in family, age relations, childhood, memory, marriage and home. He is author of several books, including *Youth and History* (1975), *For Better, For Worse: British Marriage, 1600 to the Present* (1985), and *A World of Their Own Making: Myth, Ritual, and the Quest for Family Values* (1996). He is currently researching the place of islands in the western imaginary, a book which will be titled *Islands of the Mind*.

Heather Joshi is Professor of Economic Demography at the Institute of Education, University of London. Her research interests are gender, the family, women's employment and child development using longitudinal data on Britain. She has headed the Support Programme for users of the ONS Longitudinal Study 1994–2001, and is now Director of the Millennium Cohort Study.

An-Magritt Jensen is Professor at the Department of Sociology and Political Science at NTNU, Trondheim. Her main fields of interest are demographic changes, in particular family changes, and children's welfare. She has published, among other books, *Gender and Family Change in Industrialized Countries*, Oxford: Clarendon Press, co-edited with Karen Oppenheim Mason. Jensen is presently chair of Cost Action 19, Children's Welfare.

Elin Kvande is dr.polit and a Professor at the Department of Sociology and Political Science at NTNU, Trondheim. She has written numerous books and articles in the fields of gender, work and organization and family politics.

Natasha Mauthner is a Senior Research Fellow and Deputy Director of the Arkleton Centre For Rural Development Research at the University of Aberdeen. One of her main research interests is how economic restructuring, the changing nature of work and shifting gender roles and expectations are affecting the work and home lives of contemporary households and families.

Lorna McKee is Head of Department and Director of Research within the Department of Management Studies at the University of Aberdeen. Her main research interests are in healthcare management, the management of change and innovation and the sociology of work and family life. She is Associate Director of the Centre for Research on Family and Relationships at the University of Edinburgh.

Kari Moxnes is Professor of Sociology at NTNU, Trondheim. In addition to a number of articles on parents' and children's divorce experiences she is the author of 'Kjernesperengning i familien' ('Nuclear fission in the family'), and co-author of 'Familie for tiden' ('Families at present') and 'Skilsmissens mange ansikter' ('The many faces of divorce').

Mervyn Murch has been a Professor of Law at Cardiff Law School since 1993. He is a member of the President of the Family Division's

International Committee, and Interdisciplinary Committee. He also serves on the Lord Chancellor's Task Team on Research for the new Child and Family Court Advisory Service.

Elisabet Näsman is Professor in Social and Cultural Analysis at the Institute for the Study of Ageing and Later Life (ISAL), Linköping University, Sweden. She previously worked as a research leader at the Swedish Centre for Working Life and as senior lecturer at the universities in Stockholm and Uppsala. She has a background in sociology and symbolic interactionism. Her main field of interest is the study of childhood and children's conditions primarily from children's own perspective and with a qualitative approach. She has conducted several projects on working life, unemployment and everyday economics.

Margaret Robinson is a Senior Research Associate in the Family Studies Research Centre and the Health and Social Care Research Support Unit at Cardiff University. She is a chartered psychologist, a chartered health psychologist and an experienced teacher.

Lesley Scanlan obtained her doctorate in psychology from Cardiff University in 1997. Since then, she has worked as a Research Associate at Cardiff Law School and the Cardiff Family Studies Research Centre.

Carol Smart is Professor of Sociology and Director of the Centre for Research on Family, Kinship and Childhood at the University of Leeds, UK. She is also Deputy Director of the ESRC research group on 'Care, Values and the Future of Welfare' (CAVA). She is currently researching the influence of divorce on wider kin relationships, transnational kinship, and contact and residence disputes concerning children. Recent publications include *The Changing Experience of Childhood: Families and Divorce* (with B. Neale and A. Wade, 2001), *Family Fragments?* (with B. Neale, 1999), and *The New Family?* (edited with E.B. Silva, 1999). Visit www.leeds.ac.uk/family for more information.

Amanda Wade is a Senior Research Fellow at the Centre for Research on Family, Kinship and Childhood at the University of Leeds, UK. She is currently working on a study of changing parent–child relationships over three generations and, with Carol Smart, on the effects of contact and residence orders in private law disputes. Before joining the Centre she worked for many years as a social work practitioner and manager, and her doctoral research looked at children's experiences as witnesses in child abuse prosecutions. Recent publications include *The Changing Experience of Childhood* (with Carol Smart and Bren Neale), and *Parent Problems!* (with Bren Neale).

Preface

Central to the social study of children is what Barrie Thorne has termed the 'conceptual autonomy of childhood'. This theoretical move constitutes childhood as a phenomenon in itself and reverses the tendency to study children and childhood from the perspective of some other social institution such as the school, the welfare system – or the family. Alanen addressed a related issue when she wrote about the importance of breaking open a triangle of concepts (childhood, socialisation and the family) as one of the main tasks on the new sociology of childhood. Separating childhood from the family (and indeed other social institutions) has been, therefore, a very fundamental part of constructing a distinct conceptual space for childhood.

One initial response to this, especially from family sociologists, was to deny the necessity of a separate sociology of childhood, arguing that childhood is an aspect of the family. This was, and still is, unconvincing. In the first place children and childhood remain quite empirically marginal to much family sociology and much more attention is still given to the lives and interests of adult family members. Second, childhood is clearly a distributed phenomenon. It is practised and constructed in many different social locations, including but not exclusively the family, and focusing on childhood in itself reveals this very clearly. Third, conceptually separating childhood from the family follows the logic that has disaggregated family members' interests and experiences, a step that has produced a rich and important literature on women (and latterly men) and the family.

However, insisting on the conceptual autonomy of childhood does not have to mean denying the actual, empirical importance of the family for children. This would be absurd. Most children live in families and their family relationships (with parents and other adult kin as well as with siblings and other child kin) form one very important context of their lives. More fundamentally, no social institution is independent of others but is rather constituted in relation to them. Investigating the play between these institutional settings is a very important part of the social study of childhood. In an important sense *The Future of Childhood* is about this and that fact is evident across the titles that make up the series.

Over the last decade family sociologists have increasingly come to recognise these arguments and have taken part in a productive dialogue with childhood sociologists. One result of this dialogue is a heightened interest in children's perspectives on family life and an acceptance that children's experiences cannot be read off from those of the adults but have to be investigated in their own right. The contributing chapters of this volume continue this trend and take an important step forward by presenting new research about children's perspectives on key aspects of family change: in work and employment; family composition; and in family roles and relationships. By bringing together an international group of eminent researchers to reflect on these issues the editors of this volume have provided an important service to both the social study of childhood and the family.

Alan Prout
Series Editor, *Future of Childhood*

Acknowledgements

This book is part of a collaborative effort between the United Kingdom (ESRC) and Norway (NFR) between 1997 and 2000, through the two ESRC programmes 'Population and Household Change', and 'The Children 5–16: Growing into the Twenty First Century' and the NFR programme: 'Children, Youth and the Family'. The aim of the collaboration was to promote an exchange of ideas between researchers of the two countries who were involved in research on similar issues. We thank the two research councils for supporting the activities that enabled this book. The Norwegian Research Council has provided financial support for the manuscript.

We gratefully acknowledge the support of Mrs Suzanne MacDonald who helped us to polish and prepare our final draft manuscripts. Thanks also to Ms Sue Allen who has provided unstinting backup and moral support to the team at every stage.

Thanks to our partners, Jens Qvortrup and Roger Buckland, for sharing their homes and lives with this production of this book – a Scottish–Norwegian collaboration! Special thanks to our children, Anders Tønnesen and Ellen and Hannah Buckland, for making us sensitive to changes in their lives and negotiating their futures with us.

Trondheim and Aberdeen,
May 2002

Introduction

Theorising childhood and family change

An-Magritt Jensen and Lorna McKee

The aim of this book is to explore how social change and family change are colouring the experience of childhood. The book is centred on three major changes – parental employment, family composition and ideology – focusing on children's agency as well as the boundaries of children's agency.

The subtitle of the book – 'between transformation and negotiation' – is revealing of our perspective. Our ambition is to discuss children's changing families both at the macro level – the transformation – and at the micro level – the negotiation. Within the 'new studies of childhood', children are seen as 'social actors who negotiate and participate in the construction of their daily lives' (James, Jenks and Prout 1998; Edwards 2002). In this book we demonstrate how children's families are transformed in accordance with societal changes in demographic and economic terms, and in terms of the choices parents make in response to the societal changes. How can children influence their situation given societal frames of reference and their parents' choices within those contexts?

At a societal level there is a tendency to assume that change is unidirectional, progressive and developmental. For example, increased child survival and reduced family size are seen as universal gains. While each historical period tends to be considered as an improvement on what is left behind, new challenges to children may arise from general social changes. Not all change is unproblematic, either at the social or familial level. Different social groups or household members may be simultaneously advantaged or disadvantaged. For example, divorce may provide a positive outcome to an unsatisfactory marriage for one (or both) adults, while leading to a deterioration of economic security either for one of the adults involved and/or for the children. Whether social transformation is positive or negative for children, and how this works in conjunction with children's ability to negotiate, is not self-evident.

It is the tension between, on the one hand, historical changes at the structural level and, on the other, personal change over the life course that forms the focus of the book. Modern childhood is often portrayed in terms of enhanced democratic relationships between parents and children, with the assumption that children's negotiating power has increased over time. The suggestion is that families today permit more individual choice and facilitate negotiated relationships with a shift away from collective interdependence and obvious parent–child hierarchies. Yet there has been limited empirical evidence which focuses on children's experience of social transformations: whether in terms of demographic change of household formation and compositions, work-life change or family disruption and reconfiguration. Little is known about how children react to, influence or experience social and family change. How far are children able to negotiate with adults about their broader social and familial contexts such as employment and mobility? Are children active or passive in the face of family change such as a divorce? What are the sites of negotiation between adult and child? What is the role played by parents and others in mediating and communicating transformational change to their children? Is it possible that social changes which bring gains to adults threaten children's worlds? Are our ideologies of childhood consistent with children's actual lives?

The book includes chapters from the UK, Sweden, Norway and the USA. These countries represent some features that are characteristic of childhood in rich countries, such as growing employment among mothers and growing family dissolution. The book does not aim at comparing the countries, but rather at exploring the space of childhood illustrated by case studies from these countries.

First, the issue of understanding the unexpected outcomes of social changes and the complexities of *who wins and who loses in the parent–child dyad* is crucial. Our contributors show in many nuanced ways that children's and adults' interests may be at variance. Seemingly progressive trends and ideologies – for example, the break in the chain between pregnancy, marriage and parenthood – can lead to children losing symbolic power over adult behaviour. The evidence presented in the book suggests that a social or family change can impact either positively or negatively on the individual child, or on children as a social group. Such insights compel us to revisit social and family changes with a child focus – a key theme of the book. Taking a child focus on change means that it is possible to be sensitive to temporal ebbs and flows in the quality of children's lives, now and in the past. It makes it possible to uncover contradictions in claims about society becoming increasingly child-centred. Indeed, children are becoming both scarcer and more marginalized. Now that children are no longer an economic but an emotional resource for parents there are risks as well as gains.

The second major theme refers to *children's agency in response to social transformation*. Many chapters describe stark differences in the extent of children's participation in major family life changes – for example in relation to marital breakdown, parental employment/unemployment and geographical mobility. Common issues arise throughout the book in terms of how far parents facilitate or inhibit children's agency. Overall, parental communication about change was highly valued by children. Portraits of children as 'gatekeepers' of adult secrets, ethnographers of everyday family life, diplomats in solving family crises and as conduits between the generations are painted powerfully by many of our authors. Yet such deep involvement and knowledge held by children is not always liberating and can be burdensome.

A third theme which underpins the book is a methodological one and concerns the status of children's accounts, especially in relation to abstract and often distant parental life-experiences, such as employment or intimacy. What are the methodological issues in gaining children's insights? Our authors engage with issues about children's articulacy and competencies and question whether children's accounts can be 'taken at face value'. Familiar puzzles as to whether age and developmental stage matter are also rehearsed. Challenging questions about how children garner knowledge, the accuracy of their witness to parents' lives and the quality of parent–child communication are laced through many chapters. The book is important in highlighting the need to give children a voice on parental behaviours – with many chapters showing children to be astute and canny parental observers, commentators, confidants and consultants on family outcomes.

A fourth theme, which links many chapters, concerns *time, space and continuity in children's lives*. Children's notions of 'time as love' or 'time as care' may conflict with parental conceptions. But this link can also work the other way around: where children are given the opportunity, they influence parents' perceptions of time. Understanding children's sense of the fairness of use of time and how children differentiate between quality and quantity time appears to be crucial.

A final theme which is threaded throughout the book is the need to develop the historical foundations of *ideologies of a 'child-friendly' or 'child-hostile' world*. By challenging taken-for-granted assumptions about social advancement, threats to children's place are identified: the concept of children as victims of individualization and as having a weakened social position is at odds with popular rhetoric of the idealized, empowered child. The importance of treating childhood, children and the individual child as problematic social categories in a historical context is underscored here. We now turn to each theme in more detail.

Social change and children: winners and losers

Many contributors to this volume highlight the diverse ways in which children's and parents' interests may be pitted against each other, especially when families are disrupted through divorce or separation. Parental employment and changes associated with parental work patterns or locations could also have differing effects for parents and children.

Increasingly, attention is directed towards a new and growing generational gap in poverty as described here by Clarke and Joshi. In the midst of the richer countries of the world, children's poverty rates have risen to alarming levels. The UK and the USA provide extreme examples. One feature is assumed to be responsible for this development: the number of adults bringing home a wage. This illustrates an important childhood condition: where mothers have low levels of employment (the UK), children's economic well-being is more at risk compared to those countries where mothers' employment rate is high (in Scandinavia).

Clarke and Joshi's chapter demonstrates how closely linked childhood deprivation is to changing family composition. More children live with single mothers, with unmarried cohabiting parents and with step-parents. The latter category is difficult to trace in statistics, but it is estimated that, in the case of the UK, there are about seven times as many stepfathers as stepmothers (see also Ruxton 1996).

Poor children are thus found in 'work-poor' families: children born to single mothers, in particular to teenage mothers, children who have experienced family disruption and those living in stepfamilies. Through a number of social indicators on deprivation, the main story is the same.

In her chapter on the consequences of divorce for children, Moxnes shows how divorce can not only lead to a deterioration in the economic circumstances of childhood, but also to many deprivations in everyday life, with mothers perhaps carrying heavier responsibilities at home and working longer hours, and with children having to compete for emotional time with physically separated parents, who themselves may have formed new relationships. Geographical moves and the handling of new spaces could compound these changed relationships. Moxnes' chapter is insightful in revealing what helps and what impedes children's adjustment to economic, residential and interpersonal changes after divorce. She argues (supported elsewhere by Robinson *et al.*) that children are not necessarily casualties of divorce, but can be helped by parents involving them and giving them a say over decisions, in areas such as money matters and residential moves. The skill of children in navigating and managing transactions between separated parents is also described here by Wade and Smart.

The potential conflict of interests between parent and child was also evident in relation to the child–step-parent relationship, whether residential or non-residential. As with the issue of money, the degree of involvement of the child in the process of building a new step-parent–child relationship seemed to matter. Moxnes reports that, typically, residential relationships which took longer to establish and where the child had an opportunity to influence the relationship were more positive from the child's perspective than were non-residential relationships. The theme of negotiation between divorcing parents and children is especially pertinent when residential issues arise. A number of contributors emphasize that parents can do much to reconcile parental and children's interests by involving children in discussions concerning moves. This could mitigate some of the associated loss and disruption to children's lives, friendships and relations with the non-resident parent. Many children reported obvious financial and emotional gains from step-parent relationships.

The theme of the complex interaction between parents' and children's interests in the face of social transformations is again brought to the fore in the chapters of Jensen and Gillis. Jensen raises the question of how the idea of children's proper place in marriage has influenced adult behaviour and refers to this as children's 'symbolic power'. Three aspects are highlighted: entrance to marriage, consensual unions and family disruption. Taking a long view, Jensen argues that adult behaviour used to be strongly influenced by norms of the proper place for children and the close web of pregnancy, marriage and parenthood. Young couples were expected to marry as a result of pregnancy and strong social sanctions both for mother and child could follow for those who defied this moral imperative. During the twentieth century, especially the latter part, children no longer had this symbolic power to promote their parents' marriage. A more typical convention now in the ascendancy is to respond to pregnancy by having the child outside of marriage, often in a consensual union. Marrying for the sake of the future security of the child appears to have lost its importance, just as staying together in a marriage/family 'for the sake of the children' has been replaced by an agreed wisdom that splitting up from a bad family is 'in the best interests of the child'.

Jensen interprets the shift from marriage to consensual unions and family disruptions as resulting from the changing economic value of children. She argues that the changes may not just differentially advantage or disadvantage children and parents but also discriminate between children as individuals and children as a social group. Such changes are thus perceived as highly complex and multifaceted. Individual children may be beneficiaries of more voluntary and less regulated love relationships between parents. On the other hand the substitution of stable marriages with more 'at risk' or fragile consensual unions may infect childhood with the enhanced dangers of family dissolution and financial hardship. These risks are starkly revealed by Clarke and Joshi, provide demographic evidence on the poor survival rates of consensual unions, again showing that 'freedoms' for adults may carry hidden costs for children.

Gillis likewise sees a dance over time between children's and adults' rights, needs and power relations. Historically and ideologically children and adults have occupied different spaces and in his view the pattern is not a simple one of children gaining advantage over parents. Liberalizing, incremental, linear improvements in children's welfare and social position have also been accompanied by some darker developments, both in terms of adults monopolizing children's temporal reality, constructing 'children's time' and 'living through children'. His thesis is fascinating, in illustrating how adults are colonizing children's spaces, and he contends that festivities and activities which are defined as 'child-centred' are actually serving adult interests and meeting a search for adult fulfilment, identity and selfhood. Children themselves have become a scarce resource, symbolically precious but culturally valued as parental assets in a highly individualized search for meaning. The 'commodification' of children as resources to be distributed between parents is also described by Wade and Smart in their chapter on co-parenting. Family size has dramatically reduced, the number of single adults and the incidence of childlessness are rapidly increasing and the number of adults living with children has thus dropped significantly in Western countries. Rather than a convergence of adult and children's worlds, Gillis paints a picture of separation and isolation between the generations.

Children's agency in response to social transformation

The growth in childhood research in recent decades has increasingly emphasized children's agency and many studies in this book give priority to understanding children's perspectives on social and familial change and transformation. Children's social action, argues Edwards (2002), is both shaped and being shaped by the construction of childhood. Children themselves engage with and participate in the construction of childhood, but they are also subjected to social forces transforming childhood. What are their social actions in relation to family change – and what space of agency do children have? The questions addressed here include whether and in what ways children exercise agency in relation to parental work-life arrangements, parental employment and unemployment, co-parenting and marital disruption.

In the chapters by Robinson and colleagues, Moxnes, Wade and Smart, and Berg, children's responses to and interpretations of divorce demonstrate children actively making sense of their experiences and devising multiple coping strategies. Berg shows how children are not necessarily passive recipients of marital change but engage in sense making. They draw on their common-sense frameworks on divorce as an everyday social phenomenon and create normative narratives to explain what is happening to them. Berg argues that when children report on their experiences of divorce they engage at three different levels: manifesting some aspects in their surface accounts; hinting at others, what Berg refers to as 'between the lines' and leaving out yet other features. According to Berg, the manifest stories often display a rational and pragmatic response to the divorce and, especially when compared with their parent's (father's) account, will emphasize divorce as solving family problems rather than creating them. Moxnes also picks up this theme of children seeing divorce as a way of parents removing pressure from each other, which for some children takes precedence over keeping the family intact.

While children could contrive to understand divorce at a cultural level, they were shown to be very dependent upon adult communication about what was happening at a personal level to their parents and why. Here the chapters by Robinson and colleagues, Moxnes, Wade and Smart and Berg all concur that the nature, quality and type of communication between parents and children are all crucial. Berg suggests that children cope best with divorce if they have a narrative of events. Yet, as Robinson and colleagues show, this often does not happen: adults try to bracket off children's understandings of the process, giving few explanations and excluding children from the change. Robinson *et al.* make a powerful observation that the absence of confidants can make divorce a lonely experience for children. Often, neither the parents themselves, nor siblings, find it easy to confide in each other or discuss what is happening. This can lead to hurtful, confusing silences in relation to the process of divorce. Grandparents could be a highly prized resource in breaking the barrier of silence. However children's agency was striking in judging when to keep silent, ask for information, seek guidance from relevant adults or friends. The children of divorced parents work at being the children of divorced parents and create sense-making devices. Through these chapters it is obvious that children have deep insights on divorce and have much to say to adults when given a platform. They want better information, clear communication and, when the divorce involves moving house, moving schools, or making new step-relationships they want to have a say in the changing arrangements. They also appear to want open parental recognition of their losses as well as of gains achieved. In short, many of these chapters suggest that children beg parents to recognize and grant them more agency than routinely happens in the face of marital change.

Children's responses to parental employment provide some striking parallels. McKee and colleagues show in their chapter that in the same way that children cannot directly influence their parents' decision to live together, children have remarkably little control over whether and how much their parents work or, indeed, who adopts the breadwinning and caring roles in their households. Parents were often represented as being at the mercy of the labour market and employers, with fathers' breadwinning roles especially being circumscribed. In the chapters by Näsman and McKee and colleagues children are portrayed as being very aware of economic and employment realities and accepting privations of parental time in return for economic security. At best, children felt there was token consultation over job-related mobility and working hours. They were unable to prevent workplace spillover, although they could see ways that parents were acting for paramountcy of children's interests through work and caring roles. They reported fathers trying to compensate for work-related absences with material rewards. They observed mothers absorbing work-life 'shocks' and work-related change on behalf of families.

Again, however, children's accounts suggest that they wished to gain more recognition from and better communication with parents as to how parental employment (or unemployment) 'colours' childhood (see Näsman). The insights here indicate that children's worlds are not separate and parents' failure to make or acknowledge connections between their work behaviours and changing work-life patterns and children's lives obstructs children's agency. Children do not demand control of these structural issues, but do have a valid and often well-informed, rational or pragmatic perspective on family geographic mobility, job transfers or promotions, threats of loss of income and job insecurity. Parents seem often to shy away from such issues. This could lead to some 'mobile' children never expressing feelings of loss, loneliness or risk and parents perhaps never learning of children's anxieties or experiences.

However, children do have some agency and develop several strategies of resilience in their coping with family changes. Wade and Smart discuss children's concepts and experiences of 'fairness'. While many children agreed with their parents that they should 'be shared' in a 'fair' way, over time their concept of fairness altered. Many children experienced that they were not necessarily part of the time equation – they had no time for themselves. Their parents' divorce implied keeping two households happy, where equity between the parents was more important that equality of all parties. Children often felt that their own wishes were subordinated to the larger claims and demands of their parents.

Children raise challenges to parental decisions, they demand respect and mutuality, and they sometimes use a range of resistant behaviours as part of their strategy. Their coping does not represent unconditional acceptance of parental choices. Yet it is also clear that their agency takes place within the framework formed outside their influence. The limitations for children's agency are soon reached. Referring to Hirshman's theory of 'exit, voice and loyalty', Qvortrup (1985) argues that children do not normally have all three options. They may 'voice' their opinions, but without the possibility of exerting power, because the choice of 'exit' is usually not available. Children do not have the option of leaving their families. In practically all respects, they are left with only the 'loyalty' option. Children's agency is largely a matter of coping with adults' decisions.

Gathering children's insights: some methodological issues

This book makes an important contribution to understanding how adult researchers can best capture and analyse children's experiences and narratives (Lewis and Lindsay 2000: see also Solberg 1994 and Christensen and James 2000). It penetrates issues with children concerning personal intimacy, as well as asking children to make detailed commentary and observations of more abstract parent behaviours: for example, employment and work-life arrangements. Many of the empirical chapters have deployed highly sensitive field methods, involving indepth interviews with children and other more interactive techniques (see also Harden *et al.* 2000). Berg raises challenging questions about whether we should take children's accounts at face value and using a psychosocial perspective invites us to read between and under the public scripts, where his thesis suggests that more hurtful and inexpressible fears (both a sense of loss and mourning) can be found for children experiencing parental divorce.

Many of the contributors raise vexed questions about the influence of children's age and developmental stage on the status of their testimonies. Brandth and Kvande argue that very young children have an influence on fathering, where fathers are in sole charge of their care. Fathers who are responsible for pre-school age children learn the importance of 'slow time' and gain insight into the importance of quantity time as well as quality time with children. They interpret this as active agency on the part of even very small infants to regulate fathers' behaviour, temporal schedules and priorities.

Näsman argues that, despite being aware of complexity, the statements of children from a young age have salience and can be read as accurate and powerful statements. Several authors raise an analytical point as to whether the risks for children's development from the parents' point of view are seen as such by children. Listening to children they found some of the issues to be the same, but the major difference is the emphasis that children place on the importance of being heard and involved in divorce outcomes.

In the chapters of Robinson and colleagues, and Wade and Smart, their use of qualitative methods shows powerfully that children want to be consulted and treated seriously. Children wanted to be involved in discussions that affect their present and their future. Robinson and colleagues argue that children are the gifted rapporteurs of their own lives, being articulate, reflective and constructive in their accounts. Wade and Smart also point to the resourcefulness and creativity of children in managing childhoods that involve several homes and locations. Again, by getting close to children's understandings they reveal how it is that children commit to making such separate household and co-parenting arrangements work. This invisible effort of children in ensuring equitable parental shares in their time is best uncovered in having first-hand descriptions from children.

These chapters are particularly important in showing how it is that children glean such powerful knowledge and insights. Both McKee and colleagues and Robinson and colleagues demonstrate in their chapters that children are full participants in family dramas: they are active listeners and keen observers and ethnographers and many parents or adults may underestimate this. However, such insights can be both helpful and costly, as children and adults confront everyday challenges. Much depends on the style and quality of adult–child communication and the legitimacy and respect afforded to children's knowledge.

Clarke and Joshi, as well as Jensen and Gillis, add methodological richness by challenging traditional demographic and historical data. Looking through the lens of childhood and using the child as the unit, they demonstrate that significant readings and conclusions are possible, compared with the restricted insights found in traditional demographic and historical literature.

Time, space and continuity in children's lives

Many chapters in the book are linked by a focus on the weight children attach to spending time with parents, what is meant by 'time' and children's sense of place and belonging. Taking a long, historical journey, Gillis points to the changing ideas of family time. It is not the case that parents and children spent more time together in pre-industrial Europe and America than they do today, but our way of spending time with children is adult-regulated and adult-centred. Children's spaces are increasingly 'islanded', separated from one another and from the adult world. Many childhoods are insulated from the adult world.

This book is important in drawing directly on children's views on the labour market participation or non-participation of their parents, as well as in capturing their understandings of workplace change and how parental work impacts on parent–child shared time. The role of family policy in shaping the contours of parent–child relations, time and interactions is often overlooked. Brandth and Kvande have an original angle on how the Norwegian leave arrangements for fathers (the 'father quota' introduced in 1993) have formed a part of the child discourse in public policy of Norway. The aim has been to facilitate and enhance father–child contact. Brandth and Kvande argue that when fathers utilize such leave and stay 'home alone' as the primary parent, features of caring for a young child result in men reconfiguring their concept of time, in response to children's routines and needs.

The chapters by Näsman and McKee *et al.* reflect on children's understandings of care and provider roles, the work–family and the parent–child interfaces. They reveal how children and parents negotiate these new realities and point to children's pragmatism in facing economic imperatives on parents to have a paid job and work long hours. They also explore how children experience work-based absences and separation, greedy work schedules and long working hours, parental job insecurity or loss, workplace stress and 'spillover' effects. Näsman's concept of 'colouring' is a powerful way of showing how parents mediate children's insights into the world of work. She also highlights the micro impacts of unemployment, which have seldom been documented from a child's perspective. She shows that the strategies children adopt in unemployed, underemployed and overemployed households are sophisticated. Often it is assumed that children are incorporated into and defined by the employment circumstances of their households. This model is premised on an image of child passivity and dependence. Both McKee *et al.* and Näsman counteract this view, showing how children can express resistance in small and large ways to unpalatable parental work patterns/decisions.

Both chapters illustrate the complex ways in which parental work schedules impinge on children's time and point to children's appreciation of parents, mostly fathers, being burdened by a time squeeze or deficit. In the middle-class families working in the oil sector, many fathers and children had to fit time around busy employment schedules and work absences. Fathers reported replacing time with gifts or treats, or making protected time available only at weekends or the holidays. Such scenarios could lead to conflicts in the allocations of parent time and children's demands for time. Both Näsman and McKee give examples of children's appreciation when their parents make special time available for them: at the end of the school day, for example, or through reducing their working hours. Time with children was reported by Näsman as one of the perceived bonuses for both children and fathers in the circumstances of unemployment. Gillis actually argues that we have now reached an historical point where children are on different schedules from adults. He refers to the 'hurried' child and notes the irony that although there are more dedicated times in the calendar for children today, adults do not make any more time available for their children than in the past. Family time in his view is elusive, an 'ideal' always thwarted by reality.

The impression of children as skilled time managers and as active in the apportionment of time between divorced parents is quite novel. As argued above, Wade and Smart (see also Robinson and colleagues) found that many children are active and energetic agents in making their divorced parents' access arrangements work – and this often involved extensive efforts, efforts perhaps not always recognized by parents. Similarly threaded through a number of chapters is the issue of children's sense of place and space. Several contributors show that children often face residential change in their experience of parental job moves or marriage dissolution. Such moves are not unproblematic and children speak powerfully of regret at losing friends, beloved homes and neighbourhoods. McKee and colleagues, Moxnes, Berg and Gillis all raise questions about how 'portable' children really are and whether the sometimes negative consequences of 'trailing' their parents is always understood by adults. In the same way that children valued being involved in discussions about marital breakdown, they wanted some consultation and recognition in terms of relocation. Parents could play an important role in acknowledging children's ambivalence and helping manage such transitions.

Ideology and individualization: a 'child-friendly' or 'child-hostile' world?

While large-scale transformations in composition and economic status differentiate households and children, diversity and change are also embodied in beliefs about the status of children. Public changes and changes in the context of childhood can also lead to transformations in the content and interior of parent–child relations and the meaning of childhood. Modernity has affected children's lives in two important areas, explored in this book: work–life and family composition. While large-scale transformations in composition and economic status differentiate households and children, diversity and change are also embodied in beliefs about the status of children. Children have become more symbolically precious, even as they have lost real economic value (see also Zelizer 1985).

Gillis' chapter is important in showing that parenting practices and beliefs about what is proper parenting are subject to change and variation. The link between wider social and environmental forces and parental ideologies and practices sometimes fails to be made. Gillis and others contend that maintaining children as icons has been costly, particularly to children themselves. It is adults who determine the rules. We like to think about childhood as a secret garden, but, in the twentieth century, the garden has contracted. Gillis and Jensen suggest that what we think *about* the child and how to think *with* the concept of childhood will in several situations stand in sharp contrast to children's lives. The actual child has lost its power over adult life, while the 'symbolic' child has become more precious. The symbolic child is adult-created and stands in contrast to children's own accounts of their lives.

Divorce raises the issue of place for many children and is a process of individualization of childhood, as argued by Moxnes. Several authors in the book show how children now experience their family lives as scattered between several different locations. Individual children may have different interests while getting to know their parents as individuals. Divorce and separation alter the 'taken-for-grantedness' of everyday family life. Wade and Smart argue that new ways of sustaining relationships have to be found and in the process of individualization, the idea that things should be 'fair' has become a kind of modern symbol.

Children are the ultimate dependants on family and the individualization process may leave them with heightened vulnerability.

The vulnerability of modern children is illustrated in the escalating rate of childhood deprivation (Clarke and Joshi), in the gap between the living 'with' children and living 'through' children (Gillis) and in the ways in which children's families are largely transformed outside their negotiating power (Jensen). Our authors repeatedly question whether the choice of freedom for adults is enhanced at the expense of safety and security of children. Clarke and Joshi raise the paradox of increasing poverty among children in rich countries and ask whether a polarization is taking place between children growing up in 'work-rich' and in 'work-poor' families.

Today the economy has come to depend on the surge of consumption, while two salaries are needed to keep a conventional standard of living. To a considerable degree consumption is centred on children. Gillis uses the examples of how Christmas and other festivals and tourism (now the world's largest single industry) are equally attuned to family time, while McKee and colleagues argue how parents may trade their lack of time with children with presents and expensive holidays. Throughout, a public discourse has emphasized employment (particularly mothers') in career terms, underlining that this is a matter of individual choice.

Children depend more on their parents' employment at the same time as this employment is double-edged for children. As Edwards concludes, 'Children place a great value on their parents "being there" for them ...' (Edwards 2002: 13): but it is precisely this 'being there' that is transformed through parental employment and changes in family composition.

In demographic terms, across Western societies, the population pyramid is about to be turned upside-down. As Gillis argues, lifetime childlessness has risen to unprecedented levels, yet, paradoxically, contemporary society remains obsessed with childhood. The ageing of the population implies – numerically – a marginalization of children among family members. This marginalization is also symbolic, with child-like adults romanticizing their own childhoods rather than investing in existing children. Children are getting fewer and families more dispersed.

Is there a generational conflict between adults' life aspirations and children's well-being, as argued by Jensen? Such a conflict may be easier to trace at a general level (adults versus children) than at the individual level (parents versus children). The capitalist network society needs flexible individuals with flexible families. At the same time, individualization and the personal choices of adults can leave children at the margins of society. However, to the individual child a malfunctioning family is probably no better (in most cases worse) than a divided, broken or reconfigured family: children are often positioned between 'a rock and a hard place'.

The book continues to stress that there are some broad transformations in the context of childhood, which are often taken for granted but nevertheless have strong impacts on children's lives: 'no child can evade the impact of economic and spatial forces, nor ideologies about children and the family ...' (Qvortrup 2000: 79). These are the overarching societal transformations, which cannot be underestimated. Such contexts deeply affect the contours of children's negotiating power and children's negotiating space. By marrying up insights into social transformations, changing ideologies of childhood and children's agency this book provides a three-dimensional view of the challenges of being a child in the twenty-first century.

References

Edwards, R. (2002) 'Children, home and school: regulation, autonomy or connection?' *The Future of Childhood* series, London: RoutledgeFalmer.

Harden, J., Scott, S., Backett-Milburn, K. and Jackson, S. (2000) 'Can't talk, won't talk? Methodological issues in researching children', *Sociological Research Online*, vol. 5, no. 2. http://www.socresonline.org.uk/5/2/harden.html.

James, A., Jenks, C. and Prout. A. (1998) *Theorizing Childhood*, Cambridge: Polity Press.

Lewis, A. and Lindsay, G. (eds) (2000) *Researching Children's Perspectives*, Buckingham: Open University Press.

Qvortrup, J. (1985) 'Placing children in the division of labour', in P. Close and R. Collins, *Family and Economy in Modern Society*: 129–45, London: Macmillan Press Ltd.

Qvortrup, J. (2000) 'Macroanalysis of childhood', in P. Christensen and A. James (eds) *Research with Children. Perspectives and Practices:* 77–97, London: Falmer Press.

Ruxton, S. (1996) *Children in Europe,* London: NCH Action for Children.

Solberg, A. (1994) *Negotiating Childhood: Empirical Investigations and Textual Representations of Children's Work and Everyday Lives*, Stockholm: Nordic Institute for Studies in Urban and Regional Planning.

Zelizer, V. (1985) *Pricing the Priceless Child: The Changing Social Value of Children*, Princeton, NJ: Princeton University Press.

1 Children's changing families and family resources

Lynda Clarke and Heather Joshi

Family life has changed dramatically in the past three decades in most countries in Europe. Demographic, social and economic changes have affected the living arrangements and family experiences of children. Children are now born into more diverse family circumstances and are more likely to experience a transition from one family type to another than in earlier decades. The changing nature of relationships and diversity of family types, the increase in family breakup and solo living as well as the relative importance of friends and families are often seen as indicators of family instability.

The risk of family change is strongly related to the type of family at the child's birth (Clarke *et al.* 2000). More children are being born outside marriage, both into lone mother families and into cohabiting couple families (Clarke 1992; Clarke *et al.* 1997). Children's risk of family change is higher if they are born outside marriage. Children born to cohabiting couples are more likely to experience a breakup of their parents than children in married couple families (Clarke and Jensen 1999). Children born to lone mothers are more likely than other children to experience the acquisition of a new co-resident partner to their mother, especially if they are young mothers (Clarke *et al.* 1997; Kiernan 1999). We also know that children born outside marriage are quite likely to have their natural father move in with them and even marry their mother after their birth (Clarke *et al.* 1997; Haskey 1999).

The consequences of these family transitions are now beginning to accumulate. We know that family change has implications for health and behaviour, both in childhood and in later life. Perhaps most important are the associated risks of poverty and disadvantage. We know from official statistics that half of poor children live in lone parent families and that 59 per cent of children in lone parent households are poor (DSS 2001). Also, two-thirds (61 per cent) of poor children live in households where no one is employed and over three-quarters (78 per cent) of such children are poor. The risk of child poverty is much higher when there are three or more children in the household and that over half of poor children live in social housing (local authority or housing association). Over three-quarters of poor children are white but the risk of child poverty is higher in minority ethnic groups, especially among Pakistanis or Bangladeshis.

There is now considerable evidence that child poverty has been increasing in the past twenty years or so in Britain although there have been recent decreases. This is true both for absolute and relative poverty (Bradshaw 2001; Bradshaw 2002). In 1979, 10 per cent of children lived in households with incomes below 50 per cent of the average after housing costs. By 1995/6 this proportion had risen to 13 per cent in 1979 real terms. Thus three per cent of children were worse off in absolute terms – 300,000 children were living on incomes below the 1979 real terms poverty threshold. Relative poverty, moreover, has increased more than threefold – in 1979, 10 per cent of children were living in families with incomes below 50 per cent of contemporary average income but in 1996/7 this had risen to 35 per cent. This is a period when average incomes rose by 44 per cent (after housing costs). There is also evidence that child poverty is higher than in most other industrialized countries (Bradshaw 2001). Data from the Luxembourg Income Study shows that child poverty rates (below 50 per cent of mean income) vary considerably between countries and the UK has the third highest out of 25 countries after Russia and the USA. There is also evidence that child poverty has increased more than in most other industrialized countries (Oxley *et al.* 2001). We know little, however, about other social and economic conditions of children's lives or how this relates to family structure.

Family life has changed for children in a number of ways other than increased likelihood of the loss of a co-resident parent, usually their father. There are important changes in domestic life and the modus operandi of families that are having major influences on the young today. Family life in couple families has become less gender-segregated: mothers are more likely to be employed and shared care of children by mothers and fathers (living together as well as apart) is more common than in the past (Joshi 1998). The importance of father involvement and parenting styles for children's well-being are being examined (Day and Lamb, forthcoming) and the importance of the family is beginning to be articulated in official policies (The Stationery Office 1998).

While fertility and family changes in developed countries have received much attention over the past decades, very few studies in Europe have focused on children as the statistical unit (Qvortrup *et al.* 1994). Given that the presence of children is a main reason for the concern about family changes, this is quite surprising. There has been a paucity of information about children and childhood in general in Europe, whereas the USA has a long history of treating children individually in analysis and has led the field in this change of analytical perspective (Bumpass 1984; Hofferth 1987; Hernandez 1989). Over the past decade other countries have begun to follow suit and more attention is being given to children as a focus in the study of family change. This wider theoretical focus for the social demography of children has been termed 'the sociography of childhood' (Saporiti 1994). Few such demographic studies have been carried out in Britain (Clarke 1992, 1996, Clarke *et al.* 2000). However, a refocusing of analytical perspective has emphasized treating children as active participants in social study (James, Jenks and Prout 1998).

In this chapter we set the statistical backdrop for the following chapters. We will use children as the focus of study to document the evidence on the demography of children's family location and the transitions they are likely to face, and present new data on the social and economic conditions of children. We will examine whether there is evidence of increasing social inequality among children as has been reported for adults (Oxley *et al.* 2001) and investigate how this can be linked to the family structures of children. We wish to investigate how far children's family structure at birth or later family breakdown is associated with subsequent adverse socio-economic circumstances.

In order to explore the differentials in children's socio-demographic background we will utilize data from the 1981 and 1991 censuses of England and Wales, tracing children throughout their childhood via the ONS Longitudinal Study. This allows an unprecedented insight into the living conditions of children and how these change throughout childhood. The British Office of National Statistics (ONS) links census records (beginning with 1971) with vital registration data for one per cent of the population of England and Wales born on four selected birthdays to create the Longitudinal Study (LS) (Hattersley and Creeser, 1995).

Children's family type at birth and transition during childhood

There were around 8.3 million children aged between five and 17 in England and Wales in 1991, i.e. between the age of compulsory schooling and voting age. Eighty-two per cent of them lived in two-parent families and 16 per cent in one-parent families, with 1.5 per cent not living in a family or heading their own.

The linked data from the ONS LS can be used to reveal the history of family change behind this snapshot, distinguishing (most of) the two-parent couples as either stepfamilies or as 'intact' couples who had been together since the child was born. Children's family situation at birth is shown in the registration of births on a sample birthday after 1971. The birth may be registered in marriage by two parents; jointly by two parents who are not married; or by the mother only, also outside marriage. Changes in children's family status are then detected at subsequent censuses in 1981 and 1991, by comparing the number of parents, and their dates of birth at registration and census.

As outlined above, it is already well known that children of this generation have encountered changing family structures. These new analyses of the dynamics of the process show that a large minority of the 5–17 age-group have experienced at least one change in living-in parents. However, two-thirds of the sample (65.6 per cent) were still identifiably living with both their birth parents.

Stepfamilies constitute about one in ten of the two-parent families for children in this age group. Usually the step-parent is the father: only one per cent of the children lived with a stepmother. Living with stepfathers is highest proportionally amongst children whose births were registered by a mother on her own (sole registration), although these were only a minority (one in 20). The group of solely registered children has the highest chance of living with a lone mother in 1991 (46 per cent).[1] Among the children with two parents named on their birth certificate, the married couples have a higher chance of living together in 1991 (85 per cent) than the unmarried couples who made a joint registration (57 per cent). However, since the married couples were by far the biggest group at registration, there were more children in absolute numbers experiencing non–intact living arrangements from these origins (71 per cent of children in stepfamilies and 64 per cent of children in lone-parent families were born to a married couple). In population terms, out of 700,000 children aged 5–17 years in stepfamilies, around 500,000 had been born to a married couple; out of 1,300,000 children aged 5–17 in one-parent families, around 830,000 had been born to married parents.

Change throughout childhood can be seen in another perspective if we examine the change over ten years for children under ten years old in 1981. This shows that children who were born to married parents were much more likely not to experience family breakup than children registered jointly at birth by two parents outside marriage. Over seven in ten (73 per cent) of children born to married parents were still with both parents ten years later compared with under four in ten (37 per cent) of children jointly-registered outside marriage. There is evidence of transition into two-parent families for children registered by a mother alone at birth but lone motherhood persists for many children (24 per cent were in this type of family at both time points[2]).

It might be supposed that families who part are also likely to move location, which could be an additional disruption for children. While it was more common for children in families who had experienced a change in structure than those who had not to move location it was common for all children. Half of children in intact families (50 per cent) had moved compared with three-quarters of intact families who had become stepfamilies by 1991 (76 per cent) and lone-parent families who became stepfamilies (73 per cent). More than half of children under ten years old in 1981 had moved in the subsequent ten years (55 per cent).

The varied demographic context of these children's families can also be seen if we consider the age of their mother at their birth. Children whose mothers were teenagers were most likely to be experiencing lone parenthood (31 per cent) and stepfamilies (23 per cent) by the time of the 1991 census, although some of their mothers had been, and remained, married (36 per cent were in intact families). Relatively early motherhood, between 20 and 24 years, was associated with an intermediate degree of family 'disruption', which attains a floor of around 15 per cent for children whose mothers were over 25 when they were born. This illustrates an important association between early child-bearing and family instability – both by losing a parent and gaining a stepparent, usually a stepfather.

Another source of variation in children's family structures is ethnic origin. Black children were much more likely to be living in a lone-parent family than children from other ethnic groups in 1991: nearly half (49 per cent) of black children were living with a lone parent compared with 10 per cent of Asian children and 16 per cent of white children.[3]

Family employment

The number of parents in a child's family could have several implications for the well-being of that child – the time available to pay attention to the child, for instance, but also the person-hours available for earning and bringing cash into the home. The 'workless' family, where no parent earns, accounts for one-sixth of all these children in total (17 per cent) but is more common for the youngest children, aged five to ten years. More children were living in dual-earner and no-earner households in 1991 than in 1981 as the proportion in one-earner households had decreased (from 43 per cent in 1981 to 34 per cent in 1991).

The absence of any earner in the family is relatively most frequent among one-parent families (57 per cent of lone mothers). Among two-parent families, living in a no-earner family is twice as likely for children living in stepfamilies than intact families (16 per cent compared with 8 per cent of the intact couples). Among the two-parent families with earners, cases are roughly equally divided between one-earner (around 31 per cent) and two-earners with the woman earning part time (40 per cent of intact, 27 per cent of stepmother and 24 per cent of stepfather families) and dual full-time earners (20 per cent of intact, 27 per cent of stepmother and 23 per cent of stepfather families). In other words it is more common for children to have working parents and to have mothers who work part time in families with both natural parents.

This association between family type and likelihood of family employment is emphasized in the longitudinal data if we follow children through their childhood between censuses (Figure 1.1). Children aged under ten years whose family was non-intact in 1981 and who had experienced no change at the time of the next census were far more likely to have no parent working (40 per cent) than those whose family was not intact but who had experienced a family change (24 per cent) and much more likely than those whose families were intact throughout (7 per cent).

When the number of earners is analysed by the age of the mother at the child's birth, living in a family with no earners present is highest for children of teenage mothers (34 per cent), and falls to the lowest level once their mother is 25 (11 per cent), echoing the pattern of lone motherhood. There is positive relationship between age of mother and the proportion of children with mothers in paid employment at least up to mothers aged 25–34 years at the child's birth.

Family resources

Another indicator of the family's living standards which is known in the census is the tenure of their housing. Those in public rented accommodation (23 per cent of these children) may be presumed to be generally worse off than those in owner occupation (72 per cent).[4] The children of lone parents are more than twice than average likely to be found in public ure (52 per cent) where stepfamilies are also over-represented (35 per cent). Among intact couples, 14 per cent were in public renting and 82 per cent in owner occupation. Council

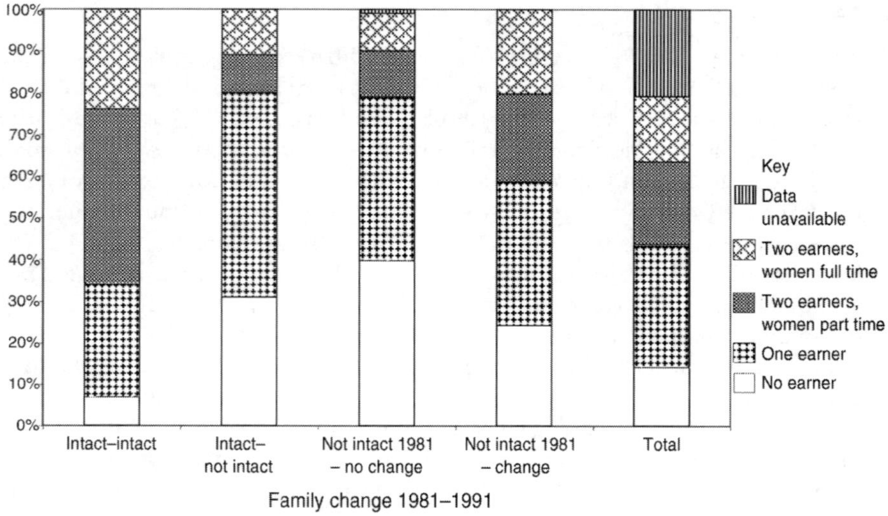

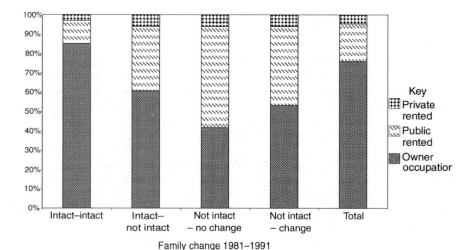

Figure 1.1 Number of earners per family in 1991 for children aged 0–9 in 1981, by family change 1981–91.
Source: ONS longitudinal study

housing is also most likely for black children (54 per cent in public rented housing compared with 22 per cent of white children and 17 per cent for Asian children).

This relationship between tenure and family type is clear also if we trace children aged under ten years in 1981 across ten years to the next census (Figure 1.2). The children with intact families throughout are most likely to be

Figure 1.2 Housing tenure in 1991 for children aged 0–9 in 1981, by family change 1981–91

in owner-occupied tenure in 1991. There is an increasing likelihood of social housing as families become less 'intact' in structure: from intact families (12 per cent) to intact families experiencing a breakdown (34 per cent) to not-intact families who have experienced a change (41 per cent), with the highest levels of public housing found for children whose family was not intact in 1981 and 1991 (53 per cent). If one examines all children whose families were in owner-occupied housing in 1981, then intact families who break down are ten times more likely than those who remain intact to move to public housing and are four times more likely to move to privately rented housing. Children in non-intact families in owner-occupied housing in 1981 are also likely to move to public or private rented housing regardless of whether they experienced a change in family structure.

Among other possible indicators of economic disadvantage we have also examined is whether the household has access to a car and housing conditions (density, type of accommodation, central heating). Car ownership became more prevalent for children's families over the 1980s: less than one-fifth of children's families (19 per cent) did not own a car in 1991 compared with one-quarter (24 per cent) in 1981. Lone mother families were the least likely and intact families most likely to own a car. Living in housing with central heating was also most common for intact families. Whereas only 11 per cent of children in intact families had no central heating and 12 per cent only partial central heating these were more common for lone-parent families (21 per cent and 17 per cent).

It is thus important whether children were from a 'deprived' family as well as whether they were living in a 'deprived urban' or other type of area. To summarize family deprivation, children were divided into seven groups on a composite score of background family characteristics (comprising an additive scale of the number of cars, tenure, unemployment and social class of the family). Children in intact families in 1991 were the least likely to be from those with the most deprived background (11 per cent) whereas those in lone mother families were the most likely to be in these most deprived areas (27 per cent), see Figure 1.3. Likewise, if one traces children aged under ten years across the two censuses, only 10 per cent of those with an intact family at both censuses were in the most deprived category in 1991, compared with 27 per cent of those with a non-intact family at both times. Thus living in a deprived area is more likely for children in non-intact families, but the majority live outside these areas.

Not only are the circumstances of the immediate household important for children's well-being, the social character of the neighbourhood is too. Neighbourhood deprivation can be roughly gauged by the social profile of the inhabitants, but it is difficult to estimate whether the proportion of children living in deprived areas increased or decreased over the 1980s as the systems used for the classification of areas changed. In Figure 1.4 we have shown only the most deprived areas – 'inner city deprived' and 'deprived industrial'. Including other areas as 'deprived' would raise the estimate of children living in

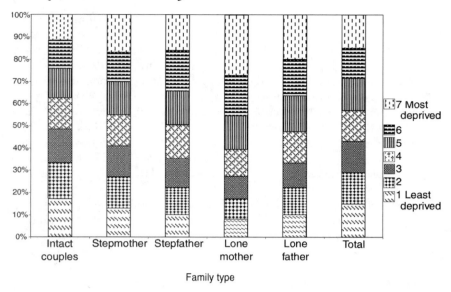

Figure 1.3 Family deprivation score in 1991 by family type in 1991, children aged 5–17

deprived areas. However, the likelihood of living in a deprived urban area is clearly linked to the children's family structure and ethnic background, as seen in Figure 1.4.

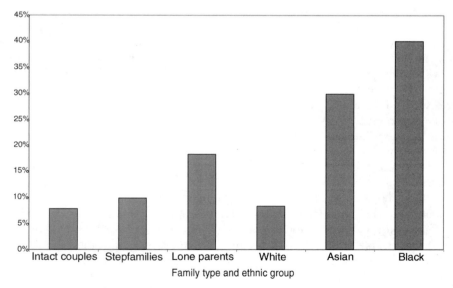

Figure 1.4 Percentage of children aged 5–17 living in the most deprived urban areas in 1991, by family type and ethnic group

While only 8 per cent of children overall were living in the most deprived urban areas, this was higher for children in stepfamilies (10 per cent) and highest for children in lone families (18 per cent). Ethnic background was also linked to living in a deprived urban area: white children were much less likely to be living in such areas. Black children were most likely to be living in deprived urban areas (40 per cent), followed by Asian children (29 per cent) with only 8 per cent of white children living in such areas. Another 17 per cent of black children were living in purpose-built inner-city estates compared with 7 per cent of Asian children and only 1 per cent of white children.

In each case of our examination of family resources there is an association between the family phenomena of early childbearing, unmarried childbearing and family breakup on the one hand, and economic disadvantages for the children's families on the other.

Conclusions

The diversity and instability in the family living arrangements of children over recent decades has meant that relatively fewer children live with both of their natural parents throughout their childhood. A growing minority of British children are being born to a mother without even an unmarried partner.

Change and instability of family forms mean increasing numbers of children are living outside a conventional two-parent nuclear family, i.e. with a lone parent or in a stepfamily. British children were increasingly likely to be born to, or living with, a lone mother, less so than in most other European countries (Clarke and Jensen 1999). The risk of family dissolution in England and Wales was also between the levels of that in the USA and Norway, and was particularly high among the growing number of cohabiting parents. The children of teenage mothers appeared more numerous (and more economically disadvantaged) in Britain than Norway. Clarke and Jensen (op. cit.) conclude that the family structures encountered by British children are inextricably connected to social stratification, and the consequent experiences affected by the nature of national welfare policy.

We have compared British children aged 5–17 in 1981 with children aged 5–17 in 1991: a falling proportion was living with both natural parents (Clarke *et al.* 2000). Lone mother families grew more than stepfamilies. The latter were more common for teenagers than children of primary school age. We were interested in evidence of social polarization among children of these ages, given the growth of poverty among families with children over the 1980s. This proved problematic, as the census indicators of deprivation (car and home ownership, and neighbour scores partly derived from them) were subject to independent trends over the decade, which means they are more suitable for cross-sectional than longitudinal analysis. There were more children living in public housing in deprived urban areas than in other area types in 1991. However, it was evident that more children in 1991 were living in dual-earner families or no-earner families. The proportion living in single-earner families had decreased. Also, children living in social housing in 1991 were more likely to have experienced family breakup than those in owned homes.

Family disruption was related to subsequent experience of disadvantage by using the LS data on children under the age of ten in 1981 and tracing them across to the next census. The children most likely to be living in conditions of social deprivation in 1991 were those living with lone mothers, those with an unemployed father, and those with a black parent. Children of disrupted families experienced more change in geographical location than intact families but there was much movement among all the families.

Trends in the family circumstances of children should indeed be a cause of concern, but less because of the absence of fathers per se than because of the absence of family social and economic resources. Children's family structures are strongly connected to social inequality amongst children. In 1991 children being brought up in council housing or in deprived urban areas were less likely to have intact families than other children and more likely to be from a minority ethnic group. Living in a deprived area or in a deprived family can have severe implications for later life achievement.

Demographic and economic indicators are clearly associated. Lone parenthood is linked to economic disadvantage. Early motherhood is a common feature of poor circumstances and non-intact families. Early motherhood is also more common for black children (confirmed in Berthoud 2001). Later motherhood and relative prosperity are more likely amongst children living with both natural parents. The growth in child poverty is related to the growth in lone mother families but it also affects two-parent families, in particular those who have no earners in the family or are stepfamilies. Children in lone mother families are also more likely to have no earners in their family, to be part of a 'work-poor' family. The consequences of a lack of income can be both immediate and long term (Joshi et al. 1999, McCulloch and Joshi 2002; Joshi and Verropoulou 2000).

The conclusion is that changes in children's families have implications for their economic well-being. Children's family structure at birth and subsequent family change have economic repercussions. More parents are employed now than in the past but non-intact families are less employed and more exposed to the risk of deprivation. The lack of a two-parent family has disadvantages for children in terms of parental employment and family resources. The consequence of the trend of an enhanced risk of the loss of a parent at some point during childhood may lead to further socio-economic polarization or deprivation of children.

Acknowledgement

This paper summarizes work done under the ESRC grant 'The Changing Home; Outcomes for Children'. We are grateful to Judith Wright of the Longitudinal Study Support Programme, then at City University, who extracted data from the ONS Longitudinal Study, and to the ONS for access to that study. Opinions expressed in this article are the authors' and do not necessarily reflect those of the ONS.

References

Berthoud, R. (2001) 'Teenage births to ethnic minority women', *Population Trends*, 104: 12–17.

Bradshaw, J. (2001) 'Poverty: the outcomes for children', *Family Policy Studies Centre Occasional Paper 26*, London: National Children's Bureau.

Bradshaw, J. (2002) *The Well-Being of Children in the UK*, University of York, Social Policy Research Unit.

Bumpass, L.L. (1984) 'Children and marital disruption: a replication and update', *Demography*, 21: 71–82.

Clarke, L. (1992) 'Children's family circumstances: recent trends in Great Britain', *European Journal of Population*, 8: 309–40.

Clarke, L. (1996) 'Demographic change and the family situation of children', in J. Brannen and M. O'Brien (eds) *Children in Families: Research and Policy*: 66–83, London: Falmer Press.

Clarke, L. and Jensen, A-M. (1999) 'Family change in Britain and Norway: a child's perspective', New York: *Population Association of America*.

Clarke, L., Joshi, H., Di Salvo, P. and Wright, J. (1997) 'Stability and instability in children's family lives: longitudinal evidence from two British sources', *Research Paper 97-1*, Centre for Population Studies, University of London.

Clarke, L., Joshi, H. and Di Salvo, P. (2000) 'Children's family change: reports and records of mothers, fathers and children compared', *Population Trends*, 102: 24–33.

Day, R. and Lamb, M. (forthcoming) *Father involvement and children's development*, New York: James Erlbaum.

Department of Social Security (2001) *Households Below Average Incomes 1994/95–1999/00*, London: Corporate Document Services.

Haskey, J. (1999) 'Having a birth outside marriage: the proportions of lone mothers who subsequently marry', *Population Trends* 97: 6–18.

Hattersley, L. and Creeser, R. (1995) *The Longitudinal Study: Technical Volume*, London: The Stationery Office.

Hernandez, D. J. (1989) *America's Children*, New York: Russell Sage Foundation.

Hofferth, S. (1987) 'Recent trends in the living arrangements of children. A cohort life table analysis', in J. Bongaarts, T.K. Burch. and K.W. Wachter (eds) *Family Demography*: 168–88, Oxford: Oxford University Press.

James, A., Jenks, C. and Prout, A. (1998) *Theorizing Childhood*, Cambridge: Polity Press.

Joshi, H. (1998) 'The opportunity costs of childbearing: more than mothers' business', *Journal of Population Economics*, 11: 161–83.

Joshi, H.E. and Verropoulou, G. (2000) 'Maternal employment and child outcomes', Occasional Paper, London: The Smith Institute.

Joshi, H.E., Cooksey, E., Wiggins, R.D., McCulloch, A., Verropoulou, G. and Clarke, L. (1999) 'Diverse family living situations and child development: a multi-level analysis comparing longitudinal evidence from Britain and the United States', *International Journal of Law, Policy and the Family*, 13: 292–314.

Kiernan K. (1999) 'Cohabitation in Western Europe', *Population Trends*, 96. The Stationery Office, London.

McCulloch, A. and Joshi, H. (2002) 'Child development and family resources: evidence from the second generation of the 1958 British birth cohort', *Journal of Population Economics*, 15, 2: 283–304.

Oxley, H., Dang, T.-T., Förster, M. and Pellizzari, M. (2001) 'Income inequalities and poverty among children and households with children in selected OECD countries', in K. Vleminckx and T. Smeeding (eds) *Child Well-being, Child Poverty and Child Policy in Modern Nations*, Bristol: Policy Press.

Qvortrup, J., Bardy, M., Sgritta, G.B. and Wintersberger, H. (eds) (1994) *Childhood Matters: Social Theory, Practice and Politics*, Aldershot: Avebury Press.

Saporiti, A. (1994) 'A methodology for making children count', in J. Qvortrup *et al.* (eds) *Childhood Matters: Social Theory, Practice and Politics*: 189–210, Aldershot: Avebury Press.

The Stationery Office (1998) 'Supporting families: a consultation document', Landau: The Stationery Office.

2 Children's perspectives on middle-class work–family arrangements

Lorna McKee, Natasha Mauthner and John Galilee

Introduction

In recent years various terms have been coined to describe the interface between work and family, including the 'work–family challenge' (Lewis and Lewis 1996), the 'reconciliation' of work and family (Children in Scotland 1998; Deven *et al.* 1997; Moss 1996), the 'work–family balance' and the 'work–life equilibrium' (Industrial Society 2000). Commentators suggest that this recent interest in work–family issues is the result of rapid social change and particularly new trends in work and family structures (Hyman *et al.* 2001; Institute of Directors 2001; National Work–Life Forum 1999). Historically work–family issues have become prominent during similar periods of flux, such as the absence of fathers from home through war, imprisonment and long working shifts/rotations (McKee 1985; Chandler 1989; Isay 1968; Lewis *et al.* 1988). More recent changes which have contributed to a growing interest in the work–family interface include: entry of large numbers of women (and especially mothers) into the workforce; changing family composition and structure; transformation of male employment; increase in single working parents; intensification of working hours; ageing population and the growing number of 'cared for' groups (Moss 1996); and the growth of equal opportunities (Brannen *et al.* 1994, 1997). Current debates about the future of work and its changing character (e.g. the trend towards contract and short-term employment (Lewis and Cooper 1996), flexible working (Rainnie 1998), downsizing, the 'feminization' of the labour market and the spread of tele-mediated businesses) also highlight the relevance of home–work issues.

One of the main objectives of the research on which this chapter draws was to provide a forum for children to discuss issues around parental work, their own work aspirations and the work–family interface more generally (see Mauthner *et al.* 2000). How are children experiencing workplace change? How are work flexibility, intensification, and the 'time squeeze' being experienced by children? How are new work arrangements spilling over into children's lives? With the exception of Galinsky's (1999) account of how American children think about working parents and Näsman's contribution here there have been few studies that have provided an arena for all family members to discuss the impact of work on their lives. This gap in our understanding and knowledge of a core aspect of children's lives is particularly remarkable in light of the acceleration in pace of work and family life over the past decade and the accompanying intensification of the work–family debate outlined above (e.g. Cooper 1999; Franks 1999; Horlick 1997; Hochschild 1997; Lewis and Lewis 1996). This is in part because the study of workplace change and family life has tended to remain as distinct spheres of investigation (Deven *et al.* 1997). In particular, research has decontextualized children, studying them in isolation from the familial, community and (parental) employment contexts within which they are embedded. However, giving children the opportunity to discuss issues around work also links in with more widespread changes in the past ten years around studying children, with for instance the expansion of the 'new' social studies of childhood (Prout 2000: xi). Rather than viewing children simply as objects of research, this new approach repositions children as the subjects of research and as key social actors (Christensen and James 2000: 3).

Little is known about how children perceive and understand the way paid employment and household work are structured and divided within their families, nor indeed how children interpret gender family roles. This chapter pays particular attention to children's interpretations of gender divisions in relation to household labour as well as the part that paid work plays in their conceptualization of parental roles. We outline children's interpretations of the 'gendered' parental roles and reflect on how satisfied children are with current work and family roles. We also comment on how the nature and structure of male occupations in a particular employment sector – the oil and gas industry – appear to shape and determine the work–life choices of these households with underlying assumptions about gender, generation and mobility.

The study

This chapter is based on a three-year research study (which was conducted between 1997 and 2000) of work and family life in the oil and gas industry in Scotland (funded by the Economic and Social Research Council). The central focus of this ethnographic study was the mothers, fathers and children of 53 families drawn from three Aberdeenshire communities with a high concentration of oil-related employees. These families had at least one parent (mainly the father, but in a few cases the stepfather or mother) employed in the oil industry and at least one child aged 8–12 years old. The sample reflected a range of employment and familial backgrounds.[1]

The children's accounts discussed in this paper are drawn from one of the three research communities referred to by the fictional name of Kingscraig (in order to respect the confidentiality of the participants from this community). The community is a small, affluent town located 20 miles to the west of Aberdeen, which has a high proportion of families involved in the oil and gas industry. During the past 20 years the town's population has rapidly expanded and it has become a popular, middle-class commuting locality especially with families drawn from the professional–managerial classes and often for returning expatriate oil families. Kingscraig is also located in a scenic area of Aberdeenshire and has a good infrastructure, especially excellent health and other amenities. There is a particularly well-regarded school at both primary and secondary level.

In depth, semi-structured interviews were conducted with each member of 17 families[2] in Kingscraig. This paper draws on the home-based interview accounts of the children from these 17 families (none of the material from the focus groups will be used in this paper). On average the interviews tended to last between 45 and 90 minutes. All of the individual interviews with the children were conducted at home. Each of the research team read through and analysed the transcripts individually and identified themes. The team then discussed the transcripts and the themes they had identified together as a group and agreed on common themes, which were evident in the transcripts. For more details about the methods used in the study to gather children's accounts see Mauthner *et al.* 2000.

Middle-class families

At least one of the parents in all of the families belong to a profession which all of the major social classification schemes would classify as middle class. For example using the government NS–SEC scheme (Rose and O'Reilly 1998), all of the fathers in the sample belong to the Managers, Professionals and Supervisors of Intermediate Occupations stratum. Eight of the 17 families had a gross household income which was at least twice the 1997/8 national average,[3] and five families had a gross household income which was at least three times the national average. Compared to the two other research communities in our study, the average household income in Kingscraig was at least £20,000 more. Although the average household income in all three communities was substantially higher than the national average, many of the parents employed in the other two communities worked in manual, temporary positions, offshore, often in difficult and non-routine working conditions. The higher wages in the oil and gas sector are often seen as a reward for the insecure and demanding nature of the work. As decades of discussion in the British Sociological Association journal *Sociology* has highlighted, higher incomes do not necessarily designate people into the middle class. Other factors such as occupation, status, education and cultural capital are equally important (see Butler and Savage 1995). Out of the three communities, all of the families in Kingscraig (using a diversity of criteria) would be more easily categorized as middle class. Surprisingly there has been very little British ethnographic, social scientific research that has explicitly concentrated on the middle classes and more specifically focused on middle-class children. In Britain social scientific research has either never explicitly discussed the social class of the children, or has been concerned principally with working-class children because of their material, educational and cultural disadvantages or because they are seen as being a 'social problem' (see Willis 1977 and Corrigan 1979).

As well as the high preponderance of middle-class households in Kingscraig, several other features made it an interesting community for exploring issues of gender roles and work–life arrangements. First, a high proportion of mothers were not in paid work in this community and second, a very high proportion of families had experienced one or more work-related moves compared to the other two communities.[4] Out of the 17 families we interviewed in Kingscraig only six mothers were involved with some form of paid work. Five of the women were employed in paid full-time work: senior manager in a large multi-national oil company (and principal wage earner in the family); solicitor currently on sick leave; childminder (based at the family home); school secretary; research nurse and business planning manager. Another worked part time in a job-share as a teacher. Evidence of women's participation in voluntary work was apparent in about four households with one mother working almost full time in a voluntary arts organisation. Other activities included sports coaching and assisting at Brownies. One mother had previously been active in the 'Meals on Wheels' organization. The relatively low levels of full-time paid work in this community were in direct contrast to the higher levels of female participation in paid work for the other two communities and when compared to national trends.[5]

In the next section we turn to explore the children's attitudes towards, and experiences of, the gendered division of labour within their families. For example, did the children perceive any pros and cons to the different work–family models? How did they evaluate their mothers' roles as carers and housewives? What were their reactions to the division of labour within their family? Did some feel that gendered arrangements suited them and their parents? How did the children regard their fathers' employment?

Children's perspectives on gender divisions of labour

Providing and caring

Many of the children from Kingscraig drew attention to and appeared to accept the traditional demarcations of men's work as providing for the family, and women's work as caring for the family unit. However they were also attuned to the contradictions in how these work roles were played out in reality. Many children, especially where the mother was at home full time, adhered to fairly traditional views of what constitutes a mother's work.

For instance, a brother and sister described their mother's role as:

> *Girl*: Erm, she just does what you think a woman would do.
> *Boy*: The housework.
>
> (Joska, aged ten, and Izzy Davista, aged eight)

Another boy went further in outlining what tasks his mother did within the family home:

> My mum normally stays home and does laundry and housework which is really nice because when we come home it's always really nice and clean and tidy and it's just nice. Everything Mum cleans just has the light shining off it.
>
> (Kyle McGuigan, aged nine)

Most children in Kingscraig, whether in dual- or single-earner households, did not view caring as an easy job and noticed that their mothers were often tired, overworked and facing heavy demands in relation to housework and mothering. As well as an awareness of creating physical work for their mothers, they sometimes cited the behaviour of themselves or their siblings as a source of emotional work. They gave examples of pressure on mothers caused by family conflict, sibling fights and disagreements, noise and the need to 'ferry' them around. For example, the youngest of three children described his mother as being perpetually 'stressed and angry'. Asked, 'Why?' he answered, 'Just when we don't behave' and explained that even on holidays the children cause their mother stress because, 'You're not at home and you're not at school' (Steve Simms, aged eight).

Father absences or non-involvement in household duties were also occasionally seen as contributing to the mother's pressure. Molly Clarke, whose father works away for six weeks at a time, notes:

> Mum gets angry sometimes that he's away and he's had to go out at nights … and she gets angry that she is stuck here with us.
>
> (Molly Clarke, aged 14)

This was echoed by another boy who observed that when his father was away:

> [It's] a bit harder for Mum because she has to take care of all three of us.
>
> (Kyle McGuigan, aged nine)

Reflecting on mothers as full-time carers, a number of children commented that their work was not all drudgery or aggravation but could also identify some freedoms in their mothers' lives. They cited examples of mothers meeting with friends during their school hours, playing sport, going for country walks and pursuing other rural leisure activities. Many children in Kingscraig described how they liked their mothers' presence at home. They mentioned how much they appreciated having her there when they came home from school, providing treats and snacks on welcoming them home from school, sharing confidences and keeping their home and lifestyles going. As one girl remarked:

> She's ready for us … she makes hot milk for me and we have a snack and then just go off and do our own thing'
>
> (Izzy Davista, aged eight)

Another girl whose mother was also at home full time expressed similar feelings:

> I like it, coming home and Mum being here so that's good. I like that.
>
> (Carla Clarke, aged 11)

While the children sometimes saw themselves as 'trials' to their mothers and could see how boring and frustrating the full-time caring role could be, they were able to see positive aspects to their mothers' roles and to identify the direct benefits for themselves. Mothers were very much viewed as performing a caring role associated with continuity and security in their lives. Working mothers were also identified with nurturing roles but in three cases where the mothers were in full-time employment, the children perceived their mothers as very overloaded and stressed. In two of these cases there was little additional support from fathers in the domestic domain and the women were described as carrying two shifts. Many children had busy after-school lives and engaged in many recreational activities. Mothers often co-ordinated transport to these activities although fathers did share this when at home and there were exceptions. As Kathy Carter, aged 11, explained, 'Mum and Dad both drive but Dad's more busy than Mum so Mum usually drives us places.' Another critical 'caring' role associated with the mother by the children was that of helping them to settle in their homes and communities after relocating. As will be explored in a later section of this chapter, there was an exceptionally high level of geographical mobility in Kingscraig. On average the children in this sample had been subject to three geographical moves during their lifetime.

Father as provider

The 'provider' role attributed to men by many of the children in Kingscraig was perceived to likewise have both benefits and costs. Children repeatedly observed fathers having to live with excessive work pressures, job insecurity, greedy schedules and unremitting travel itineraries. Yet they appreciated that this was offset against often high financial rewards, status and prestige and directly beneficial to their own lifestyles. Molly Clarke described the mood of her father when he returned from working overseas:

> When he comes back he just sleeps, like, 24 hours. He gets pretty stressed out when there's something going on at work. He can get pretty angry, well, with himself mostly when he has to let someone go, he doesn't really like it. He gets a bit stressed out when he's moving from one job to another when they've got new projects.
>
> (Molly Clarke, aged 14)

Referring to daily long hours of work (7.00am until 9.00pm) and a father who was away for periods varying from two days to two weeks, Richard Morris said:

Well, I don't exactly see him because he comes home late at night or stays away and he goes away with different companies.

(Richard Morris, aged 11)

Due to many men in Kingscraig having senior management/professional jobs and also the remoteness and global nature of the oil and gas industry, many of them had to spend regular periods away from home. The absences of their fathers were something some children had got used to, although nonetheless they missed their fathers. The degree to which the father absence impacted varied according to the pattern of absence. For some men the pattern was irregular and infrequent whereas in other cases fathers could be involved in either weekly commuting or long-distance overseas commuting, where the absence was for six or more weeks. The children's age, the mother's response to father absence, the father's own disposition to absence (voluntary or involuntary), the level of family and community support and integration all influenced how the children coped with work-related father absence. E-mail and telephone contact were often seen as vital forms of communication for children and fathers. Catherine Allan was very upset by her father's weekly commute to London and she felt her father was overworked and wished that his work responsibilities could be shared out more fairly within his company:

I think he feels unhappy for us but otherwise he feels alright. He feels unhappy leaving us and he always feels sorry to leave Mum ... I just wish his boss would give him two weeks without flying away. I think why can't they send somebody else or divide it between somebody? Whenever I think 'why can't they send somebody else?' I always feels guilty ... I think it would be nice if they could split the work between two dads.

(Catherine Allan, aged eight)

The provision of presents by the father was viewed by some children as a form of compensation for these paternal absences and stresses. Discussing the imminent return of her father who had been away on business for over a month, Molly Clarke identified one of the advantages of her father working in oil. She speculated what gifts he would bring back for her from his latest trip away:

Tomorrow he's bringing back tons. There's going to be tons of CDs.

(Molly Clarke, aged 14)

This link between parental absence and compensatory rewards was raised by another girl who said of her father:

He had to go away just about every few weeks and we didn't get to see him much. [*Interviewer:* And how did that make you feel?] A bit, erm, but sometimes he brought us presents and, erm, a bit annoyed because he always had to go away.

(Elizabeth Dawson, aged nine)

Her younger sister Ann also focused on the financial rewards of her father's work, as well as the satisfaction he acquired from his job:

> He likes it and he likes getting more money too to go on holidays with us.
>
> (Ann Dawson, aged eight)

Fathers themselves acknowledged that they tried to 'care' by providing gifts to make up for being away. The children often drew attention to the negative impact of father absence on their shared physical recreation and hobbies and gave direct examples of their leisure activities being curtailed or impoverished if the father was absent. It may be that children idealized the father's outdoor and fun qualities because at other times he was depicted by them as 'exhausted' or 'busy'. Conversely they may have under-reported their mother's contribution to physical activity and play.

As noted above, as well as mothers adopting a full-time caring role for their families in this community, they also often organized and absorbed the stresses of geographical moves. One family had moved house six times over ten years, including two moves abroad. We now explore how the children perceive these moves and the associations they make between parental work and family mobility. The children's discussions of mobility provide further insights about the formation of traditional gendered parental roles within their families.

Children's experiences of parental work mobility

The impact of parental employment patterns on children's lives was particularly evident in those families who had experienced international mobility. Here the issue of children's agency was sharply exposed, with the children often at the mercy of their parents and their parents often at the mercy of employers. Economic and employment realities were seen to dominate the limited negotiating power of the children. Of course, not all mobility was forced on parents but all of the children could be described as 'trailing' their parents. Most of the children were not given the opportunity to participate fully in the decision-making process of whether to move to an international destination, but were more typically consulted over choice of 'home' locations, for example Scotland or London. Using the concept of the ladder of children's participation referred to by Gelder (2002) in relation to family decision-making, such household decisions were largely determined by parents with at best only minimal consultation taking place with children. Children's acceptance of the almost exclusive power of parents over such decisions is captured in the comment below:

> Well, we have been told a couple of times that like if we get this [new job] we're moving and there's nothing much we can do about it. But I wouldn't like it at all. I'd prefer to stay here and get my education and decide myself where I want to go.
>
> (Molly Clarke, aged 14)

Children's accounts reveal ambivalence about whether they should be involved in decisions about moving. For example, Catherine Allan was glad to be exempted from the decision-making process to leave Alaska and return to Scotland, 'I felt I should just go along because I'm awful at making big decisions and stuff.' Older children tended to be more assertive about this issue, often citing the negative effects on schooling if they were to move. Will Carter was adamant that he would not relocate again if his father suggested another move:

> I'd obviously refuse [to relocate]. I'd say I'd live in the streets. I'd just not go because I want to finish my exams and I don't want moves to affect my performance in tests. I like living here, it's a good place and it's a nice social [life].
>
> (Will Carter, aged 14)

A dominant theme within the accounts of mobile children was the effect of such mobility on their personal friendships. Children talked about their difficulties in making friends when they first arrived at a new school or in a new country/locality. They described the pain of leaving their friends behind, as well as the anticipated anxiety of missing their friends when they next moved. The word 'sad' was commonly used to describe their feelings of moving:

> It's quite difficult because you really miss your friends and you might never see them again.
>
> (Damian Payne, aged 11)

In some cases, children had left their school in Aberdeen or Aberdeenshire only to return one, two or three years later to find that their old friends had either themselves moved to another country, or had moved on to form other friendships. In the case of Jane Allan, she felt sad when she returned to Kingscraig as she found all her old friends had moved on:

> It was easier going there [Alaska] because coming back I met my best friend and it was like we had never been best friends. And she didn't want to be best friends any more. We used to walk home from school, do everything together. And she's in my class but I don't do anything with her any more.
>
> (Jane Allan, aged 11)

Her younger sister viewed the move from a different perspective:

> I have mixed feelings [about returning to Scotland] because I would have liked to stay in America a year longer but I would have liked to come here too. In America I'd only just gotten my best friend when they said I had to say goodbye and I didn't really have much time to say goodbye.
>
> (Catherine Allan, aged eight)

In some families long-distance commuting (typically by the father) was a preferred option, enabling continuity of residence and schooling.

Children also spoke about the general culture shock they experienced when moving to countries such as Venezuela, Indonesia and Nigeria where they had to live in a secure but restricted environment. Their accounts focused on issues such as climate change, language and freedom to move about independently. Some children remarked on the schooling and quantity of homework expected when abroad. Misan Paune, who had previously lived in Norway and Holland, was relieved to return to Scotland because, 'It's an advantage because we don't have to speak any language.'

Kathy Carter also felt the same but viewed language acquisition more positively:

> Well, I knew we were moving but I didn't know we were going to South America. So Dad showed me it and I'd never even heard of Venezuela before so I was like, "where's that?" And I felt shocked and excited about going to South America and learning a new language but I was bit upset about leaving my friends.
>
> (Kathy Carter, aged 11)

Again, many of the children were highly attuned to the emotional impact and cost of moving on their parents. The need for mobility centred around the male partner's career in all but one case. As discussed above it was nearly always the mothers who took on the role of organizing the domestic move, settling the family into a new country and culture, and dealing with children's associated anxieties. Children were clearly aware of, and sensitive to, the physical and emotional labour this represented for the mothers. They were concerned not only about their own lives but also felt a sense of responsibility for their parents' adjustment. For instance Kathy's older brother Will was aware of his mother's unhappiness in Venezuela. He noted that his mother was dissatisfied with their maid's standard of cleaning, found shopping and the language difficult and was very sensitive to the heat. As he went on to comment:

> It's much easier for her. Life is much better here compared to Venezuela.
>
> (Will Carter, aged 14)

The responses to mobility varied not only between different families but also within families. One girl who had lived in Australia and Norway felt that mobility was experienced differently according to age and felt that younger children were more portable:

> I think you get more affected if you're older or younger. Say you're in the middle of exams you can't move if you're doing that and you've settled down and doin' all your tests. If you're younger like nursery or primary

one then I think it's very good fun moving to all those places. Because they don't really know and they haven't made, like, really good friends.

(Suzy Lee, aged 12)

Not all accounts were negative and a few children cited similar positive factors of mobility, which echoed many of those expressed by their parents. For example it allowed them the opportunity to experience new cultures, take up new leisure activities, make new friends and learn/improve their proficiency in other languages. The next section explores in more depth the children's perceptions of work.

Children discussing work

The contradictions of work

As this chapter has so far shown, the majority of children interviewed for this project appeared to have a high degree of sensitivity and insight regarding the negative and positive effects and consequences that work had on their parents' lives, as well as their own (see Mauthner *et al.* 2000). Children were able to see and appreciate the contradictions of their parents' work and care experiences, and were able to assess the pros and cons of their particular work–family arrangements, and the roles played by their parents within their family. The children's pragmatism and adaptability were evident in many of the accounts, with children appearing to understand and accept external constraints on their parents' lives. They could also identify the contradictory effects of work on their parents, for example the children could describe their parents as feeling simultaneously 'happy and stressed' 'or 'angry and excited' in relation to work.

Despite their sensitivity towards their parents' emotions and perhaps because of their pragmatic approach, the children rarely spoke of challenging the division of labour within their families or their parents' attempts to balance work and life. This largely uncritical acceptance of parents' work–life arrangements is open to a number of interpretations. Perhaps the children felt that they did not have the right to judge issues such as which parent worked or where they were to live in the world. They were possibly unsure about how far they could directly influence whether mothers or fathers took up paid work. Certainly the issue of economic necessity was understood as underpinning parental decisions, especially their fathers' need to work. Will Carter highlighted how children's lives are circumscribed by economic realities when he discussed how his family had little choice but to move in response to his father's job loss. In the extreme circumstance of parental unemployment, he perceived that his reluctance to move would have carried little weight. Asked if the family move was discussed with him (he was then aged 12) he replied:

No, because Dad got chucked out and he needed to find the first job and it was the first job he could find really within some consideration and nothing I could have said would have had any effect.

(Will Carter, aged 14)

This job move actually proved highly stressful for the mother and children but the children were aware that it suited their father. After living in Venezuela for a year and a half the family moved back to Scotland.

In some cases, the children's acceptance suggests they are satisfied with their family set-up, or perceive their parents to be content with such arrangements. For example, asked about what his mother felt about her long-term role as a full-time mother, one boy replied:

I think she feels good because she isn't stuck in an office with all these people around her just nagging and nagging and nagging. And I think she's happy because she isn't working. She's just like doing the dishes and stuff. She's looking out of the window. Scrubbing the dishes or watching TV. And great because we're not here to annoy her.

(Boris Grange, aged ten)

Some of the children may not have any other point of reference and lack knowledge of alternative models. For example, most of the full-time mothers in the sample had been full-time carers from when the children were born and most men had been in full-time employment. The notable exceptions in the Kingscraig families were one case where a mother had changed from full-time work to 'not working' through ill-health; another where an expatriate medical scientist had given up a full-time job when she moved to Scotland but was hoping to find paid work again; and another where the mother moved from 'not working' to working full time. As noted above there was also one case where the father had experienced a brief spell of unemployment and another where the father had 'downshifted' to a four-day week and taken a less high-powered job. Perhaps in these specific cases, the children could make some direct comparisons of different work–life arrangements.

The data also has to be treated cautiously as children are often comparing very dissimilar circumstances and seeing them from different age and lifestyle vantage points themselves. Although it is difficult to generalize, these few cases where the parental employment status changed provide some interesting insights. They suggest that children can directly experience a change in parental mood and interaction in relation to parental employment status. Children reflected on how the parents themselves felt about their changed employment status and mirrored their parents' reactions including those around conflict and satisfaction. Will Carter, whose father had lost his job, described him as 'irritable' when he was out of work as compared to 'happy and stressed' when he was employed, so he preferred his father to be employed. Kenny Riley, who had a very negative view of his mother's paid full-time job, described how things had changed with his mother staying at home full time due to ill-health. He made a number of comparisons and explained:

> It's, like, better [now mother is at home] because she does my packed lunch now more often. Like she couldn't, she sometimes couldn't do it before so I'd make it. So, like, it's different and it's better. And, like, 'cos she was unhappy [in her paid job], like she wouldn't come out of bed or something like that 'cos she was really stressed.
>
> (Kenny Riley, aged nine)

In the case where a father had downshifted, reducing both his hours and travel, his son reported that:

> He's a lot less worried. He was usually all in a rush but now he's a lot happier and he's less stressed and stuff.
>
> (Bill Hanson, aged 11)

Bill's discussion about his father's work once again highlights how the children could competently assess how work made their parents feel. Until he radically reduced his working hours Bill's father worked extremely long hours (up to 60 hours a week). Long working hours, though, appeared to be the norm for most fathers in Kingscraig,[6] with many children only seeing their fathers fleetingly, either morning or night, or just at weekends. While the children presented a picture of employers typically determining their fathers' work patterns, there were occasions when children cited examples of when their fathers had turned down or changed particular assignments, locations or posts because they were perceived as too disruptive to family life. For example, several children discussed how their parents had actively chosen moving to Kingscraig as a 'family-friendly' gesture, in the hope it would create a lifestyle compatible with a particular family life stage. This theme emerged more strongly in the parents' accounts but it is interesting that some children showed an awareness of work–life negotiations and rationales, and understood that although parents retained control over decisions, their needs as children were directly or indirectly taken into account by parents.

The way that children understood their indirect influence on parental work–life decisions is captured by the case of the Clarke family. Here the father has chosen long-distance, overseas commuting instead of the whole family relocating, but the issue of international moves recurs as the youngest daughter Carla remarks:

> My dad gets offered jobs all the time to America, Australia … usually we'd just be sitting down to supper and he'd bring it up and we'll be like, 'oh'. [Interviewer: And do you feel you have a say?] … it's usually the parents that make the decision if they're going or not but it's really what they want to do in their life.
>
> (Carla Clarke, aged 11)

The older sister also develops this theme of token consultation with little control when asked if her views were taken into account in relation to her father's work location:

> Well, they can't afford to do it. Well, they ask, they say, "How do you feel?" but they can't really afford to say, "Oh, we can't move just because my daughter doesn't want to," so you have to face it. But I think me and Carla are old enough just to accept it and that if we have to go, we can't just kick and scream and expect to stay here. So we are just going to have to accept what they say and just hope for the best.
>
> (Molly Clarke, aged 14)

That parents are not perceived as being indifferent to their children's viewpoint, and the way children have to entrust parents to act in their interests is revealed by yet a further account from Molly:

> He [father] says it's not a very nice place [Baku] and he wouldn't take us there. He might take my mum once, like, if he goes over for a long time but he wouldn't take us there. He says there is so much poverty and the buildings are run-down.
>
> (Molly Clarke, aged 14)

This theme of hostile parental work environments, in opposition to the excellent quality of life and education facilities in Kingscraig, featured prominently in children's understandings of parents' work–life decisions.

Children and their understanding of work

Again drawing on cues apparently picked up from their parents, it was apparent during the interviews that the children had already formed the view that the culture of work and having a job were qualitatively different from 'playing' and 'having fun'. They seemed to have less appreciation of the social or relational aspects of work or indeed the more abstract components of job satisfaction, although some did refer positively to their parents' colleagues and work-based networks during interviews. Parents were highly influential in shaping understandings of work both directly and indirectly but the messages conveyed were varied and often contradictory. As Christoffersen (1998) highlighted in his research, it appears that the children were able to internalize complex notions of work from an early age. Perhaps the children understood the way work was organized and patterned at home, which often involved complex trade-offs between the children, their parents and the interests of their parents' employers. It seems from the data that we collected that during childhood, changes in the structure of parental work have both direct and indirect bearing on children's lives and their understandings of the meaning of work.

The intelligence that children gain about their parents' work was again often described as having being acquired through observation, lived experience or overhearing parental or other adult conversations. There were many examples of children talking about instances when parents had been upset when shifts and rotations had been changed, holidays postponed or cancelled, and birthdays or other key celebrations had been missed. They witnessed their parents' work as being directed by external demands and beyond parental control. As many of the quotations have already revealed, the children saw the direct effects of different working cultures and flexible work practices on their parents. There were some examples where fathers did not work regular patterns or for a regular employer, had no guaranteed employment and income or contract of employment and needed to be geographically mobile. In these circumstances, children recognized that their parents had few opportunities to plan, rarely could count on any scheduled free time, nor could they regularize their personal lives. Children cited instances of this causing extreme tension and frustration within their families. Several children empathized with their parents and realised how, for instance, their fathers often missed them when away and often regretted the 'greediness' of work and its negative effects on the whole family. With the children's apparent comprehensive knowledge of their parents' work and their work-related emotions, the final section explores what effect this understanding has had on the children's own work aspirations.

Children's future work aspirations

Although we did not directly ask all children how they would configure their own work and family lives, we gleaned substantial insights into this from questions about their future work aspirations, and by asking them to choose different words to describe what would matter to them as future workers (see Mauthner *et al.* 2000). What is striking from their accounts is that most of the children wanted to be employed but also wanted the ability to control the conditions of their work. Some wanted to do something radically different from their parents' jobs, especially where they had a negative impression of that work. A minority who saw their fathers as having exciting jobs wanted to emulate them and enter similar work (this was true for both boys and girls). Part-time work was viewed as attractive by some of the children particularly when raising a family (several boys as well as girls mentioned this), and a number of children emphasized 'being there for their children' and not having too stressful a job. They mentioned the need to find a job that was 'fun' and creative, with many rejecting being 'stuck in an office' or in 'front of a computer'. The extracts pick up on these mixed aspirations:

> I'd like to do something exciting. I'd like to earn money because of all the homelessness … but I'd like to have a successful career and meet new people so one day I could get married looking on to the future and getting out of the house. I don't want always to be doing my job all the time or

cleaning the house or worrying and stuff. I'd like to get out, you know, go have fun with my friends.

(Kathy Carter, aged 11, mother not in paid work)

I just don't like the feeling of having to go on the computer every day and sending all these letters. I just don't like doing it. And like my mum, I just don't want to be all stressed out like that.

(Samantha Riley, aged 11, mother works full time but off sick)

I'd like to work in Mobil doing the same thing as Daddy. I'd get to find out what it's like and if I didn't like it the first day I would quit. I'd get to work on computers a lot to see whether there's any emails and sometimes I could work at home because that's what Dad did when Mum had an exam because Mum couldn't find anyone else to look after us.

(Alison Milford, aged eight, mother studying part time)

The way children make future career and life choices appears complex and is usually uncharted. From the interviews it was apparent that while direct familial experience could affect children's work aspirations it was not the only, or even the major, influence on their destinies and later choices. This data is useful in showing how the interaction between personal familial contexts and the intermediate contexts of parental workplaces mesh. The children's responses are obviously also drawing on other environments, such as school and other social worlds, with the data suggesting children wanted to turn hobbies into careers (for example, becoming dancers, singers, sports stars). Such aspirations could perhaps be interpreted as children expressing a new vision of work as a reaction to some of the more routine, challenging or alienating aspects of their parents' jobs and lives (see Mauthner *et al.* 2000).

Conclusion

The oil industry is often perceived as bringing affluence, creating work-rich households and offering a buoyant labour market – and indeed, the 17 families described in this chapter had high levels of income and enjoyed many material advantages. For these middle-class families work–family roles were fairly traditionally gendered, with fathers as primary breadwinners and mothers as primary carers. Despite apparent economic security, there were hidden costs to working within the oil and gas industry for many fathers in particular, such as job insecurity, long working hours, extended absences from home, long-distance commuting, job mobility, and multiple international relocations – restrictions which also impacted on the mother's participation in the labour market. While these aspects of parental work may have been accepted by the children and their families and perhaps even welcomed by some, there were clearly costs associated with them. Most of the children could recognize the negative and positive impacts of parental work–life patterns both on their own and their mothers' and fathers' lives. Their accounts have provided an insight into how their fathers' patterns of work left some family members feeling marginalized or socially impoverished in terms of poor community ties, limited social networks, cultural and linguistic barriers and frequent school moves. As the children acknowledged in relation to both their own and their mothers' experiences, disrupted friendship networks, lack of a sense of belonging, and lack of rootedness and distance from kin were commonly experienced by mobile families. Whilst hoping that their views would be considered, the children accepted that they had little control over parental work choices, especially in regards to moving. Such choices were acknowledged as being dictated primarily by employers. Within such 'mobile' families the children recognized how the emotional work of moving and settling families was borne by their mothers. However, knowledge about parental work–life arrangements, particularly that of their fathers, allowed the children to make informed decisions about their own potential career choices and life. Children did not speak of merely imitating parental work–life choices but instead interpreted and made sense of the rewards, satisfactions and costs of these choices.

The children in Kingscraig were fully wise to the realities of adult work lives and roles, the tie between work and economic security and the power of social and economic forces. They were sophisticated observers of the strengths and weaknesses of their family contexts. Parental work vulnerabilities and the advantages and drawbacks of traditional gender roles were appraised, although children could not directly influence how work and care were distributed between their parents. In both dual-earner and single-earner households tiredness and stress were associated with adult and parenting work roles. Although the Kingscraig children could be described as 'advantaged' in terms of quality of their physical environment, educational and social opportunities, they also at times experienced loneliness, sadness, insecurity and bewilderment at why things were so hard for their parents. They could not avoid workplace 'spillover', although rich compensations could be drawn down, replacing time with consumer goods and lifestyle permanence with adventure.

Acknowledgements

The authors would like to thank the ESRC for funding the study (award no. R000237243) and particularly the children and families who shared their experiences with us and the schools who granted us access. We wish to acknowledge the valued contribution of Dr Catherine Maclean who worked as a Research Fellow from 1997–9. Thanks also to the Project Steering Group who offered support and guidance throughout.

References

Brannen, J. and O'Brien, M. (eds) (1996) *Children in Families: Research and Policy*, London: Falmer Press.

Brannen, J., Meszaro, G., Moss, P. and Poland, G. (1994) *Employment and Family Life: A Review of Research in the UK (1980–1994)*, London: University of London, Institute of Education, Employment Department Research Series 41.

Brannen, J., Moss, P., Owen, C. and Wale, C. (1997) *Mothers, Fathers and Employment: Parents and the Labour Market*, Sudbury: Department for Education and Employment, Research Report 10.

Butler, T. and Savage, M. (eds) (1995) *Social Change and the Middle Classes*, London: UCL Press.

Chandler, J. (1989) 'Marriage and housing careers of naval families', *Sociological Review*, 37, 2: 253–76, Oxford: Blackwells.

Children in Scotland (1998) *Taking Account of Children and Families in the Workplace: Promoting Public Sector Action*, Edinburgh: European Commission Medium-Term Action Programme, Research Report of Phase 2, July 1997–June 1998.

Christensen, P. and James, A. (eds) (2000) *Research with Children – Perspectives and Practices*, London: Falmer.

Christoffersen, M.N. (1998) 'Growing up with Dad: a comparison of children aged 3–5 years old living with their mother or their father', *Childhood*, 5, 1: 41–54, London: Sage.

Cooper, C.L. (1999) 'The changing nature of work', *Community, Work and Family*, 1: 313–17.

Corrigan, P. (1979) *Schooling the Smash Street Kids*, London: Macmillan.

Deven, F., Inglis, S., Moss, P. and Petrie, P. (1997) *State of the Art Review on the Reconciliation of Work and Family Life for Men and Women and the Quality of Care Services*, Final Report for the European Commission Equal Opportunities Unit (DGV), November 1997.

Franks, S. (1999) *Having None Of It*, London: Granta Books.

Galinsky, E. (1999) *Ask the Children – What America's Children Really Think About Working Parents*, New York: William Morrow.

Gelder, U. (2002) *Working for Women? Family Day Care Providers – Social and Economic Experience in England and Germany*, PhD Thesis, Department of Sociology and Social Policy, University of Newcastle.

Hochschild, A. (1997) *The Time Bind*, New York: Viking Penguin.

Horlick, N. (1997) *Can You Have It All?*, London: Macmillan.

Hyman J., Baldry, C. and Bunzel, D. (2001) *Balancing Work and Life: Not just a Matter of Time Flexibility*, unpublished paper given at Work, Employment and Society Conference, Nottingham, 11–13 September 2001.

Industrial Society, The (2000) *Work–Life Initiative*, London: The Industrial Society.

Institute of Directors (2001) *The Work–Life Balance and All That: The Re-Regulation of the Labour Market*, London: Institute of Directors.

Isay, R.A. (1968) *The Submariners' Wives Syndrome*, paper presented at Annual Meeting of American Psychological Association, May.

Lewis, J., Porter, M. and Shrimpton, M. (1988) *Women, Work and the Family in the British, Canadian and Norwegian Offshore Oilfields*, London: Macmillan Press.

Lewis, S. and Cooper, C.L. (1996) 'Balancing the Work/Home Interface: A European Perspective, *Human Resource Management Review*, 5, 4: 289–305.

Lewis, S. and Lewis, J. (eds) (1996) *The Work–Family Challenge: Rethinking Employment*, London: Sage.

Mauthner, N., Maclean, C. and McKee, L. (2000) '"My dad hangs out of helicopter doors and takes pictures of oil platforms": Children's Accounts of Parental Work in the Oil and Gas Industry', *Community, Work and Family*, 3, 2: 133–62.

McKee, L. (1985) *Perceptions of Fatherhood*, unpublished doctoral thesis, University of York.

Moss, P. (1996) 'Reconciling employment and family responsibilities: a European perspective', in S. Lewis and J. Lewis (eds) *The Work–Family Challenge: Rethinking Employment*, London: Sage.

National Work–Life Forum (1999) *Looking for Balance*, London: National Work–Life Forum.

Prout, A. (2000) 'Foreword', in Christensen, P. and James, A. (eds) *Research with Children – Perspectives and Practices*, London: Falmer.

Rainnie, A. (1998) 'The inevitability of flexibility? A review article', *Work, Employment and Society*, 12, 1: 161–7.

Rose, D. and O'Reilly, K. (1998) *The ESRC Review of Government Social Classifications*, London: Office for National Statistics, Swindon: Economic and Social Research Council.

Willis, P. (1977) *Learning to Labour*, Farnborough: Saxon House.

3 Employed or unemployed parents
A child perspective

Elisabet Näsman

This chapter focuses on the work–family interface and parental unemployment from children's perspective. Increased part-time work, flexible working hours, participation of women in the workforce and change in work/family policies are all labour-market issues to be discussed. Family changes in terms of gender and adult–child relationships are also relevant.

Based on childrens' accounts, their understanding, judgements and actions are analysed in relation to their interaction with parents. The project 'Work-life and Children' interviewed 45 families with children of 3–17 years old. The project 'Unemployment and Children' interviewed children at school, at pre-school and in families. A total of about 90 pre-schoolers, 300 school-age children and 28 families contributed.[1]

These projects stress childrens' perspective and agency. Children and adults in interaction construct childhood as a life phase in the age order of society (Alanen 1992; Näsman 1995; James *et al.* 2001; Alanen and Mayall 2001).[2]

Children occupy a subordinate social position and that affects their understanding of their experiences. Children, like us all, are restricted by their limited analytical tools. In combination, these factors may cause children to adopt and reproduce adults' traditional perspective of children as fragile objects needing protection, care and control. Children may also be more content with their conditions than they would if they had a critical view of adult authority and were aware of alternative family arrangements. To take children's accounts at face value may thus be criticized (Näsman 1995).

The work–family interface

The entrance of mothers of young children into the labour market marked a major change in family patterns in the late twentieth century. In Sweden this was a matter of public policy: changes in the taxation system, publicly sub-sidised day care and parental leave increased the proportion of mothers in the labour force. Mothers first entered mainly as part-time workers, but working hours steadily increased (Sundström 1987; Jonsson *et al.* 2001: 141).

The impact of mothers' employment on child development has been an issue. 'Arguments have centred on the possible harmful effects which the increase in women's full-time participation in the workforce might be having on the social, emotional, physical and educational development of the child' (James *et al.* 2001: 78). In the case of fathers, risks for children were seen as stemming from unemployment rather than employment. This gendered focus is criticised (Smith 1981; Wyndham 1982; Näsman *et al.* 1983). That children are seen as subsumed in these worries and not acknowledged as having any agency is also questioned (Solberg 1990). The projects introduced here focus on working fathers as well as mothers and treat children as actors (Näsman *et al.* 1983; Lundén and Näsman 1989; Jonsson *et al.* 2001).

The effects of parental unemployment on children were likewise targeted for research in the late twentieth century, a time when unemployment rates increased in Europe. How unemployment affects children had largely been neglected in research (Madge 1983; Näsman *et al.* 1983). A few studies were conducted on children of the Great Depression (Elder 1974), but it was only in the late twentieth century that the impact of unemployment on children became a prime research topic in several countries (Christoffersen 1994; Näsman and von Gerber 1996; Karlsen and Mjaavatn 1995). Few studies focused on children's accounts.

The wage-earner family

Over 80 per cent of Swedish children under 16 years of age live in two-parent families and these parents are mostly wage earners. Paid labour also affects most children living with one parent, usually a mother, or alternating between households. Over 30 per cent of pre-schoolers' mothers work full time and 27 per cent of them work part time (over ten hours per week). The corresponding figures for mothers of children aged 7–16 years are 43 and 31 per cent. In both cases over 75 per cent of the fathers work full time (Jonsson *et al.* 2001: 137).

In wage-earning families the household must be organized so as to accommodate the work schedules of parents, schedules which may include shift and weekend work and seasonal variations. Families must establish a jig-saw schedule including working hours, children's hours in day care and at school, travelling time, housework, time for sleep and meals and time for other individual and joint activities. Financial issues must also be considered. The temporal schedules structure children's everyday life (Lundén and Näsman 1989).

When children are asked about parental working hours, some just answer that they do not matter or that the child has never thought about them. Some children seem unaware that the situation could be different. Older children say, 'Well, she has always been working, so I find it hard to imagine her at home' (girl, aged 14) or, 'It has become a habit. You don't think about him going to work' (girl, aged 16). Other children, however, comment upon the presence and absence of the parents.

Separation and independence

> Mum doesn't do as Dad does, because she can't. Because she works when it is night. She works the whole night. Dad works the day. We might stay with the childminder.
>
> (Boy, aged four)

From a young age, children describe their parents' work in temporal terms. They conceptualize the distribution, number and regularity of working hours when they say, 'long time', 'sometimes', 'every day', 'late', 'overtime' and 'day or night'. Children comment upon where, when and with whom they stay during the day, night and week due to the temporal structure.

Mostly working hours mean that parents and children are separated. Young children may express this negatively as missing their parents or longing for the absent parent. A five-year-old girl dislikes the fact that her mother, an assistant nurse, has to stay with the patients. 'I want to have my mother at home in the evenings.' A four-year-old boy states, 'Can't you be at home all day and not only work? Then, well, I get angry.' Some children want their parents to be present more and most often miss the father. The option two-parent families may have of taking turns at home does not always satisfy children, since some want to have access to both parents at once. They miss and long for the parent who is at work even when the other is at home. Some children are positive about their parents' working hours in general but argue for temporary changes on occasions, such as when they are ill – then they want a parent to be at home with them.

Children comment positively when parents reduce their working hours or in other ways adapt them to the children. A ten-year-old boy likes the fact that his mother's part-time work means she is generally free on Fridays. A six-year-old girl likes it when her father's shifts allow him to be at home with her.

A child may dislike a parent's absence but still be positive about the job. Young children see the link between work and money and say that work is necessary to earn a living: 'It is very important. If you don't buy any food, then you may die' (boy, aged five). The link between work and earnings may cause ambivalence. A boy wants his mother to reduce her hours and be at home more, but he also wants her to work full time and increase her income.

In the mid-twentieth century there was a debate about the eventual harm arising from children being left alone at home while their parents worked (Solberg 1990: 156; James *et al.* 2001: 78). According to the regulation of public day care in Sweden, children may need day care up to 12 years of age. The scheduling of some families means that even younger children may be without adult company either before or after school. 'Do these children perceive themselves as left alone or as entering an empty house after school? Do they feel a need for adults during these hours?' Solberg argues that these words poorly fit accounts where children are considered as actors. The term 'need' 'conceals in practice a complex of latent assumptions and judgements about children … the children appear as passive objects, recipients and victims' (Solberg 1990: 145). Solberg claims that this is an 'adultist' way of describing the situation and that the words 'alone' and 'empty' mask an adult voice (Solberg 1990: 141–57). She recommends talking neutrally about a 'vacant' house and using verbs such as 'like', 'want' or 'prefer' in order to treat children as active subjects (Solberg 1990: 142–8).

Swedish children's views on this matter vary. If a parent – generally the mother – is at home when children arrive home after school they like that and appreciate the part-time or flexible working hours that make it possible. 'I like best if she is at home when I arrive home from school … . Then I have someone who receives me' (girl, aged 11). Older children have the same view in retrospect:

> We needed Mum. We thought so. When we came home from school, she was at home. I don't think that it is good for children to unlock the door with their own key and go in and sit by themselves.
>
> (Girl, aged 16)

If the words 'alone,' 'empty' and 'need' in this context mask an adult voice, as Solberg suggests, this voice is adopted by children. Their accounts may, as mentioned, be problematized by being seen as mirroring children's subordination to adults. If these children's accounts are taken at face value, however, access to a parent at home after school is preferred. Let us turn to children who spend time on their own at home.

Children who, during their early school years, are the last in the family to leave the home in the morning or the first to arrive home in the afternoon do not necessarily see this as negative. Some say that it is peaceful and quiet at home. Others like to have sole control over their home, as described by Solberg (1990: 125–7). One girl says that the choice not to enrol her in after-school care was according to her wishes: she prefers to be free to choose the activities, company and location she likes after school, including the choice to be alone at home. To be at home on your own is preferred to institutional care. Children value freedom from the subordination to adults which prevails at institutions as well as at home. This situation is, in some cases, combined with access to adult relatives living close by.

The positive value of being on your own is to some children limited to the brighter times of the year. To arrive at a dark home and be there alone when it is dark outside can be scary even in an inner-city area. Then, it is 'good to have someone at home' (boy, aged ten). Even a teenager appreciates having his or her parents take turns arriving home early in the afternoon. To be 'alone' for a long time is 'boring'.

To young children the alternative to having a parent at home is not time on their own but outside day care. They may prefer scheduling to give them the opportunity to stay at home, for instance, in the morning. Some complain that they cannot leave the pre-school early. Young schoolchildren say that it is 'more fun' to be at home. Older children in retrospect describe the many hours in day care as 'long days' of which they tired. Schoolchildren seem to lump hours at school and in care together into a category of 'not-at-home time'.

One problem young children perceive in this context is a state of conflict linked to the bringing and fetching of them. Children may describe parents as irritated, nagging and making degrading comments about the children, while parents describe children as sabotaging the schedule by dressing and eating too slowly. Young children see time as relative to action in the present. That makes it hard to understand time pressure based on linear time. Parents thus may expect children to act according to a concept of time that the child cannot understand. This happened in families in urban areas with tight time scheduling. Fixed scheduling rules in pre-school further increase the tension.

Most young children like pre-school (Torstensson-Ed 1997). A child wants at least one parent to work so that she may go to the pre-school. However, the children ask for more flexibility to come and go when they want – a pre-school not based on their parents' working life. Children's emphasis on making their own choices is also apparent in accounts from young children who dislike being interrupted during play, when a parent comes to fetch them. Temporal regulation according to working hours is problematic.

What do children want from parents' presence? Parents have material resources and rights, including that to decide about children's activities. It is mainly via adults that young children gain access to money, transportation and formalised activities. Parents are resources who enable children to manage their lives (Jonsson *et al.* 2001: 35–42). This perspective instrumentalizes the child–adult relationship and makes parents into objects which children use. This is clearly true sometimes. The presence of an adult may be prerequisite when young children want to be at home. An absent parent during weekends and holidays may reduce the options for spare-time activities. When the father is absent the mother may only spend time with the younger siblings. When children quarrel with one parent it is good to be able to turn to the other. Children also like to get both parents' attention, talk to them and take part in joint activities. A girl wants to tell her father, not only her mother, about what she has done at school. Another child longs to share activities with the mother when the father is watching sports on TV. Some children like the whole family to be together. Those who see their family at the dinner table each day like that and to some children this is an ideal to strive for.

There is no dichotomy between working hours and time at home for children. Some children comment critically upon the time they spend with their parents. Work may intervene when parents are at home. Children of a teacher share her stress when pupils and parents phone her in the evening. Parents preparing for work are physically but not mentally available at home: 'Dad is lecturing this week and so he is totally gone' (boy, aged 17). Working at night means that parents need to sleep in the daytime.

Domestic work also takes time. Adding the hours taken for paid work, work-related travelling and domestic labour, wage-earning mothers and fathers equally work for an average of about 60 hours per week when their children are 10–18 years old (Jonsson *et al.* 2001). Mothers of young children work less but the time actually spent with children is about the same whether mothers work full or part time (Statistics Sweden 1992). A girl describes at length all the domestic duties the parents do up to her bedtime, but adds, 'Sometimes before I sleep, Mum reads a story or Dad plays cards with me' (girl, aged eight). A young child wants to play with the parents, but 'They don't want to. They haven't got the time' (boy, aged four). An older child describes how it is not until the younger siblings are put to bed that she and the parents talk together. In a survey, most 10–18-year-olds respond that their parents have enough time for them, 11 per cent say their mothers have insufficient time with them and 14 per cent say the same of their fathers. About 2–3 per cent say that their parents spend too much time with them (Jonsson *et al.* 2001: 149).

Access

Do children have access to their parents at work? Is the workplace close by and can children visit it? Openness is crucial at the workplace (Jonsson *et al.* 2001: 151), but the production process may make it hard for parents to leave their posts, or the workload may make it difficult to take a break. Travels and meetings may also limit accessibility. Children's opportunities to visit parents during working hours vary a lot. Among children aged 10–12 years, 32 per cent can gain access to their mother at work and 24 per cent can gain access to their father (Jonsson *et al.* 2001: 149). The figures increase by age.

To phone parents is a way to overcome problems of transport or workplace boundaries. Allowing employees private calls is common in Sweden and in some workplaces is seen as part of a child-friendly workplace policy. Parents frequently keep in contact with their children this way (Näsman 1997). Can children phone their parents? Children may have to get past 'gatekeepers' to reach the parent. Some cannot make contact at all due to the location or mobility of the parent. Young children may lack the necessary technological competence and numeric literacy (Näsman 1997). In general, school-age children see their parents as accessible by phone during working hours. Among 10–18-year-olds, over 90 per cent can phone their parents at work. Less than three per cent of these children are unable to contact a parent at all. Mobile phones are important, especially for accessing fathers (Jonsson *et al.* 2001: 149).

Work environment

Work conditions affect the individual's state and physical condition. This 'colouring' spills over to family life, overriding the idea of work and family as separate social spheres (Crouter 1984; Lundén and Näsman 1989). In general, 13 per cent of working mothers with children of 10–18 years old say that they are always or usually physically exhausted when they arrive home after work, while 8 per cent of the fathers feel the same. The corresponding figures for those who are mentally exhausted are 17 per cent for mothers and 7 per cent for fathers. The risk of this kind of negative spillover is higher for parents with irregular working hours, mothers with long working hours and for single mothers (Jonsson *et al.* 2001: 147). In some workplaces parental stress issues are salient and regulated. A police station and an intensive care unit may have a rule that staff are not asked to work on cases involving children the same age as their own. Debriefing processes may include specific consideration of the parental role of staff members. Reduced demands on parents' commitment may also be part of a family policy (Näsman 1997).

Children from an early age describe the condition and mood their mother and father are in before they leave for work and when they arrive home from work. Some children do that with reference to differences between working days and days off. Pre-work time pressures appear in accounts from pre-school age and children mention parents being stressed and irritated before work. Fatigue is the most frequent negative condition after work. Parents are tired but also fretful, irritated, angry, grumpy, surly, sad, dizzy, inattentive, occupied and in pain. 'Angry, irritable. He wants to be left alone. You are not allowed to be close to him. He gets so angry' (girl, aged nine). The positive effects of work are noted when a parent is described as arriving home 'fit' 'peaceful', 'glad' and 'open-minded'. Then parents may 'listen' to the child.

Children mention both the positive and negative colouring and how this either varies over time or is a regular experience. Some parents verbally describe their condition and mood to the children, while others show this in their behaviour and interaction with the children. They may close the door behind them to get an undisturbed nap, give irritated answers or make nasty remarks, refuse to talk to or play with the child or not pay attention when children try to make contact. That parents avoid contact and verbally demand time and space to relax is common in the children's accounts and related to several conditions: 'She wants to be left alone' (girl, aged nine); 'He takes the newspaper and goes to bed' (boy, aged eight); 'He gets irritated if you are in his way' (girl, aged nine).

In most cases parents and children agree as to whether colouring is positive or negative. When civil servants, however, are mentally occupied by their work at home they may see that as positive while their children do not: they complain that the parent does not pay attention and that work dominates dinner-table conversation.

Some children perceive a difference between the mood they understand that a parent is in and the way the parent appears. The interpretation is that the parents are trying to control their negative feelings and pretending to be in a better mood. Children appreciate the emotional coping, but the pretence does not fool them.

In addition to parents' condition and mood before and after work, some children talk about the physical danger faced by parents. Risk of accident when, for example, a father works with corrosive acid or a mother with violent patients and the risk of work-related diseases such as cancer due to exposure to dangerous gas, make children worry about the life and health of the parent. This means a spillover directly from work to children, not via the colouring of parents.

Understanding spillover

Children who fear for a parent's health do so based on an understanding of the parent's work conditions. Children's understanding of the causal chain of colouring varies according to the visibility of the work conditions. Visibility depends on the proximity and openness of the workplace, complexity of work organization and concreteness of work content. A child who has visited the father at a small factory, followed the manual work process and experienced the work environment himself, describes how work with glue causes the dizziness and headache that the father suffers from after work. That care-giving work is emotionally demanding is understandable to a young child. On the other hand, young children will remain uncomprehending of a large-scale factory too dangerous for them to visit. The intellectual demands of white-collar work may be hard for even teenagers to grasp.

Children who have visited the workplace describe work environment spillover in the most detail, others rely on what their parents tell them. Some parents choose not to talk about work at home, as a strategy to keep the home a protected haven free from the hardships of working life. If children experience the parents' colouring, this strategy will not work. Children who cannot see why a parent is in a bad mood after work look for an explanation, but can be satisfied by excluding any guilt of their own, 'No, he is not angry at me, fortunately' (girl, aged eight). Some children, however, seem to perceive the negative colouring to be caused by themselves. Parents who are often absent, have no time to play or who make degrading remarks to children trying to get ready to leave in the morning, were understood as treating the children as not very valuable people.

Change and action

The extent to which children see a scope for choice in family arrangements varies. The experience of friends and variation in their own experience seem to be the main sources for information concerning alternatives. Older children draw on their childhood experiences. In pre-school, others' schedules are visible in action. Two brothers refer to the different schedules of their playmates, when they question why their (single) mother does not work part time and bring them home early from the pre-school. Other children simply seem to think things over and see what resources they have for change. Two siblings suggest that their grandmother, who only works part time, could move closer to their home and make it possible for them to go directly home from school.

What kind of action, if any, do children take to change the work–family interface? Do they negotiate about the jigsaw puzzle of hours or act to cope with negative colouring?

Some parents describe their children as kind, accepting, content and disciplined; these children's own accounts, however, may reveal a different outlook. Some of them accepted the negative impact of scheduling as a matter of fact or necessity. That a night nurse sleeps in the daytime restricts children's scope for activities: 'Then you must be a bit calmer' (girl, aged 16). Others take on the role of the parents, see the problems their way and accept the situation. Still others see no problems and adapt easily to the scheduling and colouring in the family. Contentedness can, of course, be problematized as mirroring children's subordination, but I take the accounts at face value if nothing gives reason for a different interpretation. Grounds for questioning a child's acceptance may be found in the general descriptions given by that child, or by others in the family.

Some children accept the family and working-life conditions, but with expressions of low self-esteem and resignation to what they see as problems. This is adaptation to a negative situation where the child can't see any potential for change. Such an experience of lack of power is in itself negative.

Acceptance is a kind of cognitive coping. More active strategies are found in some childrens' ways of dealing with the negative colouring of a parent's moods. They try to console the parent or make life easier by helping with housework. If the child is young and the help inefficient that strategy can backlash, meaning further negative reactions from the parent. A girl, aged eight, tried to support her overstrained mother: 'Sometimes I help Mum with the food but she finds it so difficult. I am so much in her way.'

Exit is another strategy for escaping negative reactions. Children take the initiative to keep out of the parent's way under conditions where there is no chance of getting attention from them or when the parent is angry. A teenager leaves the house to demonstrate his aversion to excessive mealtime talk about work. Young children protest when they are brought to the pre-school or protest the absence of their parents, such as when the mother leaves for work in the evening, 'Then I scream so that the whole house trembles – even the garage trembles, everything trembles' (girl, aged five). Some protest when parents are occupied at home. A young boy is 'angry' and complains when his parents have no time to play with him. Two teenagers argue with their father, stating that he overestimates his own importance at the workplace and hence has no reason to work so much instead of spending time with his family. The father gives them their due, but finds their criticism hard to take.

Children may also succeed in finding their own ways to get what they want. A father who works excessively arrives home at about 10pm on weekdays. His son reports: 'Then I hear the door bang when I am about to fall asleep and I wake up. Then I get up.' The two young boys who had been put to bed pretend that they need to use the toilet and refuse to go back to bed before the father plays with them. The parents accept these strategies as reasonable, but without changing the basic problem the children have to cope with.

Against this background of working parents, we will now listen to children's accounts from recent years marked by increasing unemployment.

Unemployed parents

After a long period of high employment, Sweden experienced a dramatic increase in unemployment in the early 1990s. Unemployment rates dropped starting in the mid 1990s, but are still not back to earlier levels (Jonsson *et al.* 2001). What interests us here are the experiences and views of this issue among children 3–6 years old and 10–12 years old.

The concept of unemployment is familiar to a lot of young children. They define unemployment in terms of not having a job. Unemployment as such is understood to be negative, even though some children may experience it positively in their families. Even these children, however, want their parents to have jobs in the future. In the children's culture there is, from pre-school age onwards, an understanding that unemployment can have a negative impact on the unemployed. The following kinds of negative effects are mentioned, the first two dominating among young children:

- *Economic deprivation* – poverty, having to move and homelessness.
- *Mental distress* – such as sadness, anger, worry and restlessness.
- *Behavioural problems* – such as passivity, daydreaming, watching TV, neglect of appearance, smoking, drinking, crime and suicide.
- *Social problems* – loss of self-esteem, family quarrelling, neglect of children and public custody of the children.

Children who have had an unemployed parent generally have a less negative conception of the impact of unemployment than do children inexperienced in this.

Economic loss

Economic deprivation is the impact of unemployment mentioned by most children in both age groups. Young children sometimes see this in dramatic terms, such as homelessness and starvation.

Most of the children who have experienced parental unemployment ('experienced children') have perceived no economic impact on their personal lives, as parents generally give children's consumption priority over their own. Children get clothes, food, pocket money and spare-time activities just as they are used to. Cuts in the children's budget are made in some families, but mostly on a small scale and children do not complain about them. Children are prepared to accept major cuts in pocket money, even to the level of no money at all. In a few families, however, the cuts included poorer food, medicine and postponement of medical consultation and new glasses for the child. One boy complains that there is no cheese in the refrigerator because they cannot afford it.

Children more often see material changes in the household at large. One young girl describes how her family has to move because they cannot afford their house, saying that she will be sad to leave her teddy bears and the toys in her room, which she believes will be a consequence. That unemployment can cause family conflicts is a frequent idea among children, the main cause for such conflicts being financial hardship. Older children demand to be told if their family has financial problems, so that they can refrain from demands that may cause conflict. Children also want the chance to distribute their resources and what gifts they expect from their parents evenly over the year. They also describe strategies to reduce household costs: they may brush their teeth better so that they will not need as frequent dental care, wear secondhand clothes, take quicker showers, turn out the lights on leaving a room and reduce luxury spending on items such as junk food and sweets.

Some children want to share their resources with their parents and children in both age groups let parents borrow their savings. One of the older children was sad that her parents, who had been saving for her future, did not want to use those savings when the family was hard up.

Children also have strategies to increase income, such as selling old toys and collecting recyclable material. Though contributions from these sources may seem negligible from an adult perspective, they may comprise a large proportion of a child's pocket money. The children did not discuss contributing to the household income by wage labour. Some children were critical of their parents' discretionary spending and proposed cuts to that rather than in their own consumption.

Stress and strategies

Both experienced children and children in general described examples of the negative mental impact of unemployment on the parent and how this manifests itself in interaction with the child. We can see some similarities to the discussion of negative colouring arising from work. Young, experienced children describe how the parent is 'sad', 'irritated', 'angry' and even aggressive – 'he pulls my ears'. Some describe how the unemployed father drinks beer and sleeps during the day. Older children also describe passivity, restlessness and moodiness. Some children tell how they themselves felt when they heard about their parents' unemployment. When his mother lost her job, a five-year-old boy said that he 'felt sad in [his] whole body'. He went to talk to a friend whose father also was unemployed. Children also share the joy when an unemployed parent gets a job. This is another direct impact of parental unemployment on children themselves.

Experienced children in both age groups build causal chains in their analysis of the impact of unemployment on their parents. To describe their understanding of their parents' moods, they present their views of the situation in general or of particular events or chains of events, for instance, when the monthly bills arrive. They take the role of the parent and empathetically share their experiences without the mediating link of expressions of feeling from the parent. Children then draw parallels to how they themselves would feel under the same circumstances: 'Then I cry already because I don't have a job and I am unemployed instead' (boy, aged four). In one case this is the reason why a young child protests at being brought to the pre-school. She wants to stay at home with her unemployed father since he is sad at being left all alone and she would not like being left alone like that herself; she would like somebody to be with her.

Experienced children have several such strategies for coping with the mental impact of unemployment. They console parents or cheer them up. To dance and sing is a way for a young girl to wake her sleeping father. Some older children, however, argue that it is hard to console a father and question their ability to mediate in conflicts between parents.

Experienced children see their own behaviour as affecting how their parents are able to manage. To be 'nice', not to quarrel with siblings, to go to bed on time are all 'good' behaviours that young children in particular see as ways to make life easier for an unemployed parent, ways to contribute to the adult's coping. Older children parallel the 'good' behaviour of young children by working hard at school. The understanding is that schoolwork is important to parents, and that it burdens them if their child does not succeed in school. Some children control their own feelings of worry in front of the parents in order not to add to their emotional burden.

Some children see the social network of the family as a resource in coping with unemployment. In a single-parent family the other parent can be a resource in dealing with the financial and mental strains of unemployment. Relatives, especially grandparents, are also adults a child turns to for help and support. Neighbours are to some children crucial in helping out with food and emotional support and offering an alternative space for positive interaction, in contrast to the home. Peers are a source of support for children of both age groups, but only if the peers are close friends. Experienced children do not regard parental unemployment as shameful and may feel free to tell others about it; their main reason for not doing so is that they dislike being pitied.

Unemployment impact – a gender issue

Unemployment means that more time is available for children, even though the unemployed must seek work in order to obtain unemployment benefits. Parents and children see this as a positive aspect of unemployment. To parents, increased accessibility is primarily positive in the beginning of a period of unemployment. Others make even extended unemployment meaningful by focusing on parenting. Some fathers describe this as an important positive shift in their lives, especially when they have changed from a patriarchal family ideal. They learn domestic work and adopt a care-giving role towards the children. Also the children describe the change in very positive terms. Two pre-school children whose father spent a lot of time with them agreed that unemployment was not a problem at all in their family – on the contrary.

This stands in stark contrast to older children's descriptions of authoritarian fathers losing their status during unemployment (Komarovsky 1940). Earlier it was also common to assume that the role as housewife compensates women for the loss of a job. This belief appears in the children's culture but is not uncontested. Experienced children describe negative as well as positive impacts of unemployment on both mothers and fathers. Some families where children describe the most negative experiences are single-mother families and the most positive experiences come from a single-father family. Changes in gender roles now make unemployment harder on mothers but give fathers new options.

The welfare state

Another important change compared to unemployment during the Great Depression is the obviously important role played by the welfare state. Education and training projects for the unemployed are parts of public policy that children appreciate and they describe the positive impact of these activities on their parents' mood. The unemployment insurance system generally enables the families of experienced children to get by. Some even manage quite well and are able to save money for the children's future. Families that experience financial hardships are those that are uninsured, have had to sell their houses at a loss because they could not pay the mortgage or had got heavily into debt before the unemployment.

Public day care for children as part of the welfare state is, however, not so clearly an option for the children of unemployed parents. During the 1990s an increasing number of municipalities in Sweden made it harder or impossible for children of unemployed parents to enrol in day care, and restricted or forbade the continued enrolment of children whose parents became unemployed. Children say that they dislike being withdrawn from pre-school due to a parent's unemployment and complain very much over that. Pre-schools and schools serve as asylums for children who face a stressful situation at home. During the time spent in the institutions they can leave that behind and concentrate on other things. In several pre-schools the children may offer an opportunity to play 'unemployment'.[3]

Children acting in the work–family interface

From an early age children see themselves as actors and want to have the scope to act on their own when it comes to their personal lives. They also see themselves as family members with rights and obligations to that collective. In the negotiating family of today they want to be informed, have a voice and have their interests considered. On the other hand, most children trust their parents' decision-making in important family matters and want to leave their parents scope to act in matters affecting their own personal lives. In the work–family interface, parents' lives and children's conditions are intertwined: the working life of parents temporally structures children's everyday lives, while children at home face the mood colouring arising from their parents' work. Unemployment may mean a relief from the demands of working life, but the financial and mental impact of unemployment affects the children. This chapter has examined both children's sympathetic views and strategies for action pertaining to these matters in a changing labour market and in changing families.

References

Alanen, L. (1992) *Modern Childhood? Exploring the Child Question in Sociology*, Jyväskylä: University of Jyväskylä.

Alanen, L. and Mayall, B. (2001) *Conceptualizing Child–Adult Relations*, London: Routledge.

Christoffersen, M.N. (1994) 'A follow-up study of long-term effects of unemployment on children: loss of self-esteem and self-destructive behaviour among adolescents', *Childhood*, 4: 212–20.

Crouter, A.C. (1984) 'Spill-over from family to work: the neglected side of the work–family interface', *Human Relations*, 37, 6: 425–42.

Elder, G.H. (1974) *Children of the Great Depression*, Chicago: University of Chicago Press.

Hareven, T.K. (1995) 'Changing images of ageing and the social construction of the life course', in M. Featherstone and A. Wernick (eds), *Images of Ageing. Cultural Representations of Later Life*: 119–34, London: Routledge.

James, A., Jenks, C. and Prout, A. (2001) *Theorizing Childhood*, Oxford: Blackwell.

Jonsson, J.O., Östberg, V., Evertsson, M. and Låftman, S.B. (2001) *Barns och ungdomars välfärd*, Swedish Public Report (SOU): 55, Stockholm: Fritzes.

Karlsen, T.K. and Mjaavatn, P.E. (1995) *Barn og arbeidsledighet*, Dragvoll: Norsk senter for barneforskning, Universitetet i Trondheim.

Komarovsky, M. (1940) *The Unemployed Man and His Family. The Effect of Unemployment Upon the Status of the Man in Fifty-nine Families*, New York: Dryden Press.

Lundén, Jacoby A. and Näsman, E. (1989) *Mamma Pappa Jobb: Föräldrar och Barn om Arbetets Villkor*, Stockholm: Arbetslivscentrum.

Madge, N. (1983) 'Annotation. Unemployment and its effects on children', *Journal of Child Psychology and Psychiatry*, 24, 2: 311–19.

Näsman, E. (1995) 'Vuxnas intresse av att se med barns ögon', in L. Dahlgren and K. Hultqvist (eds) *Seendet och seendets villkor. En bok om barns och ungas välfärd*, Stockholm: HLS Förlag.

Näsman, E. (1997) 'Work–family arrangements in Sweden: family patterns', in L. den Dulk, A. van Doorne-Huiskes and J. Schippers (eds) *Work–Family Arrangements in Europe*, Amsterdam: Thela thesis 131–49.

Näsman, E. and von Gerber, C. (1996) *Mamma Pappa Utan Jobb*, Stockholm: Rädda Barnens Förlag.

Näsman, E., Nordström, K. and Hammarström, R. (1983) *Föräldrars Arbete & Barns villkor: En kunskapsöversikt om hur förhållanden i arbetslivet påverkar barns och ungdomars uppväxtvillkor*, Stockholm: Arbetslivscentrum.

Smith, Elsie J. (1981) 'The working mother: a critique of the research', *Journal of Vocational Behaviour*, vol. 18: 191–211.

Solberg, A. (1990) *Negotiating Childhood: Empirical Investigations and Textual Representations of Children's Work and Everyday Lives*, Stockholm: Nordic Institute for Studies in Urban and Regional Planning.

Statistics Sweden (1992) *Tidsanvändningsundersökningen* 1990/91. Levnadsförhållanden, nr. 80, Stockholm: Statistics Sweden.

Sundström, M. (1987) *A Study in the Growth of Part-time Work in Sweden*, Stockholm: Brevskolan.

Torstensson-Ed, T. (1997) *Barns livsvägar genom daghem och skola*, Linköping: Linköpings Universitet.

Wyndham, D. (1982) 'Why study working mothers and ignore working fathers? The impact of parental employment on children', presented at the ANZAAS Conference, Australia.

4 Father presence in childcare

Berit Brandth and Elin Kvande

Introduction

The emergence of new parental leave schemes as a system to strengthen parent–child relationships has been the most important area of expansion in the Norwegian welfare state during the 1990s. The schemes have been extended to a total of 52 weeks with 80 per cent pay, and special rights have been granted to fathers. The intention behind this granting of special rights to fathers is to encourage the father's contact with and care for their children by labelling working men as fathers. In this way, the state is acting on behalf of young children by trying to encourage fathers to take responsibility for the daily care of their children.

The leave schemes are complex, as they take various factors into consideration. Both mothers and fathers have received their *own* rights in addition to *joint* rights. In this chapter the focus is on the father's quota which is four weeks of leave specially reserved for fathers. The father's quota is based on the idea that he is obliged to take leave from work to care for the child. The father's quota is an important part of the Norwegian welfare state's time politics.

The father's quota has been considered a success as 80 per cent of fathers who have earned the right to parental benefits avail themselves of this right (RTV Basic Report 2000). As the quota was introduced in 1993, it is now important to look at the consequences it has had. Being together with infants/toddlers may perhaps be one of the most radical breaks with traditional father roles and may have long-term implications for the values and practices of fathers. Up until now, research has focused on the consequences of parental leave for the adults (mothers, fathers, parents), especially the extent to which the parental leave schemes have changed the participation patterns of fathers and resulted in a more equal division of family and work time between mothers and fathers. What type of change this represents for children has been much less in focus. One reason is that it is hard to assess the results over time. In this chapter we want to examine the father's quota from a child perspective. We primarily want to examine how young children influence fathers' care practices through interaction with their fathers in different contexts.

Theoretical approach

The topic of men and childcare is a field filled with preconceptions and myths. Due to the strongly dichotomous understanding of gender in research on women, theories have focused on differences between women and men. Differences in care rationality or care ability have made up one of these fields. This research appears to support generally accepted ideas. Care is easily perceived as an ability women have and men do not have to the same extent. In this chapter we will not examine men's care abilities or aspects of personality that make them either more or less adept at exercising care, rather we are interested in how they *practise* care for their children (Morgan 1996). Thus we ask how they act, not how they *are* as people.

Research on fathers and care has generally focused on how the care practices of the father have been shaped by the mother. Due to her activities in the labour market, she has opened the door to the father's entitlement to paid parental leave, and her negotiative strength has been considered decisive for the father's degree of participation in the family (Brandth and Kvande 1989, 1991, 1998). It has been pointed out that the mother's model power, i.e. her standards for care and housework, is also required of the father's efforts (Holter and Aarseth 1993). Whether explicit or not, in research studying the father's care in light of the mother's care, the perspective is relational. This means that what a father does is understood as a social product that is continuously defined and negotiated with the mother.

In addition to studying the care practices of fathers in an interaction perspective, research has also focused on fathers' care as a masculine practice, and whether childcare conflicts with or corresponds to masculine identity projects (Brandth and Kvande 1998).

A less used perspective in father research is how the interaction with children influences *the care practices of fathers*. In this chapter we focus on the relationship between fathers and children, and we will look for children's influence on how their fathers practise care. Theoretically, this implies that we see children as active agents who contribute to the production of the adult world and their own place in it. Seeing children as social agents contrasts with traditional socialization theory in which the notion is that children are formed by forces external to themselves in order to adapt to society (Corsaro 1997). As in this chapter we deal with very young children, their creative influence might be limited. Indeed, their births are the source of the parental leave, but children cannot directly decide whether or not their fathers use the quota, nor the ways they choose to use it. Nonetheless, in interacting with their fathers, they still exercise some influence, and in this chapter we will bring aspects of their influence on fathers' care practices into focus.

Regarding care as a relational practice means that care can be learned and developed if and when the situation so invites or demands. This in turn means that we do not consider care ability as something fixed, but rather as a potential that may be formed and developed differently depending on the relations and situations in which it is practised. Hence, we see care as situationally dependent. In this way care also becomes more ambiguous and more open to variations. Seeing care as relational also enables us to study how children influence the father's practice.

One aspect of care practice is *the practice of time*. In his book *Øyeblikkets tyranni* (*The Tyranny of the Moment*) Hylland Eriksen (2001) describes how *slow time* may be connected to safety, predictability, joy, cosiness, growth and maturation, with special emphasis on the last two. This is a perception of time that differs from the one that applies in the working life of fathers and in life in general, where time is more a matter of division and fragmentation, framed by the demand for a high tempo. The consequence may be that it is more difficult to create narratives, sequences, development and maturation.

The questions we ask in this chapter concern the contexts which provide the child with the opportunity to influence the father's practice. When is an interaction established between a father and his child where the child becomes an actor? What is the content of the practices the child influences?

Data, sample and context

This chapter is based on data from a large study on fathers' use of the parental leave schemes. The study included a questionnaire that was sent to all men who became fathers in the period May 1994 to April 1995 in two municipalities in central Norway. A total of 2,194 questionnaires were mailed and the response rate was 62 per cent. From this same sample we have interviewed 30 couples who used the parental leave system in various ways. The interviews took place when the child was between one-and-a-half and two years old.

This analysis is based on the interviews with the mothers and fathers. Thus, it is the parents who have provided information for the study. Information from the toddlers is not available, and for the purpose of this chapter, we are only able to present their perspective indirectly.

We use data from the questionnaire to provide an overview of the two main types of father practices that are investigated and the social background of the users. We distinguish between those fathers who did not stay at home alone, i.e. whose partners were at home when the father used the father's quota, and those whose partners went back to work full-time. For 53 per cent of the sample, the mother went back to work on a full-time basis while the father stayed at home on leave. For the remaining 47 per cent, 15 returned to part-time work, 9 continued their leave on an unpaid basis, 9 had their holidays and 9 were out of work. The 5 per cent who do not fall into these categories ('other') are primarily students, persons on sick leave and mothers practising various combination solutions. When we take a closer look at the mothers, we find social differences between them. The mothers with higher education, income and job status are the ones who return to full-time work when the fathers use their quota. These fathers are given the opportunity to care for the child alone during the day – thus young children in families with a high social status have a better chance of developing a relationship with their fathers in this way. In families where children are not cared for by their father alone, the mother's work status is lower, and within the couple, lower than the father's. This pattern is also distinct in the interview material.

To investigate the question of how children may influence fathers' care practices, we will focus on these two contexts. In the debate on how the parental rights should be designed, an important argument was that fathers ought to experience what it is like to have the main responsibility for childcare when the mother goes back to work. It was first decided that a necessary premise was that the mothers had to return to work before the father would be able to use the quota. However, when objections to this were raised, the government changed this initial condition so that now fathers may use the quota regardless of what the mother does after she finishes her leave. In other words, the mother may stay at home on a full- or part-time basis when the father is practising his quota. In this chapter we will distinguish between those who have had the sole care of their child under the father's quota and those who have not. We assume that using the father's quota alone, or taking it while the mother is also home, are two entirely different contexts with different opportunities for the father to be influenced by the child.

A second aspect shaping the father's quota is that it can be divided and taken part time over a longer period. It can also be shortened, for example to two or three weeks instead of one month. The latter option is particularly relevant if the mother has worked part time and thus has not earned full birth benefits. If the mother has been employed in a half-time position, she will only have earned 50 per cent birth benefits, and consequently the father will also be granted only 50 per cent. An alternative for him is then to take two weeks with full birth benefits instead of four at 50 per cent. Another aspect of the context that is of significance for children's influence is if the father has been completely away from work during the father's quota period or been at work part time. This will also constitute an important framing condition for shaping the father's care practices.

In our analysis we have therefore chosen to distinguish analytically between, on the one hand, those fathers who have been responsible for the child alone and who have also been at home full time and, on the other hand, those who have been at home together with the mother and who have not been completely off work during the father's quota period. These two contexts become a critical point for studying the change in the father–child relationship that was one of the project's intentions. We will compare the processes that arise when the father has had leave alone and full time, and when the mother has been at home at the same time and the father has had part-time leave.

Home alone

It is not only important for children that their fathers are at home on leave, but the ways in which they are at home also influence their care practices. We shall thus first consider those fathers who have been completely off work for four weeks or more and who have been 'home alone', i.e. the mother has not been at home at the same time. What we want to know is what care practices are developed and how the child influences these practices.

On the slow time track!

A common characteristic of the histories of these fathers is the experience that care work means using time. Time permeates fathers' narratives about care. The point is not only that they have understood that it is vital to spend time on their children – many fathers would agree with them on this – but that these fathers have given time to their children or used time and thus gained other perceptions of care. This is something they have done themselves; they have given their children time by taking leave. Hence, they have gained the experience that spending time on their children is important; time that is defined as being present for their children. When we consider what they do with their children while on leave, it is obvious that they are on the track of what we may call 'slow time' (Hylland Eriksen 2001). This means that the time is not spent running from one thing to another, to squeeze as much as possible into the shortest possible time. Nor is there that much that has to be done, rather the children's needs are the centre of focus. Hence, it is the child who makes the time slow.

These fathers experience that time acquires another meaning, they gain an understanding that care is about time. The fathers' descriptions of how their day-to-day lives were spent while on leave provide us with material that can help us understand this. So what was a typical day during the period of leave like? One of the fathers describes the following:

> The four weeks? It was get up early. They wake up quite early and that's more or less OK. They wake around seven and they rise and shine, so like at the weekends, they can loaf around in their pyjamas. Avoids the stress of getting changed, there's more than enough of that at other times. Then there's breakfast before the morning routines, and then get dressed and if the weather's nice, then outside. And then we would be outside in the playground or in the forest, and then perhaps go to the store for some shopping, and then home to start dinner, and then Mummy would be home, and then dinner and children's TV and then good night. Typical day.

We see here how the father describes a day that is not filled with numerous events and things to do. Basically there are very few things on the agenda. The time is spent doing such things as getting dressed, brushing teeth and going to the shop. 'Sunday time' was introduced in the sense that the children were allowed to loaf in their pyjamas. There is no impression here of a busy everyday – rather the slow rhythm of care decides. The children get him up in the morning and control his time. Their activities give him another 'perception of slow time'.

The fact that the needs of the children regulate the use of time can also be seen in the next description. This is a father who has both taken the father's quota and shared the leave with the mother. He has now chosen to work nights as a social worker so that he can be at home in the daytime with his three daughters, who are all under school age. Here he gives us a description of how days are regulated by the doings of the children and the time they need to eat:

> She gets up in the morning and gets them ready. I stay in bed a little longer, but then I get up and start breakfast for all of us. She goes to work and we eat. I clean and do the dishes. Then we usually play and read a book. In the middle of the day we have lunch, meals will usually take 45 minutes to an hour, depending on how impossible the middle one is [laughter]. Occasionally I have to feed her one small piece at a time. Then the two oldest ones go out to play, often with the neighbour kids. They'll run up to get the mail ... I'll go out and check them every half hour or so. The smallest girl usually sleeps from one o'clock until her mother comes back from work. She'll come along outside in the morning, usually with me. I'll be busy outside with various activities such as some carpentry or ... . There's not much time for my own activities, it's mostly family work.

Again we see that the child's time to sleep and eat regulates time. No strictly regulated time is described, rather flexible time that can be stretched according to need.

This is a perception of time different from the one that applies in the working lives of the fathers and to life in general, where time is more a matter of division and fragmentation, all inside the framework of the demand for a high tempo. This is what Hylland Eriksen (2001) describes as the 'tyranny of the moment', which may render it more difficult to create development and maturation. Fragmented experiences will dominate our lives.

Need-oriented care practice

These fathers have given their children time by taking their father's quota and leave, and they feel that it is important to use time with their children. As described above, they develop a care practice that is characterized by slow time controlled by the needs of the child. Thus there is also a development of competence as the fathers get to know their children by having the main responsibility and spending a great deal of time with them. It is easier for them to develop an understanding of the children's needs.

Arnfinn tells us about having responsibilities and using time:

> For my part I believe that there is a whole, like, both with the 14 days initially, and then the four weeks and my reduced hours at work in total that has given me a relationship with my children, in a way that the four weeks

are part of a whole. Now, four weeks are not that much, but anyway you get enough time that you manage to understand that it is difficult and demanding to be the person who has the total responsibility; that's what you notice during this period. But you do get quite close to your kids during that time.

and:

Sure, I believe the fact that you have so much time with your kids, you virtually learn how to read, how they tell you stuff which you maybe would have lost if you didn't have so much time. Because if you go to work and come home in the evening, the kids may be in a phase where they are tired and grumpy, and the father is also tired and grouchy, and you get this impression … and then you don't want to do anything with them. I think there is something there. But if you spend a whole day with them, then you, like, see the totality of the days that they have too, and understand why they are cross and crabby.

He points out that having the total responsibility is what makes him see how demanding care work is, and that he feels how close he gets to his children. He also claims that he has a learning experience when he points out that he is learning to 'read' his children. By spending a great deal of time with them, the day-to-day affairs of his children become a whole, making it easier for him to understand why, for example, they are grumpy and cross. He then avoids being the type of father who comes home from work and disciplines his children. Again we see how the children influence the father's care practice in this situation.

Another informant has had both the father's quota and stayed at home one day per week in the subsequent period of time with his children. He also tells how having the sole responsibility helps him to see both how care is time-consuming and that he is learning 'competence' in seeing and understanding his child. He relates the following when we ask about the importance of the leave for him:

You get so much time together with the kids and that in itself is positive, I think, the chance of following them from day to day and seeing how they behave and how they are doing in a day. And then you also gain insight into how demanding it is to have responsibility for children. That's really demanding, I must say. Actually it's much more demanding at times than being at work, I would claim. Because there's something going on all the time, and you're on guard all the time, so there's a rhythm to having responsibility for children that is quite demanding. Seeing that this is the way it is has value in itself.

From qualitative to quantitative time

These fathers practise what we have chosen to call slow time. Their experiences also help them to understand that care is about *using a great deal of time* with the children. Fathers describe that the children have initiated a process in them where focus is on quantitative time. They have experienced that care cannot be carried out in quality time, and a number of them have grown strongly critical of all mention of qualitative time. Rather, they have realized that you must be there for the child. This emerges through their responses to various questions, both regarding what they believe a good father must be and when we ask what they feel they are especially good at with their children.

Egil has found that it is important to be responsible alone, as this helps him to see things in another way. He really experienced having the responsibility alone when his wife got a job that meant she had to stay in Stockholm for long periods of time. Here is his idea of what a good father is:

> I think it is to spend a great deal of time with children, and not necessarily to have to do everything under the sun. *I have much more faith in quantity than in quality*, spending much time on your kids, being with them and just being outdoors with them so they see you. Allowing them to help and mess up the kitchen and run around, that's what I think. Both a good mother and a good father, there's no difference really between what is a good mother and a good father, simply the fact that they are there and they can be asked things and that they see that at least one of them is there generally all the time. [emphasis added]

Egil also illustrates that those fathers who have experienced the major importance of time, focus on quantitative time:

> A good father is one who has time and who can spend his time with the kids, that is I strongly believe that *we are not just talking about quality, but also about quantity*, and the fact that you are there. I really think this is important. They speak about quality and how it isn't really important how much you're together, but that it's important that when you're with them that you're really with them, but I believe that it is important for kids to have a father who actually is there. And that you do things with your kids. [emphasis added]

The outcome is that he has been with his children a lot:

> But there is always this, how we are concerned with how the kids should be close to both parents. This is essential for us, and we are always aware of this. And we have also seen results of this. Particularly our oldest kid, he's been Daddy's boy ever since he was a baby. When he was ten months old he refused to let his mother change his diapers, it was Daddy, Daddy all the

time, so he was very ... . He's only started to warm up to his mother again during the last couple of years. Yes, I sat with him on my lap every afternoon, and that was something we both loved, so he had lots of contact with his daddy, he was Daddy's boy. However, this has changed, it's not like that any more. But I think it was because he was so much with me, from the start.

This is contrasted to his own father when we asked if he had a father role model.

My father worked a lot, and when he came home we would often be in bed. What I mean is, I did see him a lot, but he didn't spend much of his time with us, and wasn't close to us. He never changed nappies, or dressed us, and I've spent lots of time doing that sort of thing. I've changed nappies and bathed them since they were infants, both of them. I think it's important, really, to have that kind of contact.

When we ask those fathers who have been home and have had the main responsibility for their children about what, in their opinion, makes a good father, many of them answer that a good father must spend time on his children. This is something they have done themselves, they have given their children time by taking leave from their jobs. Thus they have gained the realization that spending time is important. Giving children quantitative time becomes the ideal. When asked what a father should not be, one of the fathers said: 'He should ... I don't believe in just giving kids things and gifts, I believe more in giving kids time and attention.'

He is also one of the fathers in our sample who has allowed this idea to have consequences for his use of time, in that he declined to pursue a career at the expense of his children:

I want to pursue my career if this is what you call doing the best possible job in what is approximately normal working hours. I don't want to spend much more time than this at the expense of my children and my family, my wife. Thus I have less options and job opportunities. You can't work in the private sector then. If you're a civil engineer and working in the private sector then you have to expect to work around 60 hours a week. If you want to work for the university and do research you also have to expect that you'll have to work around 60 hours a week. I need to find a job which will pay me a reasonable salary and give me reasonably stimulating work, where I won't be a manager.

Home, but not alone

In this section we will look at the father–child interaction when the father takes his leave on a part-time basis and the mother is also at home. How does this situation influence father–child interaction?

Visiting in the mother's domain

The reason these mothers stay at home at the same time as the fathers is because of what childcare means to them in relation to their jobs. After they had children, these mothers adapted their working hours. Some work part time, some have extended their leave past the first year, and some have left their jobs indefinitely. For these mothers, whom we generally find in unskilled jobs, being a mother gives them greater meaning, satisfaction and self-confidence than their jobs, and this is vital for their identities. In such families there will apparently be little momentum in the restructuring of the father project. It goes without saying that the mother should stay at home. Parental leave is interpreted as a 'reward' for her. One of the fathers put it this way:

> She's the one who has carried the baby, and then she should … . It would have been wrong if I had been the one to enjoy the benefits. She had the drawbacks before (morning sickness etc.) and then that I should have the time off later. No way. That would be wrong.

It is generally thought that children have a special relationship to their mothers during the first year of the child's life (Ahrne and Roman 1997), most of all because of breastfeeding. Fathers see breastfeeding as a natural part of the relationship between the mother and the child in the first year, taking this as a sign that their own role is limited while the child is so young. 'It seems most natural to me that she's at home. She gave birth to the baby and all, and she breastfed the baby until it was more than a year old,' says one of the fathers. This appears as traditional, making it more difficult to discern any change processes. Emphasizing the bodily closeness between mother and child may be understood as an excuse for not taking more leave, but there is also an aspect of taking care of the mother. The fathers see a body that needs repair, and they interpret the leave as compensation or as a reward for the strain of pregnancy and birth. Thus this leave practice may be understood as part of the discourse on motherhood.

Father as a supporting player

The children in these families have had mothers as their main care person, and when the father's quota is due, normally towards the end of the first year, the mother has had the main responsibility for almost a year. The child and the mother have developed a close, bodily relationship through nursing, they have established daily routines together, and they have got to know each other by being together on a full-time basis. When he starts his leave, the father virtually comes into the picture like a 'visitor'. One of the fathers describes this situation: 'Because she was home, and had been home and knew everything and had the routines, I just continued the same routines. I did a bit more with the kids, but basically, it was all on her terms.'

The importance of the mother having stayed at home on leave and continuing to be home when the father is taking his father's quota emerges clearly when these fathers describe what they did while they were home. They cannot remember all that much. They describe it as being like the weekends. They participated a little more in the daily chores than if they had not taken leave, but they were unable to take responsibility and unable to 'test their mettle' alone with the child. Thus they were unable to develop the self-confidence they would have come by if they had been solely responsible. Nor can they tell the same stories about how demanding care work is. A young child generates a lot of routine work, and the role of these fathers is to be a supporting player for the mothers.

Being attentive

In contrast to the fathers who are at home alone with their children, these fathers do not argue that the most important thing is to give the children quantity time. Rather the term they use is to 'give the children attention', a term they use to designate their perception of their father project. To be attentive concerns the use of time. 'I believe they should have a lot of attention *all the time*', one of them says, specifying: 'The first thing I do when I get home then, is that the first kid I meet gets a hug and a kiss.' 'All the time', as he says, does not mean setting a priority between the job and the home. It is the time when he is at home that should be for the children. The attention is expressed by his giving the children a hug when he meets them as he walks in the door from work.

Anders, who appears to be a busy and even stressed man, describes 'attention' as follows:

> A good father, that's somebody who gives his kids attention, and who gives them attention when they demand it, and who is concerned with what they're doing, who is concerned with them *then and there* and like, well let's call it concentration. Like somebody who can bring them up, who gives them a defined framework, or perhaps clear limitations for what they should, and may or may not do. That you create some kind of framework so they know what they may or may not do, and who can answer questions and ... [emphasis added]

As we see here, there are a number of aspects to being a father that he finds important. In addition to upbringing, he wants to give them attention, 'when they demand it – then and there'. However, what kind of time is he speaking about? He continues:

> I think we give them attention all the time, *because the time is so short*. As I said, I get home at five thirty and then there is dinner, and there is very little time before they go to bed, so they have, like, well, we try to see some news, right, headlines, but they are around us all the time. We do cuddle

with them a lot, see, put them on our laps and horse around, so they probably have 100 per cent attention when we're there.' [emphasis added]

The attention he gives his children concerns the time from when he comes
home until his children go to bed. Then they receive full attention, but he also
says that during this period of time the family will prepare and eat their dinner,
and they will watch the news on television. Perhaps the children also watch children's television. Thus there is no development of the cyclic, slow time where
tasks with the children determine how the time is spent. Rather the time spent
with the children is high-tempo time. There are many things that have to be
pressed into the brief time available in the late afternoon and early evening.

Here the time question concerns whether the children are in focus during
the available time, i.e. after working hours, and not necessarily that the children
get more time. The children must be adapted to the available time, not the
other way round, where work is adapted to the children. For some of these
fathers the competition between work and children is hard when it comes to
time. But the ideal of giving children attention has yet another aspect that concerns how work shapes the father's care. Being a good father means giving the
children attention after work *even if they are tired*. Even though the job is ardu-
ous, good parents need to always pay attention to their children. If the mother
has been at home with them during the day, afternoons become particularly
important for the father:

> The question is also how tired you are, how patient. Immediately after din-
> ner it is nice to relax a little and be quiet and then it may be that … you
> simply can't manage always. And when she has them all day, then I try to
> take them as much as possible in the evening, be together with them as
> much as possible, I really feel that's right.

What these statements tell us is that not only does work take the fathers' time,
it also drains them of the energy that is necessary to be a good father and make
something of the afternoons with the children. Fathers attempt to compensate
for this through extra mobilization.

'Can't you see he's thirsty?'

As we saw above, the fathers who were at home alone developed a need-
oriented care practice precisely because they spent much time together with
the children. Those fathers who have not had sole responsibility for the
children are also able to see that spending much time with their children is
important. For example, they understand that the mother's extended period of
leave is important for her contact with the children. Magnar makes a major
point of the fact that the children are more closely tied to the mother, they
communicate better with her and she knows their signals better because she is
home with them all day. He says:

It's easier for her to 'read' them because they spend so much time with her. … she has had time to become thoroughly familiar with them for better or worse. Needless to say, I know their good and bad sides too, but not in the same way, really. She's able to interpret the children way before I can. I need more information to determine what … . Of course she has been with them in the day, and … this is what it's about, I think this is the cause.

Magnar compares himself to his wife who will be on leave for the second year running. 'She'll say, "Can't you see he's thirsty?", but I can't see this because I am not with him 24 hours a day', he says. The children thus are more easily drawn to those they spend the most time with, he believes.

Nevertheless, Magnar feels that his son got to know him better during the quota period even if it was part time. Others point to the same conclusion – that the father's quota constitutes a break with going to work every day, thus allowing for the child to become familiar with the father. The fact that the mother is at home at the same time is less important when the quota means he can avoid coming home from work and feeling too tired to give the child the attention needed from a good father.

More fun with older children

The fact that the mother has had the dominant position in the care arena at least during the first year has led fathers to move their father project a little further along the time scale. It is when they start speaking about their children when they have grown older that they get excited, feeling they can master it and cope better. 'It's more challenging and that sort of thing when they're older. It's more enjoyable and more important,' one of them says. It is obvious that these fathers feel more confident in the role of a father of slightly older children. When the children are able to start kicking a ball or doing other 'fun things', the father's role acquires more meaning for them. Therefore, when they talk about their father's project, it is care of the slightly older children that is in focus.

Because they emphasize their roles as fathers in relation to slightly older children, play has a prominent place in their narratives about how they perform their care. Children prefer their fathers for rough types of play, and fathers feel that they gain importance through this. They feel that they are better able to display their good side as fathers when the children are older. As one of them states: 'We'll throw some snowballs and stuff, see? We'll balance on the rail and jump down and do a somersault, right?' What many of these fathers like to do together with their children takes place outdoors:

What I like most is to take my kids fishing. It's not all that often, but taking them outside into the forest … .They're quite curious and … teach them stuff, that's the most fun. But we do many other things too. It's fun to play with Lego and things like that too.

Another father tells us how much his boy of four enjoys being outside, and that one of the parents has to come too, this usually being the father. Thus father and son can be found in the sandbox and on the football field. Being outside is an aspect of the daddy role where the environment gives him positive feedback. 'But I really enjoy being outside, like. I like doing small things and keeping my children happy, pushing them when they're sitting on the swing, you know, things like that.'

Playing, taking short hikes and other outdoor activities have been considered a type of care that typically concerns doing something side by side. This is a form of intimacy that is often practised among men, one that could be said to be the traditional way for men to be together. One of those keenest to hike in the woods with his children says:

> It's really important for me to tell them that I love them and ... be nice to them and hug them too. Physical contact is important to me. Yes, I think it's very important for the kids to feel that they have somebody who loves them and that they feel they can rely on you.

As this quote illustrates, even if they are not letting go of what they find very important, that is to do things together, they are enjoying each other's company and letting the children know how much they love them.

Discussion and conclusion

In this chapter it has been our aim to analyse the effect that the introduction of the father's quota has had on the relationship between fathers and their children. Our primary goal has been to focus on how children influence the care practices of fathers. This implies that we see children as active agents who contribute to the production of the adult world and their own place in it. In turn this helps us to say something about the consequences the new leave rights have had for children.

Our analysis examined two different contexts. We asked whether the influence of children on fathers' behaviour was less observable when mothers were present. Therefore we distinguished between fathers who had sole responsibility for the child during the father's quota period and those who did not. We found that when fathers were 'home alone', i.e. they used the father's quota or an extended period of leave while the mother went back to work, completely different processes would arise than when the mother was at home at the same time. When the father is completely absent from work and has the main responsibility for the child alone he becomes aware of what we have called 'slow time', where the child's needs are in focus. In this situation the father also develops a need–oriented care practice because he learns to 'read' the child. The child's agency is thus allowed to influence the father's care practices.

When the mother is at home at the same time, this type of process is not initiated. The father also continues his paid work part time. Then the mother's main responsibility for the child is not interrupted and the father acquires the role of supporting player for the mother. In these cases the mother continues her close relationship with the child, reading and translating the child's needs for the father. Consequently the child has no independent influence on the father's care practices. It is the mother and not the child who interacts with the father. The father will therefore not get to know his child in the same way and care practices based on knowing the child well are not developed. Thus he feels more at home with older children.

Thus we see that the different contexts result in quite different conditions for the development of fathers' care practices. When a father takes complete leave from his work and has the main responsibility for the child while the mother goes back to work, an interaction is established between child and father where the child more clearly becomes an actor who influences the care given by the father. When the father does not take this break from his job and the mother does not go back to paid work, the care the father gives is developed much more in interaction with the mother. If we return to one of the intentions of the father's quota, which was to strengthen the contact between child and father, we see that this primarily occurs in the context we have called 'home alone'.

The introduction in 1993 of the father's quota in Norwegian parental leave legislation came about as a result of the intention to encourage the father's contact with and care for his children. Another objective was to share the benefits and burdens of working life and family life between men and women. Our analyses show that the father's quota may also be seen as a child discourse in family policy. It reveals that if it is used as intended, namely to encourage the father to be the main care-giver, it can contribute to the welfare of young children.

References

Ahrne, G. and Roman, C. (1997) *Hemmet, barnen och makten. Förhandlingar om arbete och pengar i familjen*, SOU: 139, Stockholm: Arbetsmarknadsdepartementet.

Brandth, B. and Kvande, E. (1989) 'Like barn deler best', *Nytt om kvinneforskning* 13(3): 8–17.

Brandth, B. and Kvande, E. (1991) 'Når likhet blir ulikhet. Foreldres forhandlinger om barneomsorg', I.R. Haukaa (ed.) *Nye kvinner. Nye menn*, Oslo: Ad Notam.

Brandth, B. and Kvande, E. (1998) 'Masculinity and child care: the reconstruction of fathering', *Sociological Review*, 26, 2: 293–313.

Corsaro, W.A. (1997) *The Sociology of Childhood*, Thousand Oaks, Ca.: Pine Forge Press.

Holter, Ø.G. and Aarseth, H. (1993) *Menns livssammenheng*, Oslo: Ad Notam.

Hylland Eriksen, T. (2001) *Øyeblikkets tyranni: rask og langsom tid i informasjonssamfunnet*, Oslo: Aschehoug.

Morgan, D.H.J (1996) *Family Connections*, Cambridge: Polity Press.

Rikstrygdeverket (2000): Basic Report. Oslo: National Insurance Association.

5 Children's experience of their parents' divorce[1]

Margaret Robinson, Ian Butler, Lesley Scanlan, Gillian Douglas and Mervyn Murch

A substantial body of research has developed over recent years exploring the impact of parental divorce on the growing number of children whose families break up (see Rodgers and Pryor 1998; Haskey 1996, 1997). At the same time however, not only in the sociology of childhood (James and Prout 1997; Qvortrup 1994; Butler 1996) but also in various areas of welfare practice (e.g. Butler 1999) the critical role played by children in fundamental social processes, including family dissolution and re-formation, has been (re)discovered and acknowledged. An increasing sense of children's agency (i.e. their capacity to act positively in matters that concern them), as well as their capacity to bring new perspectives on familiar problems, has brought forth an exciting research agenda exploring children's lived experience. Increasingly, this experience is reported upon and understood from children's own points of view and challenges the narrow focus that had previously been maintained on the consequences that the actions of adults have on children's lives.

The study reported here (Douglas *et al.* 2000; Butler *et al.* 2000) was funded by the ESRC as part of the '*Children 5–16*' research programme. It is illustrative not only of children's active involvement in the process of their parents' divorce but also represents a contribution towards understanding divorce and family breakup from the point of view of those with good reason to know what this implies for children, namely children themselves.

The study sample comprised families drawn at random from the population of divorce cases (315 cases/families) heard in six courts across south Wales and the south west of England. Together these six courts gave a mix of city, town and country, increasing the likelihood of our sample being not only random but also representative. Each case involved at least one child aged between eight and 14 years. Analysis of data from court records indicates that the 70 families who finally took part in the study were representative of the initial random court sample across key variables (e.g. child's age, gender and relationship to the divorcing adults). On average children took part within 15 months (standard deviation (SD) = 2 months) of the divorce being granted (i.e. decree nisi being granted). Both qualitative and quantitative data were collected from each child and the parent with whom the child lived (resident parent). This allowed triangulation both in terms of the type (qualitative and quantitative) and the source (child and parent) of data. (See Douglas *et al.* 2000 for a fuller description of the sampling procedure and method.)

Our final sample consisted of 104 children and young people (51 girls and 53 boys) who were, on average, 11 and a half years old (SD = 26 months) when they took part in the study. Through content analysis of their interview transcripts, several broad, overlapping themes were identified: 'finding out'; 'telling others'; 'change'; 'coping and support'; 'parent–child relationships'; and 'parents' new relationships'. Using data gathered under some of these headings, in this chapter we illustrate what it is like for children to live through parental separation and divorce. In doing this, we will demonstrate not only how children revealed themselves as active participants in the process of their parents' divorce, but as articulate, thoughtful individuals able to think reflectively and constructively about their personal experience and its implications for others.

Understanding the process

The children in our study typically experienced family breakdown and the consequent disruption to their everyday lives as a form of crisis. This is not to suggest that their responses were pathological. For we, like Rapoport, simply define crisis as 'an upset in a steady state' (Rapoport 1970: 276). This steady state has also been referred to as homeostasis or psychological equilibrium and the crisis as a turning point, where 'the individual's coping resources have been surpassed and a new approach has to be developed' (Thompson 2000: 79). The attempt to regain a new sense of balance in their lives is a defining characteristic of most children's reactions to the fact that their family was breaking up.

The immediate consequences of children 'finding out' that their parents were divorcing typically included an acute sense of shock, disbelief and emotional distress. Even where children had become aware of difficulties in their parents' relationship though direct observation of arguments or even domestic violence, the effect of a parent leaving was immediate and profound. Where children had been told that their parents were going to divorce, and most (70.9 per cent, 73 out of 103 respondents) said they were told, they were given little information. Additionally, less than half of the children (43.1 per cent, 44 out of 102 respondents) were given any explanation of what divorce would mean for them.

In this sense, few children had been actively 'prepared' by their parents for the separation, even where parents themselves had planned the process. Libby, aged 13, described the feelings experienced by a number of children that divorce was regarded by parents as essentially an adult matter:

> It was like, 'Oh well, it's not really your problem, you don't have to go through all the divorce things', but no one seemed to realise I was sort of *there*. They were all concerned with what they were doing.
>
> (Libby, aged 13)

It should be remembered that for family members, divorce was a new, uncharted and emotionally charged experience. One effect of this, reported frequently by both children and their resident parents, was that they were unsure what to say or how to say it. Parents said that they did not know what was happening themselves, so did not know what to tell their children. Children, in their turn, felt that they did not know how to ask for information that they felt they needed.

Another stumbling block to communication, again reported by both children and parents, was a reluctance to talk about the divorce. This reluctance was borne out of an expressed need to protect the other person. Children and parents each wanted to spare the other's feelings and save them from additional distress and upset.

> I didn't feel like, I mean, you know it's a bit depressing to ask somebody who is getting divorced about divorce, you know!
>
> (Shaun, aged 12)

What parents perhaps did not appreciate was that in trying to protect their children, they ran the risk of compounding the child's confusion and uncertainty about the future. Most children felt information was vital in helping them understand, cope with and adapt to the crisis of family breakup and most children reported that they would have preferred almost any dialogue at all to the uncertainty experienced through a lack of information and explanation.

Oliver: I thought it was all fine, except for the fact that they were all *shouting* at each other down the phone and stuff like that and knowing that Roger [father] wouldn't let me know things, hide it all from me. I could see what was going on but he just wouldn't tell me.

Interviewer: What sort of things did you want to know?

Oliver: Enough to keep me not confused. You know, it would be all this rowing and stuff and what it would be like, 'What?! What's this about now?' And he wouldn't explain anything to me ... you know when is this going to be ended, and stuff like that.

(Oliver, aged 13)

Although children wanted to be informed about and involved in what was happening in their families, they drew a clear distinction between the formal and the emotional, the legal and the personal. Where most children (92.8 per cent, 90 out of 97 respondents) felt they had a right to be told about their parents' intention to divorce, less than half reported either that they would have wanted more information on legal aspects (49.5 per cent, 50 out of 101 respondents) or that knowing more about the legal process would have helped them cope (45.5 per cent, 45 out of 99 respondents). Children felt that knowing about legal proceedings was unlikely to help them deal with the all-important personal, emotional and practical tasks their parents' divorce had created:

I don't think I would have liked to know more [about the legal process] but I wouldn't have really minded if I didn't know anything about it ... . It's more the emotional side – how other people feel about it.

(Nick, aged 12)

These findings may relate to the fact that only five (4.8 per cent) of the children interviewed were themselves the subject of legal proceedings. The legal aspects of divorce were not directly relevant to the vast majority of children. Not surprisingly, the children's understanding of the legal process was poor. In the absence of information from parents, what most children knew about divorce was gathered from friends or gleaned from television or cinema. Unfortunately, media portrayals were a source of inaccurate, often Americanized, information.

I wasn't told, but Dad said something about they were going to court ... I thought they were gonna get, like ... arrested.

(Stephen, aged ten)

I've seen it on *EastEnders*. I've worked it out from there! I know it from there and I know it from other TV series.

(Josie, aged 12)

The lack of any parental 'explanation' left children largely unable to account for their parents' divorce in anything but superficial, 'symptomatic' terms. Overall, children expressed a strong desire to be kept informed and to be involved. The value in this of helping them obtain some cognitive control over the crisis and restore a sense of 'normality' and balance in their lives was a characteristic feature of children's accounts.

Coping and support networks

Children showed a considerable capacity to seek out and use appropriate and available help using both their own resources and the aid of other people. For many, a key strategy was to talk to someone either to gain reassurance or advice or to be listened to. Indeed less than a third (28.3 per cent, 28 out of 99 respondents) said they had told no one at all about their parents' divorce. Children differentiated the kinds of help they wanted and chose their confidants accordingly.

I think that talking is one of the best ways that helps. You can get over it if you've got some rabbits or any kind of pet. Just talk to them, they might not be able to speak but it's very good.

(Michael, aged ten)

Parents perhaps seemed the most obvious providers of information, advice and emotional support, but, as we have implied, not all children found this to be the case. Some children explained this was because their parents did not understand what it was like for the children, others that their parents had 'moved on' and did not want to be reminded of the past.

> 'My mum, because she was upset, she didn't really talk to me much … she was always upset and I couldn't really say to her, 'I'm upset, I need a really good chat with you'.
>
> (Louise, aged 12)

Children did not readily consider siblings as a source of support. They explained, for example, that siblings were too involved in the crisis themselves; were experiencing the divorce differently; were too young to provide the support and understanding needed; or simply that they did not get on that well enough to be of support to each other. Of the 97 children with siblings, less than a third (32 per cent, 31 children) said they had talked to their brother or sister; of those who had, only 20 said it had helped.

> It probably would've helped if I could talk to Jane [sister], but we're always fighting, so it wouldn't work.
>
> (Ted, aged ten)

Many children reported that grandparents were a particularly valued source of time, attention and reassurance. Grandparents' homes often provided 'safe' or 'neutral' territory where children could take refuge from what was happening at home.

> My nan … because she'd let me speak my mind and she'd let me say what I'd have to say.
>
> (Robin, aged 11)

For most children, though, friends were their key source of support. Of the 90 children who said they had a best friend, nearly three-quarters of them (72.2 per cent, 65 children) said they had talked to this person; nearly all of them (56 children) found it helpful. Close friends were chosen as confidants not only because they could be trusted but also because they were more likely to understand, more likely to 'speak the same language'. Friends whose parents had separated were particularly valued as a source of information as well as understanding.

> I told my best friend Joe because his parents are divorced and he sort of like, knew what I was talking about, he was sort of helping me a bit.
>
> (Ted, aged ten)

Children's need to confide in someone was almost always tempered by their desire to retain a substantial degree of control over exactly who found out and when. Our findings show that telling someone about the divorce and wanting to 'keep it secret' are not mutually exclusive. Whilst most children reported that they had told someone, nearly two-thirds (63.0 per cent, 63 out of 100 respondents) said they kept it secret from at least some people.

> I just told my closest friends … didn't want *everybody* to find out. I just wanted a few people to know.
>
> (Nick, aged 12)

Children's faith in their chosen confidant was founded on an expectation that neither their trust nor their privacy would be compromised. Their wish to manage and control the way in which the world at large came to know about their changed circumstances was built around concerns about being thought 'different', being teased or being made the subject of 'gossip'. In a few cases, these fears were realized.

> Well, I've kept it a secret from my worst friend 'cos he'll probably tease me and all that. I told one of my friends and he called me 'Dad-less'.
>
> (Jonny, aged ten)

As well as talking, children recognized the value of activity and distraction as ways of coping. For many, taking part in sports and playing with friends not only helped them maintain some semblance of a normal life, they also provided a safe and effective outlet for emotions.

> I make myself happy, I go out to my friends, have a laugh, go down the park and sometimes I watch a video – a funny video. I watch that to cheer myself up.
>
> (Jonny, aged ten)

> I suppose I started watching *Star Trek* round that time, you know, kind of sci-fi fantasy. I suppose it's something to escape to.
>
> (Robert, aged 13)

Whilst, at some point during the crisis, most children found crying a useful strategy, many were aware that this often had to be done in private.

Rosie: Sometimes I get really upset and I cry in my room because I think everything's gone. It's all gone away, I haven't got anything.

Interviewer: Is there any particular times when you feel like that?

Rosie: Sometimes it just happens. It normally happens when I come up and go into my bedroom.

Interviewer: Do you tell Mummy if you feel like that?

Rosie: No, I just quickly wash my face and come downstairs and act happy. Then I forget about it and then I'm normal.

> (Rosie, aged ten)

A number of children reported how quiet reflection, sometimes writing down their thoughts, helped them think through what was happening to them and put matters into perspective. This more contemplative strategy gave children some cognitive control over events and, for some, provided the opportunity to reframe their experiences in a more positive light.

> 'Well, I just thought that I'm really lucky like, I still get to see my dad and my mum. Not like just stuck with the one, and that John's [step-dad] a nice person, that he's not someone who's totally strict and nasty.'
>
> (Robert, aged 13)

As well as seeking support from others, children also reported being a source of emotional and practical support for their parents. This latter often took the form of greater participation in household chores. Emotional support usually took the form of reassurance, especially for the resident parent, and the age of the child was no predictor of the creativeness or genuineness of their efforts.

> 'I try to talk to my mother, like if she gets upset, I tell her like, 'Yeah, well, let's just get it sorted out' and things like that and she sort of perks up a bit, and then I just make her laugh about it. And say, 'Just you think how it's gonna be' if things got better, like if we were going to be millionaires, win the lottery and things like that. And I goes, 'What would you do with a million pounds?' She went, 'I'd go and buy a villa in Minorca'. We used to go [child laughs], 'Yeah, in your dreams' and we used to laugh about it, and things like that and she sort of perks up a bit and so yeah, we do help each other through it.
>
> (Claire, aged ten)

Evaluating change

Children largely viewed change brought about by the divorce in terms of loss and most (79.9 per cent, 79 out of 99 respondents) realised the separation would bring about changes in their lives. Particularly in the early stages, few children had any clear ideas about what would change, so could only speculate about the possibilities of moving house, changing school, losing contact with friends or the effects on their family's finances.

> I knew then that we'd probably have to move house ... because Dad had left we wouldn't be able to afford to keep the house on our own, so I knew we'd probably have to move house, which would be quite a big change. I was hoping we'd still be able to stay in the area because all my friends are here and everything. That's all I really thought about really. I didn't really think there'd be anything else.
>
> (Julie, aged 12)

Children expressed the belief that stability and continuity in at least some of their circumstances helped them cope with other, more inevitable changes, such as one parent living elsewhere. Not surprisingly, it was this change and the 'empty space' it created, that the majority of children felt most acutely.

> I thought, oh! It's gonna all change, we might have to move … I thought my father's going to be living miles away, I'll never be able to see him again, my mother will be upset all the time.
>
> (Daniel, aged 14)

> It's very hard at first because you just don't want them to split up. You'll be very sad at the beginning because of not having your dad around, but then it'll just come automatically that your dad lives somewhere else and life will just be normal.
>
> (Emy, aged ten)

Almost all children reported a change in the quality of their relationship with parents. Those relationships which had previously been positively regarded by children, most easily survived the crisis. Previously poor child–parent relationships were subsequently characterized by higher levels of negative effect, unresolved conflict and less satisfactory relationships between the parents themselves. Children who experienced poor child–parent relationships frequently expressed anger, often directed at the 'blameworthy' or absent parent.

Interviewer: You said in the beginning you became more angry, more aggressive. Do you think that was a result of your dad going?

Nick: Yeah, 'cos before I used to be like … like, I always used to be friendly and stuff but if someone like shouts stuff about me … like I lose my temper with them.

Interviewer: Why do you think that was?

Nick: Cos I'm like taking my anger out on people I shouldn't rather than my dad. I should be taking all my anger out on him.

(Nick, aged 12)

In a few cases children attributed their anger to the absent parent's failure to keep promises. In the following example, in particular, the child felt his father had broken his promise when he left his mother to live with someone else.

> What I'd really like to say is, 'Well, Dad, why did you break a promise?' He basically lied to me, in that sense. He said he'd keep a promise that you'll stay here with Mum and you'll never leave her. And he said, 'No, I didn't', and I said, 'You did, it's all part of marriage you mustn't leave them'. And he *promised* that he'll never leave her. So basically he's trying to keep a secret from me. Because I've never lied to him before, so why should he

lie to me? ... .Why couldn't he just say, 'No', [to the new partner] ... .You could've just kept a promise and not broken it, because you broke a promise to my mum, and I'm not going to let you know any of my secrets because you might break it. You broke the promise ...'

(Joe, aged eight)

Overall, despite children's anxieties, most found that the changes set in train by their parents' separation were not as bad as they had anticipated; indeed, some found there were benefits including their own deepening awareness and understanding of themselves and of other people and, quite often, improved relationships with parents.

Well, he's more happier and more cheerful and so I think they're better now 'cos they got a divorce. They both say that they're glad now because they're still friends now and they're getting along better and it's peaceful, more happy because they're not arguing.

(Sioned, aged 12)

I see them [parents] as completely different people now ... I don't know how they see themselves or each other. Because I've spent time with them separately I've got to know how *they* are, sort of by themselves ... . Now I know them individually.

(Helen, aged 15)

One major change children (and their parents) faced was the strong possibility that parents would form new relationships. For the children whose parents had not yet done so, the prospect was generally favourable: although they might have reservations (and many did), they said they would be pleased to see their parents happy and settled. Where one parent was already in a new relationship, typically children felt it was only fair that their other parent should find someone new too.

I cannot stand it when Mum's with somebody and Dad's not being with somebody.

(Sophie, aged 15)

However, new partners presented difficulties for many parents. Parents seemed to find it difficult to know how to introduce their children to their new partners, or even to tell their children that they had new partners. Several children recounted how new relationships which initially had been kept secret were suddenly and clumsily revealed.

Mum didn't tell me that they were going out with each other at first. But what upset me a bit was that she didn't tell me ... . Mum was going out and she said she was going out [with boyfriend] but she said she was just

going out with him like a friend. Just a friend. I watched them go, walk up
the road, and then I saw them kiss when they thought they were out of
range of the house.

(Libby, aged 13)

With Dad, it was just one day we were going into town and he said, 'Oh, you
know your mother's met someone? ... and I can find someone else ... well,
I have.' And he said, 'We're going to meet them in town now, and then we're
going to go swimming later,' or something like that. And you're sort of,
'OK', and you're all sort of in one go, meeting them and going into town.

(Rhiannon, aged 14)

In these situations (as in many others) children preferred their parents to be
open with them. They wanted to be given the opportunity and the time to get
used to the idea of their parent's new partner, as well as to the new partner
him/herself. Once acquainted with new partners, children typically were
reluctant to view them as a substitute or as alternative parents and resented
their attempts to 'act' like parents, especially in matters of discipline.

Mum started in this dating agency thing, she got a boyfriend, and he tried
to be a dad to me ... . He tried to get me to do more things, like acting
like a dad to me and I didn't like it. I told my mum that, I don't like him
... he moved in here and tried to change everything.

(Molly, aged 13)

Perhaps inevitably, children often felt a new partner resulted in their parent
having less time, and indeed love, available for them.

Sometimes when I see Heather [dad's new partner] ... I feel upset because
I feel, sometimes I think to myself, Heather doesn't belong here. My mum
should be in her place ... but I don't tell my dad, sometimes I think my
daddy likes Heather more than me.

(Rosie, aged ten)

Where parents remarried, children saw the wedding itself as a key moment.
Children were not always invited to the wedding and this caused hurt, even
amongst children who would have refused the invitation anyway.

My dad got married. He got married without telling us. He didn't tell us
for four months. So I was really upset about it. I said, 'Why didn't you tell
me when you got married?' Then Trish [step-mum] bustling in, she said,
'Well, we weren't talking at the time, there was no point telling you' ... .
Well, I wouldn't have gone, but I just felt like saying it. She said, 'Well, there
was no point, was there, you wouldn't have wanted to come.'

(Cathy, aged 13)

For the most part, children did not think that their parents' divorce had influenced their view on whether they themselves would marry or not. Having lived through their parents' divorce had made a number of children more wary, but equally they felt the experience would stand them in good stead and help them avoid the mistakes they had seen their parents make.

> It's actually given me more *things not to do* … like to discuss more with my wife, when I'm married and that, so it's actually helped me, I think. [emphasis added]
>
> (Daniel, aged 14)

Negotiating arrangements

Finally we will consider children's active involvement in managing post-divorce changes. Most children expressed the view that it was only right and fair that they should be involved in decisions, particularly questions about whom they should live with (56.9 per cent, 58 out of 102 respondents) and staying in touch with their non-resident parent (86.3 per cent, 88 out of 102 respondents), since these question very directly affected them.

> It would have been, well … not nice, but a *good* thing to be *asked*. Because if they'd asked my parents I know my dad would be saying, 'They've got to live with me,' and my mum would be saying, 'They've got to live with me.' So … I knew if I was *asked* I'd say my mum. Still, I'd feel that I said it and they didn't *make* me live with one of them.
>
> (Louise, aged 12)

Children appreciated that decisions over residence were more constrained by practical consideration (e.g. parents day-to-day availability to provide childcare) than decisions over contact:

> I think Mum probably decided [about residence] … 'cos, well, Dad had a sort of early job 'til a late job and Mum was part time so it sort of fitted in with school and stuff.
>
> (Rhiannon, aged 14)

Regardless of children's views, though, it is important to note that only a minority of children reported that they were consulted over the crucial decisions of their residence (43.7 per cent, 45 out of 103 respondents) and contact (41.7 per cent, 43 out of 103 respondents).

> *Interviewer:*   Who decided where you were going to live?
> *Joe:*   Mum did, even though it was meant to be us. She just decided that we were going to live here … so we had to stay here … it was already decided that we had to live here.
>
> (Joe, aged eight)

Children clearly understood that they could not unilaterally make decisions about residence and contact, indeed few wanted to carry that burden on their own, but most appreciated being asked.

> I was glad I was asked, 'cos I thought, yeah, I've got an opinion.
>
> (Daniel, aged 14)

> Yeah, 'cos really it wouldn't be fair if they were forced to go and live with the parent they didn't want to live with.
>
> (Nick, aged 12)

Perhaps unsurprisingly, children who reported that they had some involvement in their residence or contact arrangements also reported higher degrees of satisfaction with the arrangements subsequently made.

Contact, more than residence, was subject to a degree of continuing negotiation between parents and children. In a very real sense, contact, in both its practical and emotional senses, had to be 'learned'. Children described the practical difficulties of having 'two homes' and the tiresomeness of constantly packing and repacking bags; they commented on the lack of space at their non-resident parent's (often temporary) new home; they spoke of the difficulties in spending time with parents' new partners, either because they simply didn't get on with them or because they felt that they might be seen to be betraying the parent with whom they usually lived; they talked of how it was often difficult to find things to do that suited their brothers or sisters (with whom otherwise they might not spend a great deal of time) and how sometimes they would have appreciated seeing their parent on their own. On a practical level, children demonstrated their growing capacity to manage their 'time–maps' in ways and to a degree that children from 'intact' families seldom have to and they did so in situations that were sometimes highly charged emotionally and in which they had to develop a capacity to weigh and balance a number of competing demands.

Overall, children's descriptions of their feelings about contact with their non-resident parent highlighted the emotional 'highs' and 'lows' that they experienced as a result of spending part of their lives with one parent and part with the other. While many of the children looked forward to and enjoyed contact with their non-resident parent they often, at the same time, missed their resident parent and other elements of normal home life. Likewise, when at home with their resident parent, they missed their non-resident parent and looked forward to their next contact.

> *Interviewer:*   How do you feel if you're about to move from one home to the next home?
>
> *Maggie:*   If I'm in one I miss the other 'cos then if I'm at the other I'll miss the other one. I miss both of them really. When I'm here … whether I'm here or I'm over at my mum's.
>
> (Maggie, aged ten)

Whilst children were concerned that contact arrangements should be 'fair' to all parties, they were particularly concerned that they should remain flexible. Given what we have noted already about the importance of friends and children's desire for continuity and 'normality', it was important to children that the 'rest of their lives' were also factored into contact arrangements.

> I wouldn't like to see [Dad] every half-term because like, for a week I can stay over at friends' houses and see my friends a lot and friends are important to me and I couldn't see him every other weekend because I wouldn't see my friends then. I don't know, I would like it to be more, but it really couldn't.
>
> (Damian, aged 13)

Conclusion

Our research clearly demonstrated that children are involved in the process of their parents' divorce in that they experience the events probably on much the same emotional terms as the adults. Their initial reaction is one of disequilibrium and emotional upset. This is followed by a period of adjustment in which new domestic arrangements have to be negotiated and learned in an atmosphere that can remain emotionally turbulent for some time. The children in our study demonstrated a resilience and coping capacity which certainly might surprise parents and possibly many professionals. Overall, children wanted to be told what was going on, they needed an ongoing supply of information to help them understand, cope and adapt. They wanted to be involved in the important decisions that were made about them during this life-altering time. Being left out of discussions not only tended to increase their anxiety and upset, it also hampered their attempts to reach a new sense of balance or normality in their lives. Regaining cognitive control of events was central to most children's attempts to reach a new 'steady state'.

Children also showed how they acquired new skills in managing the time-maps of their altered lives, in maintaining a compassionate interest in what was happening to their parents, and in most cases, reaching a settled understanding of what had happened to them. All this is to point up that children do not experience their parents' divorce passively: they are involved, creative and resourceful participants.

Children are the best witnesses to their own experience and we, as adults, have as much to gain from our involvement with them as they have from their involvement with us. As one young person put it:

Interviewer: Is there anything that could be done, that would help you? By other people? Or … ?

Child: Probably, if more people understood what it was like to go through divorce, and if they knew what it was like to experience how bad it was.

Interviewer: What sort of people would need to know?

Child: Probably more children would need to know. More adults would have to understand children's feelings, others have to understand what children feel. Not what *they* feel, but what the children feel about it.

Interviewer: Do you think any adults do understand what children feel?

Child: Some of them do, but a lot think, well, they have feelings, but they don't care that much about it, because they're only kids, they don't like, care but a lot of children do suffer from it and they just don't know what to do. They're like me! They don't know what to do [laughs].

References

Butler, I. (1996) 'Children and the sociology of childhood' in I. Butler and I. Shaw (eds) *A Case of Neglect? Children's Experiences and the Sociology of Childhood*, Aldershot: Avebury.

Butler, I. (1999) 'Children's views of their involvement in child protection processes' in D. Shemmings (ed.) *Involving Children in Family Support and Child Protection Processes*, DoH/SO: London.

Butler, I., Douglas, G., Fincham, F.D., Murch, M.A., Robinson, M., and Scanlan, L. (2000) 'Children's perspective and experience of divorce', *Children 5–16 Research Programme Briefings*, Economic and Social Research Council, UK December.

Douglas, G., Butler, I., Murch, M. and Fincham, F.D. (2000) 'Children's perspective and experience of the divorce process', *Children 5–16 Growing into the Twenty-First Century*, end of award report, ref L129251014, Economic and Social Research Council, UK.

Haskey, J. (1996) 'The portion of married couples who divorce: past patterns and current prospects', *Population Trends*, 83: 25–36.

Haskey, J. (1997) 'Children who experience divorce in their family', *Population Trends*, 87: 5–10.

James, A. and Prout, A. (eds) (1997) *Constructing and Reconstructing Childhood: Contemporary Issues in the Sociological Study of Childhood* (2nd edn), London: Falmer Press.

Qvortrup, J. (1994) *Recent Developments in Research and Thinking on Childhood*, paper given at XXXI International Sociological Association Committee on Family Research, London, April.

Rapoport, L. (1970) 'Crisis intervention as a brief mode of treatment', in R.W. Roberts and R.H. Nee (eds) *Theories of Social Casework*, Chicago: University of Chicago Press.

Rodgers, B. and Pryor, J. (1998) *Divorce and Separation – The Outcomes for Children*, Joseph Rowntree Foundation, York.

Thompson, N. (2000) 'Crisis intervention', in M. Davies (ed.) *The Blackwell Encyclopaedia of Social Work*, Oxford: Blackwell.

6 Children coping with parental divorce

What helps, what hurts?

Kari Moxnes

The purpose of this chapter is to study how children cope with their parents' divorce, what children say was and is difficult and painful, but also what they consider helpful. Through analysis of children's divorce stories, my focus will be on how they experienced the changes that they had to endure during the divorce process.

Most studies of the consequences of divorce for children have used large quantitative samples comparing children from nuclear families with children with divorced parents, or parental reports on how their children have coped during the divorce process (Thompson and Amato 1999; McLanahan and Sandefur 1994; Furstenberg and Cherlin 1991). The aim of these studies has been to identify factors that can increase the risk of a negative development for the children post-divorce. A number of studies have shown that changes such as loss of economic and social capital and impairment of parent–child relations are major risks. Even though these studies have provided valuable knowledge, they are insufficient because the children are usually seen as objects of research and as passive victims of their parents' divorce (Andenæs 1995; Alanen 1992). In order to understand the consequences of divorce for children, the children must also be the subjects of research and seen as social actors who participate in their parents' divorce. With increasing age, children, whether by refusing to change residence, insisting on deciding their own visitation schedule, or by other kinds of negotiations with their parents, are actively participating in the transformation of their families (Frønes 1998; James and Prout 1997). The first question asked here is whether changes that are widely recognized as major risks for children's development from the parents' point of view are seen as such by children.

In late modernity (Giddens 1992), in what has been called 'risk society' (Beck 1992), with its increased individualization, individuals are more dependent than before on social relations: family, kin and friends. When children as well as adults are expected to 'write their own stories' the reliance on the social network for support and necessary feedback in their identity work is crucial. Divorce is in itself an individualization process for adults as well as for children. Children who before divorce were seen as belonging to their parents in one home and in a nuclear family, after divorce become individuals with legal and economic rights. After divorce the children have to 'rewrite their story', develop new relations with their parents and siblings and find a new place in their mother's and father's households. In late modernity and for children with divorced parents, I believe it is necessary to ask if weak or impaired parent–child relations do represent a greater risk to children's development and well-being than mere change.

The data

The data used in this chapter are from the study: 'Families after divorce' (Moxnes *et al.* 1999, 2000, 2001). This study consists of parental reports (questionnaires) on how their 910 children had coped with divorce (in the following referred to as 'The Parent Report'), interviews with 114 parents and interviews with 96 children. For the purpose of this chapter I have selected interviews with 52 children who experienced much change and who, in terms of theory, should be most troubled by divorce. Most of these children lived with their mother and only a few with their father. None of the children had parents who shared physical custody and, on average, they had less contact with their non-custodial parent than was common in Norway at the end of the 1990s (Jensen and Clausen 1997). The children's ages varied from eight to 18 years. Most citations used in the following are from the older children because they were the most articulate.

The children were asked to tell their divorce story. Among the topics they were asked to elaborate on were the experiences with and consequences of the following: decline in the household's level of income, change of residence, lack of daily contact with one of the parents and acquiring step-parents.

Children coping with change

As a point of departure and for reasons of comparison, a few results from one of the studies mentioned above, 'The Parent Report' (Moxnes *et al.* 1999), are used. This study, using parental reports on the consequences of divorce for their children, has shown that changes such as decline in household income levels and change of residence are major risks for children's development. On average, the children who experienced income decline and/or moved to a different house reflected more signs of negative effect and fewer of positive effect than those who did not experience such changes. There was not such a significant difference between children who had little or no contact with their non-residential parent and those who had frequent contact and between children with step-parents and those who had no step-parent. However, there was a significant difference in children's well-being as reported by the parents, between children who had residential step-parents and those who had non-residential step-parents.

Financial change in the child's household

According to the parents' reports, decline in the household income at the time of the divorce was a major risk to children's well-being (ibid.). The majority of the children we interviewed lived in households with low income.

A few children said that they had more money of their own after the divorce: either they got some of the child support money as their own, or they were eligible for a state scholarship for high-school children with parents on a low income. A few other children said that the household standard of living was better because the mother now had control over the income and no longer had to pay for the father's expensive habits. However, most of the children acknowledged that their household income was low, and that it was worse after the separation. Some children said openly, 'we are poor', and expressed worries about the household's financial present and future. The older children explained why the income was low. In most cases it was because their mother did not earn much. She had little work experience, an unskilled job, worked part time, had gone back to college, or her income was a disability or a single-parent allowance. Other causes for the low income included the father not paying child support, paying too late, or paying less than he was supposed to pay.

The majority of the children said that their family's low income never had serious consequences for themselves. None of the 52 children reported that they could not participate in activities because of lack of money, but many said that they did not get pocket money and many told of a heavy workload at home. I understand these children's stories as expressions of solidarity with their residential parent. Instead of saying that they could not take part in snowboard skiing or continue playing in the school band because it was too expensive, they said they did not want to, or that they had lost interest. Instead of saying that they had to take responsibility for household chores because the mother had to work long hours, they said it was only fair that all family members shared the housework. And instead of complaining about not getting a weekly allowance, they said they did not need one, they got the money they needed when they asked. They expressed solidarity with their parent and took responsibility for the financial situation. The children had learned to be responsible in money matters. The interviews can be read as stories of how, through negotiations with parents and siblings, they became informed about the family income. But there are also stories of how, through discussions and self-reflexivity, they learned to see their own part in the family's financial situation and that there were alternative ways for coping (Finch and Mason 1993). For example, when Robert's bike had been stolen and he needed one badly, he also knew that he could not raise the money for a new one:

> First my mother, sister and I discussed it, we agreed that my sister's shoes had to come first … . Then Mother talked to Dad, he agreed to pay one third. We decided that when I had worked and saved one third, she [mother] would pay the last third. I hope to make that before the summer is over.
>
> (Robert, aged 13)

Through negotiations the children not only became informed and learned to be responsible, they were also given the right and possibility to influence their own situation. When children feel that their voice is heard, that their interests are given the same consideration as those of others, and the lack of money is seen as a shared family problem, then it is seen as fair and just and easier to accept. Having a say in money matters is one reason why few of the children considered themselves to be passive victims of the family's tight financial situation. Furthermore, they developed ways of coping. Among those children who were old enough, many earned their own money. They delivered newspapers, cut grass, took on babysitting duties or did housework in their own home. They had shown much initiative and creativity and were proud of it. However, some of the children told us that it was very difficult to be poor.

> It is awful, not to have money, my mother worries, and we all fight, not about money, but because everything is so difficult … I don't know any way to make it better.
>
> (Berit, aged 17)

In the months, sometimes years, after the separation some of the children tried to understand and solve the money problems by arguing with their parents. Most of them gave up after a while. Instead they withdrew and avoided any discussion about money.

Low household income was also a problem for children whose parents were fighting over money and especially for children with fathers who did not pay the requisite child support. These children expressed more anger and/or sadness and little, if any, of the solidarity toward their parents mentioned above.

> My father often doesn't pay [child support], he delays the payments, or pays less than he should. My mother thinks this is so because he wants to punish her, but he is punishing us at the same time … . It isn't fair, a few times we have not had money for food, and twice my mother has had to go to the social security office to ask for money … I have seen the way my father and his new family live, they have plenty, we have nothing … he has said many times that if I lived with him I would get more.
>
> (Tom, aged 14)

Tom told us that he often wondered if his father really loved him and his sister, and that because of his father's behaviour, he would never move to live with him, he would rather be poor and live with his mother. Tom was hurt, so was Janne:

> All the fights and worries about money make me feel that I am the problem, I should not cost anything … if I did not exist they would not have anything to fight about.
>
> (Janne, aged 15)

According to most of the children a low household income was a problem – it caused stress and living with it was hard. Thus the children supported findings from the parental report study, that decline in the household income is a risk for children's well-being. However, there was considerable variation in the extent to which lack of money was a problem, and in how the children coped with it. The children's stories must be understood in the context of the household's income level. The stories of children living in households which usually had some money left (often very little) after the bills were paid, differed considerably from those told by children living in households that had no money left, only piles of bills they were unable to pay. The first group of children were usually well-informed and understood the financial situation; they knew they had a say in money matters and that made them feel responsible. They presented the lack of money as a shared family problem. The second group of children, living in families where there was no money about which to negotiate and where parents often fought about money, had no way of influencing the use of money and felt powerless. Some were ashamed of being poor, withdrew socially, or felt rejected and unloved by one of the parents. For these children the lack of money was a practical problem, but more important, it had become a personal problem. This became damaging to family relations, socially devastating and threatening to their self-esteem. After divorce, the older children learned that they were economic subjects with the right to support from both parents. For some children this was a positive experience – they got their money and increased freedom. For others who had a mother with little money or a father who was unwilling to pay, economic rights became an empty formality with no consequence and this felt like a devaluation of themselves.

Residential mobility

The Parent Report showed that change of residence was a risk to children's well-being (ibid.). With few exceptions, the children we interviewed had changed residence when their parents separated or divorced, and some of them had moved more than once. Some had moved two or three times either because their mother was dependent on the local authority for housing and had to take what she was offered, or because their residential parent had found a new partner and together they had moved to a new home better suited to the needs of the extended household. Many of these families lived in an apartment that they rented.

Even if most of the children did not move far from the pre-divorce home, they said that it had been hard to leave. For some it was hard because the original home had been nicer and bigger than the new home and/or because the new home was in a less attractive neighbourhood. For others it was difficult because they moved so far from the old place that they could no longer have frequent contact with friends. But if leaving the pre-divorce home was bad, finding new friends and becoming included in the new community was worse. It was worst for those who knew nobody who could facilitate integration into the new community. Few of the children mentioned the parents as facilitators. The parents usually were away at work most of the day, had friends in other parts of the town and had no time or need to acquire friends in their new neighbourhood. Integration was something the children often had to cope with alone. Some children were angry with their parent and felt that she or he had failed them by moving and/or not helping them to stay in contact with old friends and integrating into the new place.

> I never wanted to move, that was what my mother and her boyfriend wanted. But they do not live here, I mean they are away working, and when they come home, they never leave the apartment. I am the one living here … I have to go to that stupid school and take all the shit.
>
> (Britt, aged 13).

The stories of Anna and Lisa, who both moved twice, illustrate the difficulties that changing residence can lead to and the differences in choice of coping strategies. Anna lived in East-town until she was nine. Her mother could not afford to keep the pre-divorce home, so they first moved to an apartment in another part of the town, where they lived for two years. The mother then met a new man and together they moved to a third place in town.

> I have no friends here, but that does not matter, I do not like them, they only think about boys … . No, I do not go to the youth club … nobody talks to me there … I used to play football at East-town, but not here. Here the team is bad.
>
> (Anna, aged 13)

According to Anna, absolutely everyone and everything was positive and fun in East-town, while everything was stupid and negative at the place where she had lived for the last two years. Anna went to school alone, was alone in school and returned home alone. Very seldom did she do anything after school except bake and prepare dinner for her family. She had become mother's little helper and was praised for her work. Lisa's story is similar. The first time she moved, Lisa changed school, but the second time she refused to. Her mother wanted her to change school because of the expense and the time it took to travel across town. Lisa was fighting to keep her friends and threatened her mother by saying she would move to her grandparents, or ask for a foster-home if she was forced to change school.

> It was terrible to move from The Hill. I lost all my friends. It took a long time before I got to know anybody … not before I started playing in the band … . Most of my friends play in the band, but we do a lot of other things too.
>
> (Lisa, aged 12)

Neither Anna nor Lisa could do anything about the relocation of the home, but their ways of coping with the second residential move were different. Anna, as I understood her, felt it was too painful to actively seek new friends and became an unhappy and isolated child. Lisa stood up to her mother and spent a lot of time and energy on keeping her friends. She was satisfied and proud that she had managed to take charge of her own social life.

Changing residence at the time of divorce is considered a major risk factor for children's well-being, and the children's stories supported this. How great the loss and how much sorrow was caused depended on the distance between the old and new home and to what degree the parents were willing and able to help during the transition. There were striking differences in the stories of children who had taken part in the family negotiations as to when and where they should move. These children were usually well-informed and prepared when they moved and often they had made a deal with one or both parents that they should be helped so that they could keep in contact with old friends. Many children, even some who had to travel for more than an hour, continued at their pre-divorce school for some months, while others continued to play football or some other game with their friends in the old club. For children whose parents could not help them keep in contact with old friends, or who moved so far away that staying in contact was impossible, changing residence was more difficult. Many of these children's stories reflected months, even years, of being excluded from other children's activities, of being treated as invisible or of being pestered by the other children. Difficulties finding new friends often led to social isolation and developed into a personal problem because it forced the child to question his or her own attractiveness as a friend. Changing residence also made the individualization of the child more pronounced. Children who moved and/or had a parent who moved, had to develop new relationships and construct their own space in the new neighbourhood without much help from parents.

Loss of contact with parents

No large quantitative study has been able to show any relationship between the amount of contact children have with the non-residential parent and the children's well-being (Emery 1999). Neither did the Parent Report (ibid.). However, I do not believe that this indicates that the amount of contact with the non-residential parent is without importance for the child's well-being.

Most of the children who had frequent contact with their father were satisfied. A few children complained about the long distance between the parental homes, of having no friends at the place the non-residential parent lived and/or lack of flexibility in the visitation arrangements. Travelling long distances was tiring, having no friends at the father's place made staying there boring and rigid visitation schedules made it difficult to take part in important social activities.

Most of the children who had little or no contact with their father were not satisfied, but their emotions in regard to their father's absence and their ways of coping with that absence differed considerably. A few of the children who had infrequent contact were satisfied because they were used to not seeing their father much: he had worked far away or he had never taken much part in their life.

> It's OK, I never saw my father much … . He works in Africa, he helps poor and sick children … . Next year I will go and see him. He has promised me that as a present for my confirmation.
>
> (Ben, aged 12)

Others were relieved when they seldom or never saw the father because his behaviour had too often made them feel ashamed or frightened.

> I am afraid when I have to go and see my father. I never know if he or my grandmother is drunk. When they are I try to leave, but that is difficult, they will not let me … . My brother never goes to see my father [he refuses to] that is unfair … . But if I do not go to see him he comes here to fetch me, and everybody in the building will see how awful and drunk he is.
>
> (Anna, aged 13)

Anna tried to keep contact with her father at a minimum, but at the same time she missed him and was very hurt by his behaviour. Before the divorce she used to be 'Daddy's girl', but at that time she did not know that he was an alcoholic because her mother had done her best to keep that from the children.

Reduced or lost contact with one of the parents had been a problem for many of the children and is a risk for children's well-being post-divorce. How much of a loss and how painful reduced contact was depended on the amount of that contact and the reasons behind it. Children living in households where negotiation between parents and children was part of the normal communication usually had the necessary information as to why they had a certain visitation schedule. Visitation was flexible and the children felt free to argue for both more or less contact with the non-residential parent. These children knew that their voice was heard, that the parents considered their needs and wishes to be important, and therefore felt that they had both responsibility for, and control over, the relationships with their parents (Schultz-Jørgensen 1999). The majority of children presented the lack of contact as an unfortunate but necessary consequence of the divorce, the parents' work situation, lack of money and/or the distance between the parental homes. They did not present the reduced contact with the non-residential parent as a personal problem, but rather as a shared family problem and as nobody's fault. It was those children who seldom had contact with the non-residential parent who seemed most hurt and disturbed when they talked about that relationship. In these cases one or often both parents were unwilling or unable to negotiate a schedule for the child's contact with the non-residential parent and therefore the child could do little to influence the relationship with the father. Regardless of whether the children wanted more or less contact, it was those children who could not understand why they seldom had contact with the father who were most unhappy. These children were unable to provide a personally and/or socially acceptable explanation as to why, and that troubled them (Dahlhaug 2001). For these children the relationship with the non-residential parent had become a personal problem: they wondered if they no longer were lovable since the absent parent treated them as he did.

> The saddest thing with the divorce was getting used to having two differ-
> ent parents.
>
> (Karin, aged 15).

Karin's statement is an illustration of divorce as a process of individualization. Instead of relating to the parents as a set, it becomes, to an increasing degree, the child's responsibility to develop a relationship with each parent and to keep those relationships separate.

Extension of the family with step-parents

The Parent Report showed no significant differences in well-being between children with and without step-parents (ibid.). However, I do not believe that this is because step-parents have no effect on the child's well-being. The same study showed significant differences in well-being between children with a res-idential step-parent and those with a non-residential step-parent, the former group on average doing better.

The children told of a stressful period when they got a new step-parent; they were worried about what she or he would be like and if this new person would make a negative change in their lives. Per expressed what most of the children were afraid of at that time:

> You know what is said about step-parents, they are awful towards step-
> children.
>
> (Per aged 13).

However, after a while most children recognized the importance of step-parents and the economic and social resources they had brought to the household. In time most step-parents, especially residential step-parents, were considered to be a gain.

There were differences in the stories of children with residential and non-residential step-parents. Of most importance was the difference in process. While having a residential step-parent was usually the result of a long process of negotiation in which the child had time to get to know the step-parent, and the child's opinions as to when and under what conditions she or he could share the home were crucial, having a non-residential step-parent was another kind of process. In that process, only few children had a say and many did not meet the step-parent before she or he was living with the non-residential parent.

Among the children we interviewed who lived permanently with a step-parent, all but two lived in their mother's household. Most of these children told of a good relationship. They talked about their stepfather as someone who belonged in the family, a friend who was often of help, and many like Per stressed the financial importance of the stepfather's presence in the household:

> If he had not earned that much money we could not have kept the house.
>
> (Per, aged 13)

Only some very few called the stepfather Father or Dad. On the contrary, a number of children stressed that even though they liked the stepfather, he was not a father. We were told many stories about children's resistance when the step-parent tried to behave as a father and make decisions on their behalf. The stepfather's status in the family was dependent on his relationship with the mother. As long as the children could see that their mother was happy, that the stepfather contributed to the household tasks and did not interfere too much in the children's own lives, they accepted him, or were happy that he lived with them. Otherwise, they openly expressed their dissatisfaction or distanced themselves from him. In the five years that had passed since Lisa's mother separated from her father, four men had lived with them. Lisa had learned to distance herself from her mother's boyfriends.

> Women have to have a man, it is natural, but he has nothing to do with me. He is not my stepfather, he is not a father, he is only my mother's boyfriend … . Luckily he is gone a lot, because he is a truck driver … . If he is here and my mother is away I stay in my room until she is back. I have promised my grandfather, I shall not be alone with her men.
>
> (Lisa, aged 12)

Lisa knew that there was nothing she could do to stop her mother from bringing men into the home. Instead, she built a 'wall of politeness' between herself and her mother's boyfriends.

Among the children who had non-residential step-parents all but three had a stepmother. The stories about the step-parents in the non-residential parent's home differed more widely. Some children expressed happiness that their father had a new cohabitant or wife. They related how their father had become happier and more fun to be with since she came into his life. Others disliked their father's new partner, usually because she made them feel like an outsider, and not welcome, or because they seldom got to spend time alone with the father. A few children disliked the stepmother so much that they refused to visit their father.

> Sometimes I have to be together with her [stepmother] and her kids, but if I have been with them one weekend, I can force him to go away with me alone.
>
> (Eva, aged 14)

Other studies have indicated that it is more difficult to be a stepmother than a stepfather and that children are often more satisfied with their stepfathers than with their stepmothers (Robinson and Smith 1993). Such discrepancies are usually explained by the higher expectations placed on stepmothers as compared to stepfathers. That might be true, but according to the children it is also a question of gains and losses. Because most of the children did not spend much time with the non-residential step-parent they really did not know her. Therefore, they had difficulties seeing that she had anything to offer them. Instead, they saw and felt that she and the step-siblings took the attention, time and money that the father used to give to them. For these children the step-parent represented no gains, only losses. Even if most of these children blamed the stepmother and excused their fathers for this, by doing so they presented their father as weak, as someone unable to stand up to his wife.

According to the children, acquiring step-parents had been a stressful process. However, having parents who, from the child's point of view, gave priority to the new spouse and step-siblings, became a personal problem. It was damaging to the parent–child relationship and painful to the children who wondered why the step-parent and/or step-siblings seemed to be more worthy of the parent's love than themselves. Having step-parents also increased the individualization of the child. We were told many stories of new love-relationships that took so much time and space that the child felt as an outsider or lonesome in both parents' homes.

'Not good enough parenting'

The dominant theme in many children's stories was that the difficulties they had when coping with changes during the divorce process were made worse and even more painful when the parents did not co-operate and/or give the child sufficient support. What is called 'not good enough parenting' includes a high level of conflict between the parents, lack of parental involvement and incompetent parenting. Other studies have shown that the parent–child relationship is often impaired during the divorce process (Emery 1999; Gittins 1998).

Most children told of a close and good relationship with both parents before and after divorce and of an improved relationship with the residential parent post-divorce. After the separation they got to know their mother better, their respect for her increased and they felt she was treating them with more respect. The mother–child relationship had become closer, friendlier and more democratic. Only a few children told a different story about the residential parent. These children had a mother who had not coped well with the divorce. She was still mourning the loss of her spouse and/or had not managed to reorganize the children's or her own life. Some of these children felt deceived, or abandoned, by the mother. They felt sorry for her and pictured her as a weak person for whom they had lost respect. Katrina was one of the children who had to 'parent her own parent' for years after divorce. When describing her mother she used words such as 'nervous', 'afraid', 'sad' and 'depressed':

> She does all kinds of things to make me stay at home, rents movies, makes food she knows I like … . When I leave she often cries quietly, that makes me feel terrible … . I have to see friends.
>
> (Katrina, aged 13)

Children 'parenting their parents' was a common phenomenon in the first month following the separation. Many children told stories about how they put the parents' needs above their own and tried to comfort, care for and do practical chores for unhappy parents. Most of these children were proud of being able to help their parents. However, when the parent was unable to behave as a parent for a longer period of time, then 'parenting the parent' became too heavy a burden. Children were parenting both residential and non-residential parents. Anna (cited previously) also tried to 'mother her dad'. In the first year after the separation she visited him, cleaned the house and made lists of what he needed to buy. She even tried to control his drinking. She gave up trying to help him when he moved in with his mother, who also was a heavy drinker.

As already mentioned, some children's stories were about losing contact with their non-residential parent, in most cases the father. He was no longer involved in their life, at least not in the way they expected a father to be. Many children presented their non-residential father as weak because he was dependent on drugs, had an antisocial lifestyle or was unable to stand up to the new spouse. The unhappiest among these children were those who could not understand why the father who once loved them dearly no longer made an effort to see them.

Most children had no recollection of quarrels or fights between their parents during the divorce process, but a significant minority of children said that the parents had frequent arguments before, during and/or after divorce. Every child who told that the parents were still arguing or fighting also said that this was a painful problem, which made them sad or angry. While children with parents who were friends or friendly towards each other felt free to continue and strengthen their relationship with both parents, children with parents in conflict felt caught in the middle of the conflict. Parental conflicts, which were hard to cope with when the parents were married and lived together, often became more of a burden after separation when the child was the only link between the parents – the link through whom all the harsh words, blame, accusations and threats were passed (Öberg and Öberg 1992). In order to handle the hostility between the parents many children erected an 'information-proof wall' between the two homes. By never carrying any information, positive (which often was the worst) or negative, between the two households the child could avoid accusations of favouring, defending or taking sides with one of the parents (Lian Flem 2001; Christensen 1999). It was hard for these children to live with parents who were constantly fighting, often for their own parental rights, and who paid little attention to the child's needs and desires (Smart 1999). Likewise it was hard to live with parents who were weak or so self-centred that they did not recognize or acknowledge the child's need for love and caring. However, incompetent or insufficient parenting is not always, even in most of these cases, a result of divorce: often it is the reason for divorce. According to the majority of the children who told of conflict between parents and incompetent or insufficient parenting, such parenting had been a problem long before divorce (Block *et al.* 1986).

Coping successfully with parental divorce – a matter of negotiation or resignation

The children's stories supported the results from the Parent Report, namely that decline in the household level of income, change of residence and having step-parents, especially non-residential step-parents, are difficult, stressful and therefore a risk to children's well-being. The children's stories did not support the finding from the Parent Report that the amount of contact with non-residential parents was without importance for children's well-being. On the contrary, children who had little or no contact with their father were in most cases unhappy because of that poor relationship. According to the children, separation and divorce was a stressful process and adjusting to all the associated changes was both difficult and painful. However, these were changes, stress and loss of resources the children learned to cope with when given sufficient time and support. Such problems seemed to be easier to cope with when they were shared, defined as a family problem and as an unfortunate, but necessary, result of divorce. The children living in families where there was no room for negotiation, where the children were seldom heard and their needs and wishes not given due consideration, often felt neglected by the parents, and lonely and unsure about their identity.

Divorce is a process of individualization of family members. In our culture individualization is seen as positive and understood as producing increased autonomy, independence and freedom – all positive concepts from the point of view of adults and youth. But to children who are dependent on their parents, individualization can mean increased vulnerability and loneliness. Some of the stories told by the children showed that they had been able to benefit from the increased individualization. They were conscious that the divorce was a realization of their legal and financial rights and they got their own money as part of the child support payment or through a scholarship. More important, they were part of a reflexive discourse in which problems, disagreements and the division of responsibilities were solved through negotiation. Reflexive discourse and negotiation are both conditions for, and consequences of, individualization. Family negotiation is an expression of the individualization of the child and the democratization of the parent–child relationship. It is a recognition of the child as an individual – not an equal to the parent in all matters, but often in matters concerning the child. Family negotiations seem to be the best means for helping the child through the divorce in a healthy way. By negotiating, the children got necessary information, shared their point of view with their parents, learned to see the world from different points of view and, finally, by so doing, discovered that they could choose alternative ways of coping. The stories told by children who lived in families 'drained' of economic and social resources, where there was no room for negotiation, showed that they had not benefited from individualization. In their stories, self-determination or freedom of choice was almost never mentioned. Even though some had fought for their needs and wishes in the beginning, passive acceptance, resignation and withdrawal eventually seemed to be their only options.

References

Alanen, L. (1992) *Modern Childhood? Exploring the 'Child Question' in Sociology*, Publication Series A, Research Reports 50, Jyveskylä: Institute for Educational Research.

Andenæs, A. (1995) *Foreldre og barn i forandring*, Dr. polit avhandling, Trondheim Psykologisk Institutt: SVT fakultet NTNU.

Beck, U. (1992) *Risk Society. Towards a New Modernity*, London: Sage.

Block, J.H., Block, J. and Gjerde, P.F. (1986) 'The personality of children prior to divorce', *Child Development*, 57: 827–40.

Christensen, E. (1999) 'Børn i familier med alkoholmisbruk', in L. Dencik and P. Schultz Jørgensen (eds) *Børn og familie i det postmoderne samfund*, København: Hans Reitzels Forlag.

Dahlhaug, T.E. (2001) 'Fjerne fedre – hva gjør barna med det?', in K. Moxnes, H. Kaul, I. Kvaran and I. Levin (eds) *Skilsmissens mange ansikter*, Kristiansand, Høgskoleforlaget: Norwegian Academic Press.

Emery, R.E. (1999) 'Post divorce family life: an overview of research and some implications for policy', in R.A. Thompson and P.R. Amato (eds) *The Post Divorce Family. Children, Parenting and Society*, London: Sage.

Finch, J. and Mason, J. (1993) *Negotiating Family Responsibilities*, London: Routledge.

Frønes, I. (1998) *Den Norske Barndommen*, Oslo: Cappelen.

Furstenberg, F.F. and Cherlin, A.J. (1991) *Divided Families. What Happens to Children when Parents Part?*, Cambridge, Mass.: Harvard University Press.

Giddens, A. (1992) *The Transformation of Intimacy. Sexuality, Love and Eroticism in Modern Society*, Cambridge: Polity Press.

Gittins, D. (1998) *The Child in Question*, New York: St Martin's Press.

James, A. and Prout, A. (eds) (1997) *Constructing and Reconstructing Childhood. Contemporary Issues in the Sociological Study of Childhood*, London: Falmer Press.

Jensen, A.M. and Clausen, S.E. (1997) 'Barns familier', Samboerskap og forelderbrudd etter 1970, Oslo: NIBR, Prosjektrapport 1997–21.

Lian Flem, A. (2001) 'Det er liksom mamma og pappa som kommer først, da.', in K. Moxnes, H. Kaul, I. Kvaran and I. Levin (eds) *Skilsmissens mange ansikter*, Kristiansand, Høgskoleforlaget: Norwegian Academic Press.

McLanahan, S. and Sandefur, G. (1994) *Growing Up with a Single Parent. What Hurts, What Helps*, Cambridge, Mass.: Harvard University Press.

Moxnes, K., Haugen, G.M.D. and Holter, T. (1999) *Skilsmissens virkning på barn*, Rapport, Trondheim Allforsk, NTNU.

Moxnes, K. and Winge, A. (2000) *Foreldresamarbeid etter skilsmisse*, Rapport, Trondheim Allforsk, NTNU.

Moxnes, K., Kaul, H., Kvaran, I. and Levin, I. (2001) *Skilsmissens mange ansikter*, Kristiansand, Høgskoleforlaget: Norwegian Academic Press.

Öberg, B. and Öberg, G. (1992) *Pappa se meg. Om förnekande barn ock maktlösa fader*, Stockholm: Göthia.

Robinson, M. and Smith, D. (1993) *Step by Step. Focus on Step-families*, London: Harvester Wheatsheaf.

Schultz-Jørgensen (1999) 'Famililiv – I børnefamilien', in L. Dencik and P. Schultz Jørgensen (eds) *Børn og familie i det postmoderne samfund*, København: Hans Reitzels Forlag.

Smart, C. (1999) 'The 'new' parenthood: fathers and mothers after divorce', in E.B. Silvia and C. Smart (eds) *The New Family*, London: Sage.

Thompson, R.A. and Amato, P.R. (1999) (eds) *The Post Divorce Family. Children, Parenting and Society*, London: Sage.

7 As fair as it can be?

Childhood after divorce

Amanda Wade and Carol Smart

> Family life no longer happens in one place but is scattered between several different locations.
>
> (Beck and Beck Gernsheim 2002: 92)

Introduction

In this chapter we will address what it means for children to experience their family lives as scattered between several different locations and how they manage the inevitable problems and challenges of sustaining relationships through the apportioning of time and space. Our focus is on post-divorce family life where parents live in different locations and parent–child relationships are maintained in large part through the dividing of children's time more or less equally between households. We refer to this practice as co-parenting after divorce or separation. Our main focus will be on the accounts of the children we have interviewed in two studies[1] in which they talk about what it is like to be shared between their parents and to live their lives across different households with different kin and step-kin. But the context in which this empirical data is discussed is an ethical one, namely the concept of fairness. We draw this concept of fairness from the narratives of the children themselves and we shall pay attention to the ways in which they conceptualize this moral concept, and also what it means when they actually set it into operation. However, before we turn to this data, we shall focus on the idea of fairness and why it seems to have entered so powerfully into the imagination of the children of divorced parents.

Fairness and families

As Beck and Beck Gernsheim (2002) argue, 'the family' is no longer understood to be a unit with homogeneous interests. They suggest that this is largely because sociologists recognize that men and women have different interests, are positioned differently in the family and may have very different life trajectories. Sociological work also increasingly acknowledges that children are players in family life. This means that we begin to appreciate that each child may have different interests, be positioned differently in the family and may have different life trajectories when compared with adults or with each other.

The thesis put forward by Beck and Beck Gernsheim is that the process of individualization is affecting relations between family members and creating a new dynamic. This thesis has been much debated (Giddens 1992; Beck and Beck Gernsheim 1995; Smart *et al.* 2001) and we will not repeat these debates here. However, it is clear that current rates of divorce and separation, as well as the trend towards cohabitation, are transforming families. This means that:

> More and more co-ordination is needed to hold together biographies that tend to pull apart from one another. At a number of levels, the family thus becomes a daily 'balancing act' or a permanent 'do-it-yourself' project ... more and more things must be negotiated, planned, personally brought about. And not least in importance is the way in which questions of ... *fairness between members of the family, have come to the fore.*
>
> (Beck and Beck Gernsheim 2002: 90–1, our emphasis)

The argument that provides the basis for this assertion is that relationships are no longer likely to be sustained by the power of outside forces alone. So community expectations or legal regulations or religious teachings alone do not keep people bound together if the quality of their relationships is impaired. It follows that once the quality of relationships becomes the central issue, 'expectations' and 'negotiations' become very important – at least in adult relationships. Thus it becomes more unacceptable to take it for granted that women will take on all the domestic labour in a relationship; equally it is harder to assume that fathers will not be involved in childcare activities. In situations where there is a serious mismatch of expectations and where negotiations do not resolve the incongruency, it is likely that husbands and wives will feel that the contract they have entered into is not 'fair' and they may become increasingly discontented.

The rise in rates of divorce in the UK since the 1960s has also contributed towards this trend, while also being a consequence of the changing mentalities of men and women. The process of divorce requires couples to divide their matrimonial assets from the home down to the last photo album. This now common division of property (as well as division of memorabilia, shared biographies, pain and hopes) and of course the division of children, means that few couples can be unaware that what has been pooled may need to be disassembled according to a 'new' set of principles. 'Old' principles may no longer suffice. Thus the idea that women should keep the children while men keep most of the economic resources no longer seems 'fair' (Delphy 1976). And the even older idea that the 'innocent' party should keep the children as well as the financial resources now seems to be a moral anachronism. New ideas of what is fair (at least in principle if not in everyday practice) are developing all the time. The idea that things should be 'fair' between men and women in their domestic and economic relationships has therefore become central and has also become a kind of modern symbol of how good gender relations are. But with children the situation is not exactly the same. Children do not choose their relationships with their parents and they do not enter into these relationships even as putative equals. The appropriateness of the concept of fairness in the parent–child relationship is therefore tempered by other factors such as the parents' responsibilities to protect and nurture the child, and to socialize the child into the moral order in which very concepts like fairness reside. A child is likely to be aware of issues of fairness in relation to self, to siblings or to other children, before s/he is conscious of issues of fairness between parents/adults.

Notwithstanding this order of things, we found in our interviews with children after divorce that the question of fairness *to* and *for* parents was paramount. It was as if these children were already well versed in the negotiations that are part of adult family life and marital separation. We cannot tell whether the children of divorced parents are different in this respect to other children. They might have become sensitive to issues of fairness between adults in family matters through participating in and/or overhearing adult discussions of what is fair in the face of divorce. Or they might have been extrapolating from the principles they use in their relationships with other children in the sharing of objects like toys. Or they might be fully versed in modern expectations of gender equality and thus be extending these principles to new circumstances. Our research cannot explain the cognitive processes these children experienced, but we can comment on the social context in which fairness has become such a paramount concept in their understanding of post-divorce relationships.

Children's concerns about fairness *to* and *for* their parents suggest that they stand in a particular relationship to the divorce process. Although many children are upset and worried for themselves when their parents separate, the emphasis on fairness suggests that they still have a strong moral awareness of the position of both their parents in relation to each other. But what is most significant is that the 'thing' that they want to be most fair about is the apportionment of themselves between their parents. In principle, children seem to think that it is fair if they are divided equally between their parents on divorce. It would be fascinating to know whether 20 or 30 years ago children with divorcing parents would have voiced the same adherence to the principle of equality-as-fairness. One wonders whether, had they been allowed to speak at all, they would have spoken in terms of the dominant moral concept of the time, namely within the doctrine of matrimonial fault or possibly the tender years doctrine.[2] Would they have said that children should go with the innocent party? Or might they have been more influenced by the equally powerful ideology of maternal love within which it was assumed that young children needed most to be with their mothers rather than fathers? In suggesting this we are not implying that children are mere ciphers, rather we are implying that they may be much more sensitive to the ebb and flow of moral and cultural values than is generally recognized. Like adults, they may be engaged with contemporary moral debates and seeking answers that are compatible with modern thinking about the morality of relationships.

But we can only surmise how children might once have answered questions about post-divorce family life. What we do know is that at the turn of the millennium they are apparently thinking in principle in terms of equality for mothers and fathers – even when this turns them into a form of 'commodity' for sharing under the tenets of distributive justice. Their emphasis on equality suggests that they are active social democrats who see justice being achieved through the redistribution of goods and material resources. It should not surprise us that children in England at this moment in history would resort to such a philosophical solution given that, as Fraser (2001) argues,

> The redistribution orientation has a distinguished philosophical pedigree, as egalitarian redistributive claims have supplied the paradigm case for most theorizing about social justice for the past 150 years.
>
> (Fraser 2001: 21)

What is perhaps surprising, though, is that children come to define themselves as one of the goods or material resources that is up for redistribution and/or sharing. Why and how have children come to define themselves in this way? Do they see themselves as the most precious of all commodities or as mere possessions of their parents? Does their view of themselves reflect the view their parents have of them? If so, is this view one that comes into play through the process of divorce? In other words, do children come to objectify themselves because the divorce process means that parents themselves come to treat them as objects or marital assets? In saying this we do not mean that parents become cynical, nor that they cease to love or appreciate their children, rather we are suggesting that objectively children start to number amongst the things that are fought over and thus they become thing-like – at least at some stage in the divorce process.

Of course if children do come to see themselves as a resource for redistribution at the time of divorce, this self-perception may not last long. One of the interesting features arising from the interviews that are explored below, is the way in which once children start to experience this equality *in practice*, their unalloyed support for it may begin to evaporate a little. In terms of the contemporary politico-moral debate over redistribution versus recognition (Honneth 2001) we might say that children move away from accepting the designation as a resource to be shared equally between parents, towards seeing themselves as persons who deserve respect from their parents and recognition of their own needs and interests. The moral journey that these children make is an interesting mirror to these larger philosophical debates about whether redistribution or recognition would be the best foundation for a moral society (in our case a moral family). Honneth (2001) argues that one of the key elements of recognition and respect is characterized by love in which reciprocal needs are acknowledged and emotional security is achieved. The journey made by the children we interviewed took many of them from a place in which they saw the redistribution of themselves as a means of being fair to parents on to a place where they saw it as necessary for their parents to recognize that they too had needs. This recognition, if widely acknowledged, would mean that parents would have to become willing to give up 'equal shares' in the 'thing-like' child in order to accommodate the needs of children-as-persons. In this moral journey we can see children move (metaphorically) from being objects to becoming persons. Put another way, they stop being self-defined resources available to secure their parents' happiness and become other-recognized persons with their own needs and desires (which are likely to include the ongoing need for parental love).

We have argued elsewhere (Smart *et al.* 2001) that children are moral agents and that they think ethically about their relationships and the obligations that flow from family ties. We have suggested one problem that children face is that adults do not recognize this agency sufficiently. Of course, children do not often speak with the language of moral philosophy, nor do they necessarily reason in an abstract fashion, which seems to be the mark of acknowledged philosophical thinking. However, the accounts we offer below suggest that even young children are philosophers and they are capable of trying to live out their philosophy and modifying it as the limitations of particular moral categories become apparent to them.

Fairness and the care of children after divorce

The importance of fairness as a core principle was confirmed by our study of family transitions carried out in four primary schools in Yorkshire (Wade and Smart 2002). The schools reflected differences in class, religion, ethnic mix and urban/rural location, so we managed to interview children who had very different life chances and differential access to cultural capital (Coleman 1988). Fifty-five children, all of whom had some experience of parental separation, discussed their views on family change during detailed conversational interviews. Their experiences were highly diverse, as were their family circumstances. But, irrespective of whether the children were from economically secure or disadvantaged homes, or were from minority ethnic backgrounds, co-parenting emerged as a concept familiar to almost all of them. A vignette that we gave to 47 of the children asked where a child we called Lee, whose parents were splitting up, should live. The largest single group of responses (27) favoured a traditional 'custody and access' arrangement, with children proposing that Lee should live with his mother and see his father at weekends. However, the next most popular option[3] put forward by 20 children was that Lee should spend equal amounts of time with both parents. This suggestion came not only from the more middle-class white children in the sample but from black and Asian children, and also from economically deprived children.

> Why don't they have goals? Like, Mum has him for a week and Dad has him for a week. That would be good if they fight.
>
> (Makeda, aged six)

> They should go to court or something, where Kevin and Sally [from *Coronation Street*] went. Then, the dad can see them, like, four days, and the other one can see them three days.
>
> (Lizzie, aged ten)

These findings suggest that even though the 'old' moral order, which defines mothers as the proper primary carers of children, is still active, there is also a growing presumption that 'equal' parenting is the moral or fair solution. Moreover, the children's comments reveal that it is not seen as an arrangement applicable only to non-conflictual separations.

In what follows, we explore how it is that the idea of being 'shared' between parents appears attractive to children, and then how they find it works in practice. Here we will draw on our ESRC study (Smart *et al.* 2001) in which 65 co-parented children[4] took part.

Why should children want to be shared?

The principle that both parents should remain equally responsible for the care and upbringing of their children if they separate, as emphasized by the Children Act 1989, is clearly attractive to many parents. Although the ethos of shared parenting promoted by the Act was not originally envisaged as meaning that children should have two homes (DoH 1991: para. 2.28), realities such as changing employment patterns for mothers have meant that shared physical care may be becoming more popular than originally intended. Many mothers now expect their former partners to share childcare responsibilities, not only by supporting children economically but by playing a direct part in their upbringing. Even mothers who would prefer to raise their children alone may now be persuaded that it is only 'fair' that fathers should remain closely involved with their children, and that their children have a 'right' to an on-going relationship with their father. For many fathers, children may now represent less a financial responsibility and more a lasting and reliable source of emotional attachment when adult relationships founder (Smart and Neale 1999). Moreover fathers have become increasingly vocal[5] in asserting their 'right' to parent their children on divorce (Burgess 1998; Secker 2001). But the question that is more intriguing is how it is that children have come to accept that they should be 'shared'. This is especially the case when it means that they have to give up a single, settled home for a peripatetic lifestyle which, as one child we interviewed said, 'is like putting your life in a couple of carrier bags every week'.

One answer lies in the fear felt by many children that they will 'lose' one of their parents on separation (Smith 1999; Dowling and Gorell Barnes 2000). This is not a baseless anxiety. Some research has indicated that children in contact/residence arrangements regret the loss of ordinary day-to-day contact with their non-resident parent and that contact is in many cases infrequent and diminishes over time (Eekelaar and Clive 1977; Furstenberg *et al.* 1987; Seltzer

1991). Co-parenting does not prevent children from feeling loss but it may mean that an approximation of an 'everyday' relationship can be retained with both parents:

> Dad at one point said, 'To be fair on you, I'll move away', and we were like, 'No, we don't want you to,' 'cos, like, you can't have a real father or mother relationship when you're just going off for tea once a week. And neither me nor [my brother] wanted that 'cos we were close to *both* of them and we wanted that kind of, like, the normal, everyday relationship with both of them. And then that [co-parenting] was the only way, we just started splitting the time.
>
> (Selina, aged 16)

Children do not set out, then, only with an idea of being fair to their parents when they opt for co-parenting. It seems that they may also be thinking of themselves. Co-parenting may attend to children's need to remain close to both parents, while also allowing each parent to remain a 'real' parent.

However, when we came to look at what children had to say about the structure of co-parenting arrangements, it became clear that being fair to their parents was very much embedded in their thinking about how cross-household parenting should work. From the outset, they thought predominantly in terms of being 'shared' between their parents on an equal basis because this avoided discriminating between them:

> I think pretty much when they split up they decided that I should spend equal time at both houses or else it wouldn't really be fair. [This way] nobody's got an advantage with me.
>
> (James, aged nine)

> I'm equally attached to both parents, so if I didn't see one of them as much as I saw the other, I suppose I'd feel guilty, really, for spending more time with one parent than the other.
>
> (Andrijka, aged ten)

Being fair to parents

Dividing a seven-day week into equal parts is not straightforward and there was considerable ingenuity in the co-parenting arrangements that children and their parents set up. Some worked over a 14-day period and this could be arranged to ensure alternate weekends in each home:

> We started to think of how we would share the time and Mum and Dad suggested quite a lot of things and then it was brought up, a week with one, a week with the other and that was far too long without seeing the other parent. So then we started splitting the week up and we thought that

> two days, two days, three days would be the best one because it's equal and it swaps round so you get the weekend with both parents.
>
> (Tom, aged 11)

Others split the week into two parts, with the half-day changeover usually occurring at the weekend while another option was for children to rotate between homes on a week by week, fortnight by fortnight, or even daily basis. The principle common to all of these, however, was that neither parent should have more of the child than the other. In practice, of course, it is difficult to ensure that time is divided with such precision so some families adopted a 'tight-structure/loose-fit' arrangement:

> [The arrangement] is not equal time to the day, to the hour, I mean that's stupid, but it's pretty equal days.
>
> (James, aged nine)

Nonetheless, children went to elaborate lengths to ensure that the principle of equality was not compromised. If a holiday or a visit from grandparents meant that they spent time in one household which 'should' have been spent at the other, this was seen as 'screwing up' the rota. Balance was restored by compensating the parent who had missed out and any inequities had to be morally justified:

> It's really even, it's really fair. We go week to week and usually my dad sees me the same as my mum. Well, my mum sees me a bit more I think but [hesitates] we can't sort that out really unless my dad doesn't work as much – but he wants to.
>
> (Elizabeth, aged nine)

Anniversaries and family celebrations created particular dilemmas. The significance of events like birthdays and Christmas meant that they had to be meticulously planned to avoid the risk of one parent having an advantage, leaving the other feeling hurt or slighted. However, the children's desire to ensure parity between their parents was not demonstrated simply through their efforts to share out their physical presence 'fairly'. We heard how they worked to ensure that the number of birthday or Christmas cards delivered to each house was roughly equivalent, or would scrupulously alternate which home housed new drawings or models made at school. Even in their thoughts they were conscientious to avoid appearing to favour one parent above the other:

Interviewer: Say you closed your eyes and thought about home, where would you think of?

Thomas: I'd think of a house with the upstairs being my mum's or something, and the downstairs being my dad's.

> (Thomas, aged 11)

Becoming fair to themselves

We discovered that some children's concepts of fairness altered over time as they confronted the practical and emotional demands of moving between households and apportioning themselves between their parents. In trying to be even-handed in their dealings with other family members they found that their own needs were sometimes neglected. For a number of children this gave rise to a more fluid and complex understanding of what a fair co-parenting arrangement might look like. We discuss these shifts in understanding under the subheadings of time, effort and space.

Time

Time was an important factor in children's detection of a lack of rightness at the heart of the 50–50 model of co-parenting. They found that the principle of equal apportionment between parents meant that they were not part of the equation but only the object to be shared. This problem frequently took the form of a dilemma as to how to combine a social life of their own with their desire to 'give' their time to their parents. Independent time is, of course, an issue that generates tension in many households, irrespective of a parental sep-aration. The dilemma for co-parented children is more complex, however, because their time is already heavily committed in keeping two households happy.

Thus some older children wished that they had more time for themselves or sometimes wanted to reduce the time spent with one parent:

Chrissie: At first all three of us would go routinely to see Dad. And then it changed so that I wouldn't be going as the routine and now it's got to the stage where … James [brother] is sort of in the change because –

Bob: He, only recently, had a problem with sleeping here.

Chrissie: I'm not sure if it's an excuse because he's finding it difficult to tell my dad he doesn't want to come. … I mean, it's just he's got an active social life. I think if Mum and Dad lived closer we'd be able to be at either place and keep the social lives going but because of the distance, certainly James, and Bob actually, all their friends are out near my mum, and it's very difficult.

(Chrissie, aged 19, and Bob, aged 12)

Effort

Children also became increasingly aware of the effort involved in maintaining a life across two households and their own contribution to this effort some-times felt disproportionate. They were the ones who were constantly moving and however committed they were to living with both parents, they found it hard work. Bags had to be packed and unpacked, school books and games kit had to be organized so that they were at the right home at the right time, and homework had to be co-ordinated with changeovers. The constant displacements were demanding and tiring. 'I never actually feel like I just sit down and just relax totally', said one child, 'I always seem to be doing something.' Parents, on the other hand, always had half of their time to themselves. They could unwind from being a parent and focus on other aspects of their lives. Children recognized that their parents had to cope with emotional changes – that the shift from being a parent to being 'themselves' might not always be straightforward, or that sometimes parents might be lonely when the children left. Nonetheless, parents could stay put and this, above all else, gave the impression that they had an easier time of it.

But it was not simply that moving backwards and forwards was demanding of children's time and energy. It could be emotionally draining too. Changeovers were often trigger points for intense feelings of irritation or sadness, and children needed time to adjust:

> I'd rather have it a week on, a week off, because basically I get a bit, I don't like moving a lot. I get used to living in one house and then in a short time I just have to move on to my next house. On the very first day I don't like it, I don't think I'd like it on the very first day on week-on/week-off, but it'd be easier, I'd be able to get used to it and stay used to it for a bit.
>
> (Sam, aged 11)

In these circumstances it was important to see that everyone involved was making a similar commitment to the co-parenting enterprise and where there was some imbalance it could lead to open arguments or hidden resentments in parents or children:

> I'm at my dad's house from Monday evening from about six o'clock when he gets back from work till Tuesday morning going off to school, and on Friday nights from about six o'clock. At one point Mum got cross because Dad did a course on Monday evenings and she was like, 'Honestly! Getting a baby-sitter, it's not fair, he should have you on a different day.'
>
> (Beth, aged 14)

Space

Space was a significant issue for the children, from the geographical landscapes they crossed as they journeyed between their homes and schools, to the different emotional terrains in which they had to live out their relationships. The physical spaces of their homes could become enmeshed in these emotional spaces because they contributed to whether the children felt settled, or felt that they had a real home. It was not so much that the economics of post-divorce family life meant that they had to adjust downwards their expectations about the types of homes their parents lived in, as that they sometimes questioned whether the spaces they inhabited 'belonged' to them:

> I probably feel more settled at my mum's house because, I mean it's partly because my dad's not brilliantly organized and … I haven't got my own room that I could really call my own. I mean, there's a cupboard in there which has got all my dad's clothes in it and there's a chest of drawers with my stuff in it. It doesn't seem quite mine because I haven't got anything that's specifically mine in there.
>
> (Karl, aged 15)

However, it was in relation to new family members that the issue of space tended to become especially significant. A number of parents used the intervals created by co-parenting to keep their lives with new partners separate from their children. But this was often a temporary expedient. Re-partnering invariably meant that children had to accommodate themselves to seeing their parents in relationships that absorbed much of their time and attention. Space and proportionality were the metaphors through which they often described the effects of the entry of new parents and new children into their lives, and apprehended the complexity of achieving a liveable balance between their own interests and those of their parents:

> I don't like Mum's new partner, I'm not overly fond of what he did to us. … now when we go out he's always right next to her and my brother's on the other side of her and I'm walking behind or in front of all of them and I don't get much attention now. And they're thinking of having a baby and if that happens I'll only get like a quarter of the attention and so I'm going to say that I'm going to spend a lot more time with my dad if they have a child.
>
> (Thomas aged 11)

The importance of recognition

None of these issues necessarily sapped children's commitment to co-parenting. Many of them saw the physical and emotional demands of their new lives as an unavoidable price that had to be paid if they were to retain 'real' relationships with their parents. But some children sought adjustments to the 'contract' they had entered into, to achieve a better accommodation of their needs. In these cases parents' willingness to recognize the validity of their children's perspectives became a critical factor in their overall happiness and the quality of relationships. Many parents took account of children's views (even at some emotional cost to themselves) and adhered to democratic processes of negotiation in which the opinions of children and adults alike carried weight. There were some children, however, who were reluctant even to broach the issue of altering a 50–50 arrangement because this was intimately linked to a fragile truce between their warring parents. Other parents simply brushed aside children's requests as inconsequential:

Rob: My dad really wants me to stay more at his house. And my mum wants me to stay at my mum's house more. And I do. And I don't get a choice to say if I want to …

Interviewer: Has there been a time when you didn't want to go [to dad's]?

Rob: Yes. My mum told me a day before I was supposed to go, that I was going. And I said, 'Do I have to go?' My mum said, 'Yes, because I've got to do something' and I said to my mum, 'I'm not sure if I want to go 'cos it's a bit noisy there'. And my mum said, 'Just tell them not to be too noisy' which I did. But they sometimes don't listen, and that's one of the times they didn't listen.

(Rob, aged eight)

The extent to which parents were willing to see their children as separate persons with their own needs and perspectives strengthened or undermined the 'real' relationships which the children sought. The children appreciated that their wishes often had to be subordinated to the larger claims and demands of their parents' lives, but when parents consistently refused to allow them room for negotiation, or eroded their sense of personhood, children sometimes abandoned the effort to make co-parenting 'work' by voting with their feet, and reducing, or even terminating contact.

Bound up in these processes of negotiation were children's concepts of fairness. A parent who was obstructive, or who held rigidly to their 'right' to an equal proportion of the child's time, was invariably designated 'unfair'. But over and above this, the core constituents of a fair agreement were recognized by many children as infinitely more complex than they had initially imagined. For these children fairness became associated with equity rather than equality. What they sought was to achieve a settlement capable of accommodating the varying needs of different family members in as flexible and reasonable a way as possible. This sometimes meant recognizing that a better fit would be achieved if children spent more time with one parent than another:

Dad doesn't feel it's really, really fair but it does work good for him because he's got all his meetings to go to and I'd be really bored. He might not realize that but I'd be totally fed up and I'd just want to go home or see my friends. It works for Mum because she's got some time with Ian [new partner] when they can eat fish and stuff, 'cos I hate fish, and it gives her a break from worrying about me. But it's also good for me 'cos it means I don't have to spend too much time with my dad, but I've still got him, I still see him.

(Beth, aged 14)

Conclusion

The children in our studies of post-divorce families live complex lives. We do not claim that their lives are *more* complex than the lives of children before them, but the complexities they experience now seem more open to articulation. These complexities may also be more 'felt' simply because, as Beck and Beck Gernsheim have stated, family life no longer happens in one place. Moving out of the conventional place and space of family life in the UK in the second half of the twentieth century – namely the single household – to living across households with kin and step-kin distributed more widely than in the recent past, gives rise to new forms of family life. This in turn brings new expectations, disappointments and challenges. In navigating these new terrains, children and young people appear as actively engaged moral philosophers. They employ moral principles (especially the principle of fairness) to set the parameters of appropriate behaviour. But their philosophy is not Kantian, in the sense of being based on abstract reasoning. Rather they appear to modify their philosophy according to lived experience and, arguably, they develop a relational philosophy in which there are no absolutes, but rather accommodations based ultimately on mutual respect and recognition. Divorce or separation alters the taken-for-grantedness of everyday family life. Before divorce the sorts of principles governing parent–child relationships might not be clarified, defined or acknowledged openly. They may simply be lived but unnamed. Divorce (or separation) ruptures this moral universe and gives rise to new possibilities and experiences. One of the most significant issues for children is the new challenge of relating to parents separately in separate households in a context in which they may feel that they have a duty to treat each parent as fairly as possible. This is something of a role reversal – at least as contemporary sociology might see family relationships. The typical presumption has been that parents should treat children fairly, and also that parents have duties and responsibilities towards their children. Our work on post-divorce family life suggests the reinvigoration of an older vision of how families operate, with children assuming duties in relation to their parents and with children feeling responsibilities for the fair treatment of adults. It may of course be that mainstream family sociology[6] has simply failed to see that children have often (always?) felt a sense of duty and obligation towards parents. So much discussion on the family has been caught up in the rhetoric of moral decline and worsening behaviour that the idea that children may be active moral agents has become almost unthinkable.[7]

In arguing this point, it may be felt that we are overstating the sophistication of the children's moral reasoning. Certainly, our terminology may be more elaborate that that of the children themselves. But it is in the context of ordinary, everyday family life, with its competing claims and demands, that the children we interviewed developed a strong sense of how parents and adults should behave in relation to one another. These children were reflexive beings who were attentive to the needs of others and not only to their own desires and preferences. As they grew older it became important for them that their parents respected them as separate individuals and, in this sense, they wanted *recognition*. They also gave recognition to their parents because the divorce they had lived through meant that they could see their parents as separate people too. In this chapter we have concentrated mainly on the way in which the principle of fairness (interpreted initially as equality) was modified by experience, and in particular by children's growing awareness that simple equality was fair for parents but not necessarily for themselves. The shift away from fairness-as-equality to fairness-through-recognition could be a painful process, and in some instances led to a breakdown in relationships. However, it was through this process that the children themselves were able to show that post-divorce family life really cannot be construed as a simple form of redistribution of assets between parents. Their experiences form the basis of an important critique of overly simplistic visions of how to create fairness after divorce or separation. As long as policy discussions focus on what is fair for parents, the complexity and the importance of the quality of relationships between parents and children will continue to be overlooked to the detriment of adults' ability to recognize children as people.

Acknowledgement

We wish to acknowledge the work and collaboration of Dr Bren Neale, grantholder with Carol Smart on the ESRC project on which this chapter is based. Dr Neale is an integral part of the team at the Centre for Research on Family, Kinship and Childhood and many of the ideas expressed in this chapter have been produced in collaboration with her.

Reference

Allan, G. (ed.) (1999) *The Sociology of the Family*, Oxford: Blackwell.

Beck, U. and Beck Gernsheim, E. (1995) *The Normal Chaos of Love*, Cambridge: Polity Press.

Beck, U. and Beck Gernsheim, E. (2002) *Individualization*, London: Sage.

Burgess, A. (1998) *The Complete Parent*, London: IPPR.

Coleman, J.S. (1988) 'Social capital in the creation of human capital', *American Journal of Sociology*, 94: Supplement S95–S120.

Delphy, C. (1976) 'Continuities and discontinuities in marriage and divorce', in D. Leonard Barker and S. Allen (eds) *Sexual Divisions and Society*, London: Tavistock.

Department of Health (1991) 'The Children Act 1989 Guidance and Regulations', vol. 1, *Court Orders*, London: HMSO.

Dowling, E. and Gorell Barnes, G. (2000) *Working with Children and Parents through Separation and Divorce*, Basingstoke: Macmillan.

Eekelaar, J. and Clive, E. (1977) *Custody after Divorce*, Oxford: Centre for Socio-Legal Studies.

Fraser, N. (2001) 'Recognition without ethics', *Theory, Culture and Society*, 18–(2–3): 21–42.

Furstenberg, F., Morgan, S. and Allison, P. (1987) 'Paternal participation and children's well-being after marital dissolution', *American Sociological Review*, 52: 695–701.

Giddens, T. (1992) *The Transformation of Intimacy*, Cambridge: Polity Press.

Gillis, J. (1996) *A World of Their Own Making*, Cambridge, Mass.: Harvard University Press.

Honneth, A. (2001) 'Recognition or redistribution? Changing perspectives on the moral order of society', *Theory, Culture and Society*, 18 (2–3): 43–56.

Jagger, G and Wright, C. (eds) (1999) *Changing Family Values*, London: Routledge.

Secker, S. (2001) *For the Sake of the Children: The FNF Guide to Shared Parenting*, London: FNF Publications.

Seltzer, J.A. (1991) 'Relationships between fathers and children who live apart: the father's role after separation', *Journal of Marriage and the Family*, 53: 79–101.

Smart, C and Neale, B. (1999) '"I hadn't really thought about it": new identities/new fatherhoods', in J. Seymour and P. Bagguley (eds) *Relating Intimacies: Power and Resistance*: 118–41, Basingstoke: Macmillan.

Smart, C., Neale, B. and Wade, A. (2001) *The Changing Experience of Childhood: Families and Divorce*, Cambridge: Polity Press.

Smith, H. (1999) *Children, Feelings and Divorce: Finding the Best Outcome*, London: Free Association Books.

Stacey, J. (1996) *In the Name of the Family*, Boston: Beacon Press.

Wade, A. and Smart, C. (forthcoming, 2002) *Facing Family Change: Children's Circumstances, Strategies and Resources*, York: The Joseph Rowntree Foundation.

8 Children's stories of parental breakup

Lars-Erik Berg

Introduction

Children's reactions to parental divorce or separation are here studied along the continuum from 'divorce as misery' to 'divorce as problem-solving'. The text builds on selected material from research on divorced fathers and their children in the mid-1990s, carried out in Göteborg, Sweden, by Berg and Johansson (1999). It concerns the emotional wrestling performed by fathers and their children during and after the divorce process. We used semi-structured interviews, and conversations and narratives were encouraged.[1] In this chapter attention is given to the children's stories, with few comments from their fathers.

'Divorce as misery' has been studied intensively. Smart and Neale (2001)[2] (also see the *Economist* 2001) discuss some of this work where the tone is one of understanding rather than dismay. To this we can add fairly positive attitudes as indicated by our interviewees. We shall try to understand what happens psycho-socially to children during divorce. Some of the fathers' versions and more detailed references to the international discussion are found in Berg (2001).

Theoretical background

The theoretical basis for our interpretation is found in symbolic interactionism. Nancy Chodorow's (1978) cultural neo-Freudian theory was also taken into account. We did not confirm Chodorow's scenario of high gender differences in parental involvement. On the contrary, we found that both fathers and children were unwilling to differentiate the two parental roles. This can be seen as due to historical/cultural changes during late modernity, possibly combined with emancipating national political trends.

Another influence is taken from Giddens' discussions (1990, 1991, 1992) of a steadily growing reflexivity. This hypothesis was confirmed to a high extent at all levels of our study, both for different social classes and for different generations. The same held true of Bauman's (1991) sociology concerning post-modern conditions of ambivalence and ambiguity that prevail in a society characterized by pluralism, great variability of expectations and considerable freedom of choice.

Bauman can be interpreted in both light and dark ways: ambivalence can create feelings of freedom and strength in a deliberate wrestling with problems; it can also work subconsciously, thus confusing the mind. It is not a precondition that enhanced reflective capacity will lighten the burdens of ambivalence. We found evidence for both interpretations.

We start with the conscious reasoning and attitudes manifested by the children. Then we present our understanding of what is being told between the lines, of expressions given unconsciously and some interpretations of what is not told at all.

Children's rational reactions

Stories told by the children are not copies of their fathers'.[3] However there is often an affinity – some common themes but with variations.

One theme is the children's attitude to the legal conditions of divorce. Should divorce be free or legally restricted? Is divorce a sign of failure, or should it be regarded more positively? A story told separately by a father and his daughter (now aged 16 but 13 at the time of the divorce) will crystallize the most typical difference between fathers and children.

The divorce for this particular father was a disaster. His wife had fallen in love with another man. One of the toughest events was telling his own parents of the failure of his marriage. He could not manage it but began weeping. The matter was solved by his daughter telling her grandparents about the divorce. The father relates this with a mixture of feelings, where the comic aspect of the reversal of relations of strength and authority is clearly visible. He recognizes his weakness and appreciates his daughter's capacity to be a support for him, although he is a healthy, strong man with a good, traditionally masculine job.

His daughter tells a simpler version of the story, where difficult feelings are apparently absent. It is natural to her that she told her grandparents, because her father could not do it without weeping. She picked up from where he left off when he could not bear it. It is as simple as that!

Although the disparity in this case is greater than normal, the differing attitudes of the two are typical: the degree of *rational reasoning* about problems of divorce is more pronounced in children than in their fathers. Children regard the situation as a case where problems have arisen. The solution should be worked through sensibly, not subsumed in irrational feelings of anger, mourning and inferiority. Unhappiness may present itself, but it should not determine the problem-solving process.

This particular girl scores high on the scale of pragmatism and her attitude is typical. Remaining with her story, we find an effort to solve another problem which stirs her emotions more. Her mother had a lover before the divorce, and she made her daughter her confidante. The girl comments that this is too heavy a burden to place on a child. She blames her mother not for having a love affair before divorce but for taking her as a confidante. She does not moralize to her mother. She is rational, stating that if the relationship between the parents is enduringly bad, they should divorce – however, they should avoid involving the children in their relationship problems.

This attitude of rationality and pragmatism surprised us. The tendency is clear and it also crosses age differences. Amanda (now aged eight, aged five at the time of the divorce) already knew at five about divorce, because she had 'seen it on TV', and now she says that, '… if you don't like … to live together … then …'. She means that divorce is the natural remedy for marital conflict. She is among those children who say that the two worst things about divorce are having to move and seeing Daddy too little when he moves out of the child's home.

Some children adopt an analytical attitude. Erica (now aged 13, aged six at the time of the divorce) argues that if parents cannot 'give each other support and if they do not like to do the same things', they should divorce. If there is any moral evil it would be to insist on keeping such a family intact. Freedom from socio-emotional constraint is the better alternative, even if life in separation is filled with uncertainty and difficulties. And children will not be hurt too much if the parents can manage to carry their parental responsibility even in the acute phases of divorce. Keeping the family together is not most important, but that people do not exert extreme pressure on each other.

How do we account for these differences between fathers' and childrens' attitudes? The cultural system of norms that regulate marriage and family has a long tradition in which avoidance divorce is taken for granted. This tradition is questioned today. Fathers have their roots in the old tradition, but they have not transferred it to their children. Children see a lot of divorces taking place, and do not make a fuss about it. Divorce is normal, both statistically, culturally and emotionally. Mass media also perhaps contribute to the 'normality' of divorce.

A complementary solution is to assume a tendency in children to let consciousness work with the problems until they are minimized. This follows Giddens' reflective approach. Children may invest a lot of energy in such work. Anne (now aged 13, aged nine at the time of the divorce) gives us a vivid picture of a divorce filled with anger and even violence. She says her parents and the whole household were 'totally sick' for a while. 'But I didn't care,' she adds, 'because it was sick.' We can interpret this in different ways, one of which is that children invest much attention in belittling the tragic and dramatic dimensions of divorce. Anne in reality tells us that she felt terrible, but that she consciously worked very hard to minimize bad feelings.

Minimizing the trauma may also have a subconscious counterpart. Perhaps Anne's older sister, telling us about the unfaithfulness of her mother, had worse feelings than she expressed, although she seemed genuine enough. She worked on herself in order to tolerate or accept her mother's behaviour. Perhaps part of this emotional work was done on a subconscious level. This girl's father tells us that she is considering moving in permanently with him, as he has eventually found a decent place to live. Is there an issue of showing solidarity with her 'offended' father against the 'offending' mother? The girl herself has no more criticism against her mother than that mentioned above.

Between the lines: anger and mourning

Two emotions are discussed by many children: mourning and anger. Both of these are realized and discussed manifestly and clearly, but children also express themselves 'between the lines' in important ways. For reasons of space and clarity we choose to illustrate both aspects together.

Many children tell us there was a short period when the emotions of mourning and anger were sometimes heavy to carry. When we scrutinize more closely, we find that it is not the divorce per se that is the worst thing: their anger focuses on their parents not coming to a conclusion in harmony but having a period of quarrelling and of difficulties in communicating. It can also concern external problems like moving to another place.

> I didn't care, but that we were forced to move ... !
>
> (Anne)

It is peculiar that the parents' violent quarrels were nothing to talk about, but the fact of moving was. Anne exaggerates the hardships of moving to another home, in order to find an emotional outlet for feelings properly belonging in another psychic location – a simple illustration of how the mind works in a partly subconscious way to rationalize emotional problems.

The concept of mourning is even clearer for all the children, and concerns the *part-time disappearance* of the father. He used to be there every day, and then suddenly the child sees him at best every second week, or much less. And the more time you spend with your father, the less you see your mother! Divorce invariably leads to experience of loss.

The father's 'invisibility' is a big problem. When we ask, once new routines have been allowed to settle, 'What is the worst thing after the divorce?' children say broken agreements over meeting times. When Daddy says that he cannot see you on the agreed day, but that you must wait a day or two, or that the trip to Granny's cannot be made, that is upsetting. A clear message emerges that regularity in managing limited time together with the father is of great importance. Children from ten years to the lower teens stress this. An example is Erica (now aged 13, age six at the time of the divorce), who is one of our most eloquent and rational subjects. She is one of the few who talk freely about feelings of sadness, and who shows it during the interview. She regards postponed meetings as a source of sadness in the first instance, and then of anger. Anger comes if the postponement is repeated. However, it seems that fathers are always readily forgiven. Children's capacity and readiness to take the father's working conditions into consideration is great.

To summarise, children have a great capacity for analyzing and discussing divorce rationally in a positive and penetrating way. Each child negotiates between expectations and reality and with the father. This is true to an astonishing extent. How can we account for this, in the light of the 'misery' research on family dissolution? We will suggest two explanations here, the latter of which takes Freudian aspects of unconscious thought into account.

The first explanation deals with identity as a social narrative. It was revealed most explicitly by a grown child (Ivan now aged 23, aged ten at the time of the divorce). Ivan regards his mother and father as very good parents. He has nothing to blame either of them for. Since the divorce he has lived mostly with his mother, who has not remarried. His father already had three daughters when he met Ivan's mother, and after the divorce, he inherited two more children.

Ivan's account of the divorce stresses first that his parents told him, at a very early stage, what was going to happen. Second, they told him why it would happen, namely that, 'my mother could not carry on living together with Daddy, because they were so different'. Third, they explained that he had no part whatsoever in the divorce. And finally they confirmed that he would go on seeing his father on a regular basis, mostly one day every week.

Compare this with what is often reported in studies of divorce, where children are informed very briefly about the divorce and about the father leaving home only a short time before he actually leaves. It is also common that the father is very seldom seen after leaving, especially when he becomes involved in a new family, or when he is unemployed or has poor living conditions.

These are important points. Ivan is well-informed a long time before things actually happen; he is reassured that neither of his parents will disappear but will be regularly available, no matter what else happens, and he knows that he carries no responsibility for the divorce. Ivan stresses that these points are pivotal for him not to have experienced the divorce as a catastrophe, but instead as a sensible way of solving problems of family life.

In our theoretical traditions, the phenomenon of personal identity construction is problematized, for example by pointing to its *narrative* character. This comes to mind when analysing the difference between the 'misery' version of divorce on the one hand and the 'problem-solving' version on the other. This difference is sharply illustrated by our different subjects: Ivan, with his verbal analysis of positive experiences; Berit (aged 19) with her bad experiences of her parents' divorce; Erica (aged 12) with her correspondingly good experiences; Tor (aged 15) with very varying experiences of several divorces that his father went through with him; and Marc (aged 12), whose principal impression of divorce is the positive one of gaining siblings and other relatives.

Our point is that divorce seems to have been woven into the narrative of identity and everyday life for these children to a high degree, even in the majority of the unhappy cases, whereas the opposite is true in the 'misery' material in which there is – at worst – practically no narrative at all. Daddy just moves out. There is a 'snapshot' of the divorce, a statement at one specific point in time, and then the subject is left. *Identity* for a child has an intimate link to the *character of the parents*, and it is built up within a *narrative*. Thus, if the narrative is absent or abbreviated, and if one of the parents practically vanishes, we can easily see a link to severe socio-emotional problems for the child. We conclude that parents must help the child with the narrative. The problem is that they do not always do this.

The *how* question seems to be much more important than the *why* question, as far as the children's stories are concerned. We need no further psychology than this seemingly simple one, taken from a sociological version of social psychology.

Whose fault? Responsibility or guilt?

Children tend to feel guilt when they experience emotional distress between the parents. They can even feel guilty when they are victims of incestuous acts or other forms of abuse. Psychoanalysis theorizes such experiences. Klein's (1937) theory of 'the good and the evil breast' is used to explain feelings of guilt.[4] Such theories are also applicable to divorce. Wallerstein and Kelly (1980) use them for their empirical material, but find the support weak and ambiguous.

We took up the question. Some of the teenage children, viewing the divorce with hindsight, had thought of themselves as partly causing the divorce, but had not thought in terms of responsibility or guilt. These children develop theories using themselves as examples for theoretical reflection, mostly feeling reassured of their innocence when theoretical examination has been carried through. It seems as if they have read Wallerstein and Kelly! This is one of the points where we were struck by the mature theoretical abilities that these children possess, often more so than their fathers, who are also good philosophers.

We asked, 'Is a divorce something where anybody does anything wrong? If so, who did most wrong in your particular case?' Most children did not even understand the question. With thought, they could understand that a divorce is something bad, and that somebody could be more responsible for it than someone else. However, the concept of guilt does not enter their minds: they actively deny this way of thinking. Divorce has no direct relation to guilt. It is not even a problem. It is more problem-*solving* than problem-*creating*.

Our material actualizes the distinction between the concepts of *guilt* and *cause* in this question. Some of the children can see themselves as partly causing the divorce, but theories of children's feelings of guilt are not relevant in our material.

This still leaves the question of *cause* to be explored. Piaget's theory of childish *egocentrism* can be used to carry our interpretation back to the points that Ivan made so clear above. Piaget maintains that children make judgements from their own standpoints. They cannot easily imagine that there are judgements other than their own. They are forced to make egocentric evaluations, having no capacity of taking the position of the other person or of abstract thinking. An easy example would be: Jack knows that he has a sister, Jill, but when asked if Jill has a brother, Jack says no. He can see no brother around Jill, centred as he is in his own being.

Linked to Ivan's points of the communicative capacity of the parents, Piaget can be used to illustrate children's feelings of guilt and/or cause in divorce cases, and this can be an adequate starting point for theorizing. If the child has *no access to information* on the subject, he or she must invent their own theory. Their own locus of action is highlighted: the child must be the cause of the divorce. Why else should the parents divorce, as they have married out of love, and as they have not announced that love has ceased? Of course it must be that the child is impossible for Daddy to live with!

There is still another aspect of egocentrism: as the child is an *actor*, most events seem to be caused by the child him or herself! And if we add the Freudian theory of the *omnipotent* child, this theory becomes even clearer.[5] Finally, add also an interactionist aspect of *narrative* in identity construction, and the confused child theory becomes obvious.

However, what is striking to us is that these theories are not confirmed in our material, neither among older nor among younger children. Most of them are well-informed − by their parents − that they are not the cause of the divorce. Divorce is a question of deciding rationally about alternative ways of living. This interpretation is stronger among children than among fathers, although it prevails also among the latter. Thus we find a positive relation between a high level of information and a commitment to rationality. However, even children with a low level of information make a good attempt at handling the divorce rationally. As we shall see, failure in this endeavour is due to the double burden of a low level of information and hostility between parents.

The rational management of tough emotions

Nonetheless, thoughts related to the feelings of guilt are still cultivated. Children can experience their own relation to the divorce as deeply problematic in some way. This emotional experience is clearly displayed in some interviews. Eskil (aged 15), enjoying the fact that he can always see his father regularly, feels relaxed: Daddy wants to see him after all! Eskil sometimes thought that his own behaviour had something to do with the divorce.

Didrik (now aged 17, parents divorced before birth) is a clear rationalizer. His parents lived in different countries. He lived for about ten years with his mother. Then he was visited by his father and decided some years later to go to live with him. A few years later his mother followed him, and from about the age of 15, his parents have lived in the same town and have a reasonable relationship. Didrik is deeply reflective about himself. He finds that he is 'emotionally cold and withholding', more so than his parents. He also believes that this trait is hard for his parents to see. He keeps cool and tries to have a good, friendly relationship with both parents. In the past he was able to believe that his own behaviour had a bad causal influence on the relationship between his parents; not so nowadays. He likes his life. He does not feel dependent and does not like having intimate relations with anybody.

Didrik is an illustration of the tragic aspect of Giddens' late modern reflexivity, and of Bauman's ambivalence. He distances himself to such an extent from his emotional sufferings that he can rationally analyse them almost professionally. But at the same time he expresses in many ways the condition of ambivalence − his own and his father's. Didrik has set out to carry emotional problems which were introduced in his life even before his birth. His parents are communicative with him, have enabled him to develop the capacity of reflexivity and to carry the burdens of ambivalence.

The same capacity of exerting reflexivity and carrying ambivalence is also shown by other respondents. We asked Eskil about his parents' new partners.

Eskil: You know … I didn't think of it. Mostly … I thought … that it isn't good to sit alone at home. Good for Daddy to see another woman, when Mother met another man and divorced. That's what everybody thinks, you know!'

Interviewer: But you said that you felt that somebody came and sort of took your father from you?

Eskil: Yes, yes, I did.

Interviewer: And you don't feel this way any longer?

Eskil: No.

(Eskil, aged 15)

Eskil has trained himself in social competence and empathy by placing himself in the position of other children: he comments on the fact that the sons of his mother's new man thought the same of him in regard to their father. He also judges himself as childish when moving from his father's house with his mother into her new man's house, when the father introduced a new woman some time afterwards. Eskil likes this woman and her daughter, but he remembers that he felt a stranger in his own home, especially when a new half-sibling was born. Now he has worked out a position in the new family, being fond of and attentive to his new little sister. It has been hard work for him.

> … I felt bad some years ago, but that's the case with all divorce children, who think that … that … . It's the same for all. It's only childish, what all … what most of us think …

(Eskil, aged 15)

Repression and rationalization

Daddy moves and the rest of the family may move to another home: these are the worst things about the divorce. But there is more to be explored. Children do not mention quarrelling as the worst problem, yet it is tragically evident that this is the toughest thing for them to cope with.

Sometimes quarrels are mentioned in direct and open terms, but briefly and in a low voice. Eskil's usually clear thought is confused – there was and was not quarrelling. He expresses ambivalence, ambiguity and contradiction. Or is he persuading himself that it was not so bad, after all?

Eskil is one of the most articulate respondents, yet quarrels are difficult for him to talk about, because they give rise to difficult emotions not only for him, but also for his parents. They have not been able to be clear about their problems. This incapacity transfers itself to Eskil. Heavy material becomes heavier if not talked about. Language is the prerequisite not only for mature reflexive capacity, but even for elementary levels of conscious thought. The capacity to shed light on emotional problems between members in a closed group requires trained skills of expression. Eskil did not get enough help with this.

Berit (now aged 19, aged ten at the time of the divorce) illustrates this even more tragically. She has a younger sister and an older brother. Their father often worked at home, in close contact with the children. Berit's mother fell in love with a neighbour, her father grew furious and her mother answered this with anger. Their quarrels never reached a solution, but ended in silent antipathy. Her mother continued to live with the neighbour. Her father, wretched, drifted for a period before pulling himself together. Some time later he also found a new partner, with whom he still lives. All his children spend more than two days a fortnight with him. But he wants no contact with their mother.

Significant others build up the fundamentals of identity in the child through mirroring processes. Some sort of language must be used in this process. No consistent identity, good or bad, can be built without expressions and reflections.

Berit shows us two related traits – she provides a narrative with a low degree of consistency: unrelated facts coexist side by side. And she shows a high degree of ambivalence and contradictory thought. Reflexivity cannot illuminate her mind. Darkness is impenetrable, knots insolvable.

Berit oscillates between not knowing much about her parents' divorce and knowing much. Her attitudes and memories are incoherent. And she recognizes contradictions in her own story: she says that she does not remember much, but that she still remembers almost everything. We interpret this that she remembers traumatic, isolated events but she has no coherent narrative because she was not given one.

The oscillation also applies to Berit's feelings towards her parents and their new partners. She feels both good and bad feelings for them. And she does so at different times and at the same time. Berit says that she liked father's new woman a lot in the beginning, but that she nowadays regards her as a 'bitch', because she is too harsh to her younger sister Bodil. Bodil thinks that the new woman 'is great, especially talking about emotional problems'. But Berit claims that the new woman is bad to Bodil.

Oscillation is still more evident concerning their mother's new man. Berit told him, 'You can't try to be my father, don't think of trying, because I'll ...!' She goes on: 'Perhaps there was some quarrel with him in the beginning, but after that it was fine.' She keeps a distance, but at the same time she tries to appreciate him because he is her mother's man, and she thinks she is far more similar to him than to her own father.

We interpret that Berit's wish to please her parents also forces her to accept and love the new adults in the family. And this is happening at an age when she feels the need to develop her own identity. She should work on her own emotions instead of being a support for her parents, but this is not possible for her, the divorce being violent and laden with silent hostility. Berit answers by trying to 'swallow' the whole situation, an attempt which is doomed to failure. And nobody is there to help her in her confusion.

Confusion becomes still stronger when looking at Berit's attitudes to her parents. Of her mother she says that she does not blame her for falling in love with another man during her marriage with the father, but in fact she does:

> I asked Mama, 'Why did you do it? …' meeting another guy! … I blamed her for that … I have a friend … who is unfaithful. I get furious and I blame him, but Mama has done the same thing, why don't I blame her?
>
> (Berit, aged 19)

Berit tells us that she *blamed* her mother, but yet that she *did not blame* her, but *should have* done so, just as she blamed her friend. These internal contradictions are symptomatic of her way of talking.

The contact with her father 'is not so good, but still quite good, I think. I'm not here to see him very often, but it's still good; he is my daddy, so I often long for him.' She presents her father's character thus: 'He is greedy, kind and clever … I don't really know. Perhaps I don't know him too well. Don't know really.' But she knows one thing, her father's home is a place stamped with sociality. She likes this trait, which is not directly connected with him.

What is Berit's logic? She reveals the silent conflict between her parents. Talking about the early, explicitly aggressive period, she says, 'No, I never heard them quarrel, or perhaps I heard them quarrel, but I don't remember.' Berit says yes and no in the same sentence, but she does more than that. She says first that her parents did not quarrel, then she says second they did quarrel and finally she says she does not remember. By saying she doesn't remember, the facts about whether the parents did or did not quarrel become redundant. Clearly by admitting her inability to remember she is hinting that there is a deep emotional involvement and that there is something to dig up and remember.

Perhaps the best conclusion is to quote Berit herself. Asked whether there is anything potentially good with divorce, she answers:

> There is probably no good way to do it … I think that … afterwards, parents should still have good contact. Not be enemies and refuse talking to each other, as my parents have done.

This is – for once, in Berit's narrative – clear enough, although it constitutes another contradiction. She means that meeting each other even after times of hard conflict is necessary. For Berit the silent, aggressive attitude that she has witnessed has created within herself contradictions and oscillations between incompatible emotions and points of view. This has become a subjectively logical condition of life for her: contradiction is the basic logic of life.

Such is Berit's burden. Verbalizing problems and social–emotional work would help her to understand that there are also fundamental conditions of life other than contradiction and avoidance.

Verbal therapy: the healing effect of narrative

It should be clear by now that explicitly verbalizing conflicts helps children to master emotional problems. Conversation between father and child should be of even greater help. Gustaf (aged 30) and his daughter Sara (now three, aged six months at the time of the divorce) provide an illustrative case. Here we present a story partly manifestly told, but according to our interpretations the healing effect of conversation is not told, not even between the lines.

The past three years have been tough. Gustaf says he has experienced sabotage on the part of his ex-cohabitant but also lack of interest and suspicion from the authorities. The mother is the custodial parent. He has thought of contesting for shared custody, as he thinks the girl's mother is not capable of fulfilling the role of a single parent, for example sometimes leaving the home unattended at night. However, he has chosen not to disturb relations more by engaging in such a battle, and things have been working out better lately. But the emotional strength and health of both parents have been under severe pressure.

Still Gustaf insists on sharing responsibility but feels that he is prevented by the mother and authorities. At the time of separation, which followed a period of worsening conditions, Sara was only six months old. These are the preconditions for the development of the relationship between father and daughter.

Gustaf already felt strongly for his child when they planned the pregnancy and that affection grew as time passed. Father and daughter established a deep relationship through day-to-day contact and his practical involvement. We give one example which is relevant here because it shows the girl cultivating aspects of social competence, e.g. the capacity to solve conflict through facing the conflict without anxiety.

They were talking about the bad relations between the parents, and Gustaf told Sara about the reciprocity of good and bad feelings. 'We can't cope with each other because Mama thinks I'm silly with her, and I think she is silly with me!' He also told her that this was his opinion, and that her mother might have another. Sara handled the problem in her own way. Immediately upon coming home, before her father left, she told her mother, 'Mama, you shouldn't be silly to Daddy!'

This is not mature adult behaviour. But it very clearly demonstrates what is lacking for Berit, namely the possibility to create social and emotional order. According to Gustaf, Sara has a moderating effect on both parents. They can communicate better when Sara is present.

This situation illustrates psycho-social processes going on for Sara and her father (and hopefully mother). It shows that first the girl is attentive to her father and feels that his problem of communication with her mother is urgent; second, she can form an opinion of the problem and how it should be handled; third, she feels capable of helping her parents by her own actions, of exerting influence on them; fourth, she can freely express wishes and arguments in an atmosphere that is tolerant; fifth, she dares to criticize her mother who is vitally important to her, and on whom she is totally dependent most of the time; and finally she also dares to oppose her father, who did not want her to talk of this matter with her mother – she feels secure doing so.

This little girl demonstrates a considerable social trust and competence. This is all the more clear if we make another definition of social competence: the capacity to influence a group of people in a constructive way, departing from a firm knowledge of the (subject's own) Self and its characteristics, and the place of this Self in the group.

The human Self has a social origin in situations where the subject confronts other subjects, which react to it. The Self is born in this social process of receiving the reactions from the Other/s and in turn reacting to these. The expressions from the individuals involved constitute the conditions for the emergence of the Self.

Thus Sara is rapidly cultivating a competent Self, given that she is not threatened by repression from either of her two parents for taking and express-ing her standpoint. She demonstrates a wish to exist in harmony with her parents, in spite of their conflict, and she shows the insight that she may influ-ence her parents, to stop quarrelling. This is made possible only because of communication, in spite of the conflict.

Gustaf and Sara's story was chosen to juxtapose that of Berit. There is one important similarity and one important difference between them. Both situa-tions demonstrate bad communication between the parents. But the Gustaf/Sara situation is not silent. The atmosphere is openly social, even if bad emotions prevail between the parents. In the case of Berit the situation soon grew silent, and she grew bewildered about the nature of all the heavy emo-tions and other impressions. Critical communication (within limits that are not too frightening), as the case is for Sara, is much better than none at all, as for Berit, who has bad communication with her mother as well, on top of it all. Sara seems trusting even at three-and-a-half years old. Berit had no trust in her parents when they divorced; today she has only fragile trust in them and in her-self. Her picture of the drama is fragmented by contradictions and lack of knowledge. The tragedy is not *hostile* communication: it is *no* communication.

Our argument is supported by a developmental psychological cornerstone: in order for the child to grow intellectually, there have to be (mild) frustrations which permit communication, transcendence and problem-solving. Using G.H. Mead (1969) in combination with this we can deduce that one outcome of these 'mild frustrations' is the Self itself – it would not emerge, were it not for the individual's confrontation with the other Selves.[6]

The case of Berit grows deeper in this interpretation. What she exhibits is not only the emotions of her parents' shortcomings of conflict-solving: she also shows us the tragedy of a partly dissociated Self or identity.

Summary and conclusions

What do children say about their parents' divorce? One theme we have han-dled is divorce as problem-solving rather than problem-creating. The rationally pragmatic attitude of children, even at a young age, is demonstrated. Then we shift focus to see what is told more or less indirectly between the lines. In this way we can study a variety of social/emotional problems experienced by children. The most usual negative feelings are transitory anger and mourning. The other side of this coin is the great tolerance shown to the parents' shortcomings. Intensive distress and guilt are rare. We then pass on to the dark area of traumas and dissociation created by hostility and silence. Finally we return to conceiving divorce as cultivating a special sort of social competence. Children seem to be maturely reflecting on the problems of divorce, given that they are afforded a fair chance by being supplied with the relevant information. Creating a coherent narrative may be more important than the question of whether it is 'true'.

References

Bauman, Z. (1991) *Modernity and Ambivalence*, Oxford: Polity Press.

Berg, L.-E. (2001) 'Divorce and fathering in late modern Sweden', in T. David (ed.) (2001) 'Promoting evidence-based practice in early childhood education: research and its implications', *Advances in Applied Early Childhood Education*, vol. 1., London: JAI Elsevier.

Berg, L.-E. and Johansson, T. (1999) *Den andre föräldern (The Second Parent)* Stockholm: Carlssons Bokförlag.

Burgess, A. (1997) *Reclaiming Fatherhood. The Making of the Modern Father*, London: Vermillion.

Chodorow, N. (1978) *The Reproduction of Mothering*, Berkeley: California University Press.

David, T. (ed.) (2001) 'Promoting evidence-based practice in early childhood education: research and its implications', *Advances in Applied Early Childhood Education*, Vol 1., London: JAI Elsevier.

Economist (2001) 'Home Sweet Home: the debate about family values', in A. Giddens (ed.) *Sociology, Introductory Readings*, 2., Oxford: Polity Press.

Elkind, D. (1994) *Ties That Stress: The New Family Imbalance*, Cambridge, Mass. Massachusetts: Harvard University Press.

Fürstenberg, F. and Cherlin, A. (1991) *Divided Families*, Cambridge, Mass.: Harvard University Press.

Giddens, A. (1990) *The Consequences of Modernity*, Cambridge: Polity Press/Blackwell.

Giddens, A. (1991) *Modernity and Self Identity*, Cambridge: Polity Press.

Giddens, A. (1992) *The Transformations of Intimacy*, Cambridge: Polity Press.

Kearney, Manson, and Plantin, (2000) *Fatherhood and Masculinity*, University of Sunderland, Centre for Social Research and Practice.

Klein, M. (1937) 'Love, guilt and reparation', in M. Klein and J. Riviere (1964) *Love, Hate and Reparation*, New York: W.W. Norton.

Lund, M. (1987) 'The non-custodial father: common challenges in parenting after divorce', in C. Lewis and M. O'Brien (eds) *Reassessing Fatherhood*, London: Sage.

McLanahan, S. and Sandefur, G. (1994) *Growing Up with a Single Parent*, Cambridge Mass.: Harvard University Press.

Mead, G.H. (1969) *Mind, Self and Society, from the Standpoint of Social Behaviourism*. Chicago: University of Chicago Press.

Smart, C. and Neale, B. (2001) 'Constructing post-divorce childhoods' in A. Giddens (ed) *Sociology, Introductory Readings* (2nd ed.), Oxford: Polity.

Wallerstein, J. and Kelly, J. (1980) *Surviving the Breakup*, London: Grant McIntyre.

Winnicott, D.W. (1964/76) *The Child, the Family and the Outside World*, Harmondsworth: Penguin.

9   For the children's sake

Symbolic power lost?

An-Magritt Jensen

Many will argue that the negotiating position of children within the family has augmented. Children are listened to and have a say in contrast to the more remote relations between the generations in previous times (Hendrick 1997). In mass media the negotiating power of children is frequently portrayed as a problem. Indeed children are depicted as greedy, demanding consumers. Concern is surfacing over fading discipline and exhausted parents doing their best to satisfy their children's neverending demands.

While public discourse often envisions the individual child's enhanced power, I shall raise an issue of children's diminishing power in family matters. It is the symbolic, not the actual, child power that is the focus of this chapter. My argument will be that children have possessed a symbolic power over adults' behaviour which has disappeared.

Transformation and negotiation

A few clarifications are needed on the intersection between transformation of family structure at the societal level and negotiation at the level of the actor. The relationship between structure and agency is at the core of sociological controversies. Where does agency start and how does it interact with structure? From Marx and Durkheim onwards, sociological legacy tells us that individuals do not choose their life in a vacuum. They choose it, says Marx, within a system of social relationships that is determined by the material forces of production, while Durkheim accentuates the division of labour. More recent sociologists, such as Beck and Beck-Gernsheim (2002) argue that the process of individualization undermines the traditional social institutions to the advantage of the individual as a basic unit of social actions. In most Western countries the family is a core social institution where struggles between new individual desires and old collective demands are now taking place. Family changes provide a particularly interesting case of changes in the relationship between structure and agency because it goes without saying that the agency in question belongs to the adults. Adults, not children, are seen as linkages between structure and agency in the broad transformations of families. This raises the question, is choice and freedom for adults enhanced at the expense of safety and security of children?

I shall argue that children have possessed a power to influence adult behaviour which has gone astray. I understand power as the ability to produce a certain occurrence (Gould and Kolb 1965: 524). Children's 'power' was based upon societal norms about the family. At the symbolic level, children can be seen as having had a symbolic power to produce and uphold their parents' marriage. Hence, the kind of power discussed is a symbolic power, a power that has impact because it is recognized and through this given a value (Bourdieu 1999). Symbolic power gains power because it is not openly recognized as power. It rests upon its 'taken-for-grantedness'. Children could influence their parents' behaviour as long as this influence was not questioned.

My argument is that historically, children imposed constraints on parents' choices in relation to the family as a social institution. Young people married in the expectation of having children, stayed together and accepted a certain division of labour within the family, 'for the children's sake'. It was not openly recognized as a kind of 'child power', but functioned at the symbolic level as such. Children's symbolic power was the collective consciousness about marriage as the only place for having and rearing children. This power vanished during the 1970s and beyond.

The collective consciousness about the kind of family into which children should be born and raised has dramatically shifted. We may discuss the degree to which people, men and women alike, are free to choose their family form. In spite of the process of individualization it may be argued that adults' choices are also subjected to structures such as the mode of production and the division of labour. This is not elaborated in this chapter. More attention is given to whether children's power to influence marriage patterns and durability is to the benefit of children or not. Many accounts are given of children growing up in misery, in fractured or damaging families, where their best interests would have been a marriage split. On the other hand, are we sure that the substitution is compatible with children's interests?

In this chapter I shall highlight how changing adult behaviour seems to reflect the lost symbolic power of children in family matters. I shall then discuss some consequences for children's lives and reflect on whether the declining marriage may be described as a generational conflict where the interests of the parents conflict with those of the children. A main source of data is the Children's Families Survey (CFS) which was carried out in Norway in 1988 and then repeated in 1996 (Jensen and Clausen 2002). The surveys used children aged four, ten and 16 as the unit of observation in national representative samples covering about 6,500 children. A parent in the child's household provided information about family type at the child's birth and changes during childhood. The surveys covered the period from 1972, when the oldest cohort from the 1988 round was born, to 1996 when the youngest cohort from the 1996 round was four years old. This is the period when consensual unions spread rapidly from being almost non-existent to being as common as the married family. We can follow the marital status of parents at the birth of the child and whether they married, stayed together or moved apart at a later stage. I shall supplement this with information from the UK and other countries where available and relevant.

The areas to be explored here are how the symbolic power of children is diminished in the having of children, marital status at the birth of a child and the durability of the conjugal family.

Childfree zones in adult life

In contrast to pre-contraceptive times when children, to a large degree, were a part of what is taken for granted, having a child now involves an active choice. At stake is emotional satisfaction, balanced against long-term investments in money and time (Hobcraft and Kiernan 1995). However, a progressive part of adult life is lived before (or without) this long-term investment. Young people will typically approach their thirties before even considering having a child. Children have turned into one of the major issues of negotiation among young couples: the so-called 'child question' (Beck and Beck-Gernsheim 2002). The wish to have a child conflicts with the wish for an independent adult life. The age of entrance into parenthood is delayed, the number of children reduced and the proportion of childless years enlarged. The lifestyle of the SITCOMs (Single Income, Two Children, Oppressive Mortgage) is contrasted to the THINKERs (Two Healthy Incomes, No Kids, Early Retirement).

A drive towards single life is traced in the European Fertility and Family Surveys.[1] Among men and women aged 25–9 around 1990, one in four women (23 per cent) in Central Europe were living without a partner or a child. Among men, this was true for close to every second (42 per cent). Even at age 35–9 almost one in five men (17 per cent), were living alone. The European Value Studies confirm ambivalence towards children among young people. In 1995 only 17 per cent of European women aged 25–39 and 14 per cent of the men stated that children were an essential value in life (and an additional 51/43 per cent stated that children were 'very important') (Jensen 1999).

Negotiations about when to have a first child and whether or not to have a third child are growing in intensity. Many will argue that a postponement is to the benefit of the children since parenthood is better prepared. But first and foremost the delay echoes how children have to be fitted into the life-planning of adults. Subsequently, most people do have children but they are postponed to later in life. Postponement of having a first child may be seen as an indication of young people's ideas of children. Children are postponed until other life goals – education and employment being typical examples – are under control. The having of a child is judged against the having of other aspects of life and in this 'competition' adults choose to live an ever-expanding part of their life in a child-free zone. Postponement – and avoidance – of having a first child is a first indicator of children's lost power over adult behaviour.

From shotgun to non-marriage

In the nineteenth century marriage gained a hegemonic position as an institution in which children should be born and raised. During the last part of the century, when statistics was gradually established as science, the mediocre social position of the unmarried mother and her child surfaced to general knowledge. Such children were more likely to die, they were poorer, socially rejected and had fewer life chances in general. Linguistically they could be named bastard, illegitimate, whoreson.

Historically the collective consciousness grasped children and marriage as a unity, supported by social condemnation of deviants. Until the mid-1900s the only proper place to have and rear children was in marriage and the proportion of the ill-fated children born to unwed mothers was kept at a low and surprisingly stable level. In Scandinavia, until 1970 this level did not exceed 10 per cent of all children born since 1800[2] (Jensen 1999). However, it is estimated that two out of three children born in the eighteenth century were conceived before marriage. Norwegian priest and sociologist Eilert Sundt was travelling in Norway around 1850 and found that sexual intercourse before marriage was the norm. Similarly, Goody (1994) describes how illegitimate births and pre-marital pregnancies could be very high in northern Europe in general. This was a common feature until the latter part of the twentieth century.

Pregnancy was a common reason to marry. In Norway in 1950, when only three per cent of the children were born outside marriage, almost every second child was conceived before marriage and this pattern prevailed until 1970 (Dyrvik 1976). For England a similar picture is given (for example in McRae 1997). Marriage statistics reveal a large variation and not-formalized family relationships existed along with formal marriages in the UK. Nevertheless, extramarital births constituted only 5–7 per cent of children born between 1800 and the 1970s (Stone 1990).

From 1970 a new era began, but there were still variations between countries. Norway and Britain had very similar and low levels of extramarital births, 7 and 8 per cent respectively, swiftly escalating. In 1997, 48 per cent (Norway) and 37 per cent (Britain) of children were born outside marriage (Clarke and Jensen 2001). Almost every second child – in the case of Norway – continued to be conceived before marriage, but unlike previous times, the pregnancy no longer led to marriage. 'Shotgun' marriages of this kind were a potent demonstration of the symbolic power of the (unborn) child to influence their parents' behaviour. By contrast, pregnancy has now turned into a reason to avoid or at least to postpone a wedding ceremony. The idea of marrying as a pregnant bride seems to conflict with the new meaning of a wedding, a symbolic and often costly rite of passage to the celebration of the couple, in contrast to formalizing impending parenthood (McRae 2000).

The escalation in extramarital births has given rise to a new family arrangement – consensual union. In Norway the rise in extramarital births is absorbed into the rise in consensual unions, while births to lone mothers remain at approximately the same level as in the 1970s. Hence, no change has taken place in children's probability of being born into a two-parent family. The only change is that children are increasingly born into a not-formalised family. They are born 'illegitimate', but into a family consisting of two parents. It is the formalization not the family structure that has changed.[3] From a child perspective we may ask whether this is a trivial change, with no consequence to children's lives. I shall argue that it is not.

A private deal

Unlike marriage, which is a social institution with legal rights and duties, consensual union is a private deal. A young couple moves in together often with no social ceremony and with no public registration. Even if public authorities gradually seek to regulate consensual unions in terms of public services, taxes and pensions systems, the very idea of consensual union is its non-formalized nature (initially in Norway characterized as 'paperless union'). Nonetheless, the rapid social acceptance of consensual unions in Norway has been remarkable. Until 1972 living together without being married was actually prohibited by law. Although not practised, the 'concubinage paragraph' (as it was named) could imply a prison sentence of three months (Penal Code of 1902 §375). Since the 1970s, consensual unions have become the norm, practised in most groups of the population.[4] It has become exceptional not to live in a consensual union before parenthood and it is increasingly common to continue this after the child is born, as we shall see in the next section.

The question is whether the shift from institutionalized marriage to a private deal in consensual union can be characterized, with any degree of reasonability, as children's lost symbolic power over family formation and duration? On the surface there is no difference between a married family and a consensual union in Norway and, in public opinion, they are families on equal terms. Most young people will state that they see no reason to marry since what matters is love, not formalities.

The Norwegian Children's Families Survey (CFS) demonstrates the rapid emergence of consensual unions. We can use the 1996 survey to illustrate this. It includes children born in 1980, 1986 and 1992, who were 16, ten and four years old respectively in 1996. Focusing on the circumstances around the birth of the oldest (1980) and the youngest (1992), striking divergences emerge in parental behaviour prior to the birth of the child. In 1980 consensual unions were augmenting but it was still rare to have a child without being married. Four out of five children had parents who cohabited before they were born, while only 12 per cent were born in a consensual union. Even if the child was born in such a union, the parents were likely to marry after the birth (in every second case). Consequently, in 1980, most children had parents who cohabited before they were born, but only a small minority had parents who did not marry later. One decade later, among children born in 1992, the picture had changed. By now a very small minority of the children had parents who did not live together before they were born (7 per cent), every third child was born in a consensual union (34 per cent) and fewer had parents who married later (less than one in three). These children were relatively young (four years old in 1996) and some parents may have decided to marry later, but the trend is quite clear. Consensual union is developing into a permanent kind of family in which children are born and raised.[5] In the course of just a couple of decades, from 1972 until 1992, the hegemonic position of marriage evaporated. Consensual unions were decriminalized and social attitudes reversed. Most people across cohorts, regions and class will defend living together in consensual union, whereas only a couple of decades earlier unmarried cohabitation was associated with shame and social disgrace.

Based upon the CFS, we are able to tell that considerable changes took place concerning the marital status of the parents in the family into which children were born but is this a significant change, or is it rather a change in formality with few other consequences, as suggested by several commentators (among them Trost 1978). I shall argue that the shift from marriage to consensual union is significant for children in several ways. There are in particular two related consequences. They are the risk of family breakup and its impact on the relationship between children and fathers. However, children's risk of family breakup in consensual unions is part of a larger transformation of family durability that is also taking place in marriage and we shall turn to the overall increase in parental breakups before returning to the father question.

The collapse of marriage: children as the vanishing marriage glue

The birth of a child is less likely to lead to marriage and even when it does, the probability of divorce is enhanced. As described earlier, young people entered marriage often with little time for exploring the relationship. Shotgun weddings had to take place often in a big hurry, but they did last, in contrast to the post-contraceptive planned marriages that followed. Divorce rates were relatively low until about 1970 when a sharp increase occurred in several European countries (Haskey 1993).

Children experience a high risk of parental separation, in particular when we look at the combined effect from divorce and dissolution of consensual unions. In Norway, this development may be illustrated by looking at children aged 16, comparing the CFSs from 1988 and 1996. The 16-year cohort of the first survey was born in 1972, while the same cohort of the second survey was born in 1980. At age 16, 14 per cent had experienced a parental breakup by 1988, compared to 19 per cent by 1996. The overall increase is marked – five percentage points – but not dramatic. However, when children from the CFS 1996 are subdivided according to their parents' marital status at their birth (married or cohabiting), we find that 15 per cent of those born in marriage had parents who had divorced 16 years later, compared to 35 per cent among those born in consensual unions. The difference is even larger for the younger children (6 per cent of four-year-olds versus 17 per cent) (Jensen and Clausen 2002). Both marriages and consensual unions are fragile, but it is the consensual unions that surface as a vehicle for parental breakup. It is also consensual unions that are expanding at the expense of marriage.

Over the entire period covered by the two CFSs, 1972 to 1996, consensual unions became more common. The so-called 'selection effect' – indicating that those who cohabit dispose of characteristics that would anyhow produce a higher risk of family dissolution – is expected to fade as consensual unions become more widespread. In accordance with this, one might also expect that the gap in risk of parental dissolution between consensual union and marriage be narrowed. Such an expectation is not supported by data. Even though consensual unions have become more widespread, the higher risk of parental breakup compared to marriage remains stable (Jensen and Clausen 2002). This suggests that a higher risk of dissolution is a permanent characteristic of consensual union, also when its distribution in society is large. To children consensual unions represent a more fragile family, a finding that is common also in Britain and other countries (see Clarke and Jensen 2001).

Hence, at first sight, no indications were found that consensual families differed from married ones. However, as these unions have become widespread one important difference has emerged in research across countries. Consensual unions have proven to be more fragile than marriage. As a result, children born into a consensual union have a much higher risk of parental dissolution compared to those born in marriage.

A paradoxical development also became apparent: as fertility was becoming controlled by the contraceptive revolution and as a consequence, the possibilities of planning the arrival of a child improved, parental breakups emerged as an escalating feature of modern childhood. Children have lost their 'symbolic power' to keep their parents together in general. But this ability is even weaker among children born in consensual unions, which is the fastest growing form of family. The weakening of children's symbolic power over parental marital behaviour has taken place through a double effect: first, through their weakened ability to influence their parents' marriage and, second, through their weakened ability to influence the durability of their parents' relationship.

Family change and the marginalization of children

While children had been a 'taken-for-granted' reason for marrying and keeping marriages going, in the 1970s the situation reversed. Children were no longer a 'taken-for-granted' issue and less so in consensual unions than in marriages. A study comparing married and cohabiting women and men aged 20–29 years asked, 'What would contribute to a successful marriage?' (Lesthaeghe and Moors 1996). The most striking difference among a large battery of answers was found in relation to children. While two out of three married people regarded children as an important feature of a successful marriage, less than every second cohabitant thought so. Similarly, very few married people stated that having children was *not* very important for a successful marriage (8 per cent), while a considerable share of the cohabitants thought so (24 per cent).

In contrast to previous ideas of parenthood, marriage is no longer seen as prerequisite to establishing a loving relationship. Among the reasons given for cohabiting rather than marrying, are a sense of freedom and an easier exit in case things do not work out (McRae 2000). The description is similar in several industrialized countries, but most pronounced in Scandinavia, the UK and France. French demographer Toulemon argues that children, as a reason to establish and keep a marriage, have moved from the centre to the periphery, in contrast to the importance put on the love relationship of the parents. It is, says Toulemon, 'marriage, rather than the birth of a child, which appears to be a better guarantee of the stability of the couple' (Toulemon 1995: 183). Hence, marriage still has a symbolic value, but its justification has shifted from children to the love relationship of adults.

Given that the trend continues, it is estimated in the case of Norway that 36 per cent of the children born at the beginning of 1990 will experience a parental breakup during their childhood. If we add the 4 to 5 per cent of children born to lone mothers, we may well see that 40 per cent of these children will not live with both parents throughout their childhood. Change in family structure may indicate a weakening of children's symbolic power to 'glue' parents together.

Parallel to changes in family formation and duration is a change in family functioning as a nuclear family. Mothers' employment is a prime example. Unlike pre-1970, most children in Norway now have an employed mother (between 60 and 90 per cent depending on age of child and marital status of mother). Mothers in general have joined in the breadwinner role, but more so among mothers in consensual unions. Furthermore, it is now common that parents share the expense of children, but in marriages fathers contribute more, while in consensual unions mothers supply more. Consequently, children seem to be less of an economic responsibility to fathers in consensual unions even if parents live together. Finally, family conflicts may echo a more ambivalent sentiment towards several aspects of family life. In consensual unions parents have conflicts between each other about the child and there are more conflicts with the child than in marriage (Jensen and Clausen 1999).

These findings indicate that consensual unions represent a different family type to that of married families. Both the high level of dissolution and the high rate of employment indicate lifestyles with emphasis on individual choices – the choice of leaving an unsatisfactory family and earning your own money. Having said this, it is time to soften the argument. In actual life the boundaries between married and consensual families are more fluid than depicted here. Some parents marry after a while and among those who don't a contracted marriage will not 'cure' the family problems. More likely, we may regard consensual unions as a reflection of the priorities of our times, where living with children (if not the idea of children) increasingly conflicts with adults' life aspirations (see Gillis, this volume, and Beck and Beck-Gernsheim 2002).

Public fatherhood in decline

'Child-free zones' are more common among men than women. Men's age at entering fatherhood is on average three years more than the mother's age and their likelihood of not living with the children after a breakup is much higher. This implies that non-married births and parental dissolution affect children's relations to fathers more than mothers. Throughout the fundamental family changes over the last decades, and despite their supposed links with female emancipation, no change is taking place in the likelihood that children live with their mother. In Norway, 98 per cent of children live with their mother, with or without their father present. The increasing likelihood of children being born outside marriage, albeit in a consensual union, and of experiencing a parental breakup has had no impact on the likelihood that children will live together with their mother throughout childhood. By contrast, children live with the father if the father lives with the mother. In fact consensual unions, often regarded as a modern way of forming a family, reinforce the mother and child linkages for two main reasons.

As a private deal, consensual unions avoid the legal rights of fatherhood embedded in the 'pater est' rule of marriage. According to this, a child born in marriage is considered as the husband's offspring disregarding the biological connection. By contrast, a child born outside marriage is automatically under the mother's sole legal authority. As long as the father stays with the mother, his lack of legal rights has few consequences. However, at the time of parental breakup – which happens more often to these fathers – he realizes that he has no parental legal rights (unless he has informed the authorities otherwise, an option that few are using). At the moment of maximum conflict between the parents, these fathers realize that the child will live with the parent who has the legal rights – the mother. This general pattern, whereby children tend to stay with the mother after divorce, is reinforced in consensual union. Since these children are also often younger at the time of separation than children of divorcing spouses, the chances that the child will stay with the mother are further enhanced.[6]

Few children live with the father only, while most keep in contact. Two out of three have regular visiting schedules, leaving one in three with infrequent or irregular patterns of seeing each other. On average there is little difference between children's contact with married and cohabiting fathers after dissolution. However, the factors influencing visiting frequencies differ. In the case of married fathers, contact is more regular. In the case of cohabiting fathers, social factors play a more decisive role. The father's education and income and, most significantly, his relationship to the mother are vital. There is more disparity in these fathers' visiting schedules (Jensen and Clausen 1999).

In several respects, consensual unions seem to leave children in a more marginal position than marriages. The shift in fatherhood from a public to a private role is an indication of this change as will be argued below. The loss of children's symbolic power is gendered.

The foundations of symbolic child power: economic transformations

Why should children have symbolic power to influence parental behaviour in one historical period and not in another? Why should this change surface in fatherhood more than motherhood?

A suggestion is promoted by Goody (1976) who notes that family organization is a function of the 'power bank' in a society. In historical Europe the 'power bank' was based upon property and a well-defined line of transmission of heritage from one generation to another. Where property is an ascribed resource distributed largely through the family, children are vital to those in charge of economic resources for the attainment of power and prestige. In the course of time two important changes have taken place. First, property inherited through the family line is now, if not substituted, at least supplemented by education. Second, with the process of individualization the fulfilment of personal needs has gained in importance relative to the fulfilment of family needs (Giddens 1992; Beck and Beck-Gernsheim 2002). Both changes have been preceded by a decline in the economic value of children to parents.

Historically marriage was based upon its importance to the social order. Foucault (1984, vol. III) describes how marriage was gradually institutionalized way back in the Hellenistic and Roman civilizations before Christ. The institution of marriage was useful not only to the family itself, but also to the city and the state. Marriage had legal implications for the status of the child, 'handing down a name, instituting heirs, organising a system of alliances and joining futures' (Foucault 1984, vol. III: 74). Marriage involved 'a hidden economy of kinship', with regulated rights and obligations (Goody 1994). Far from being a private deal, marriage was crucial to the social order. Historical accounts confirm the roots of marriage in perceptions of the value of children. As children's influence as the focal point of mariage has faded, there has been both a change in the justifications for marriage and an upsurge in alternatives to marriage as a hegemonic form of union.

Why can we trace the changes more in fatherhood than motherhood? The question leads us into the very foundations of marriage. Foucault discusses how marriage, from Aristotle onwards, is a means for men to obtain legitimate descendants. Wives 'were under his power; it was to him that they had to give their children, who would be citizens and heirs' (Foucault 1984, vol. II: 145). In a society in which men are in charge of the power structures, they also have an interest in controlling important resources in the distribution of wealth, argues O'Brien (1981). The focal point for O'Brien is the need for a social substitute for biological uncertainty: 'Obviously, the most persistent and successful form is marriage' (O'Brien 1981: 56). Marriage was necessary to men, says O'Brien, because children were a resource in the power structures of society.

Gillis (1998) describes pre-modern Europe as a society where bachelors had no social position. Being a family-father was the basis upon which property, power and prestige rested. With the advent of industry, monetary capital – not 'child capital' – gained priority as the principal unit of wealth. Through mass education, the economic value of children to the family was turned into a cost and the direction of the generational wealth flow shifted from an upward to a downward trend (Caldwell 1982). This is the foundation, I shall argue, as to why children have moved from frontstage to backstage, to use Goffman's old metaphor. As stated by O'Brien, in a modern capitalistic society, 'True potency appears only in the marketplace' (O'Brien 1981: 160). These impacts are reflected more in fatherhood, I suggest, because it – unlike motherhood – is socially defined. When the family position has no bearing upon the prestige system, those with fewer family ties are more in accordance with the demands of the global 'market managers'. Bachelors and single people will be better able to meet the demands of mobility, contract work and flexibility, men having better access to these options than women.

It seems reasonable to suggest that children's symbolic power over adults' marital behaviour has changed in stages over time. There was not a sudden decline in marriage as children ceased to yield power, because it still played a role in the gendered division of labour, providing women with economic support and men with service at home (Becker 1993). During the first part of the twentieth century children were already a drain on the family budget, while marriage peaked around 1950–60. But turmoil had begun and increased divorce rates from the 1960s were the first sign. Still, the married family maintained hegemony as the only acceptable institution for having children until the 1970s, when young women were able to support themselves. Once the steps to break the hegemony were taken by the 'pioneering' cohabiting parents, the justification to marry and stay married 'for the children's sake' broke down with amazing speed.

In the public discourse children's symbolic power was lost while attention was directed towards their increased negotiating power within the family. But, at the end of the day, this power too is subject to adult choices, as suggested by the Australian demographer John Caldwell: 'the speed of fertility decline can undoubtedly be explained by ever more successful demands by children for a more equal share in family consumption and pleasure ...' (Caldwell 1982: 254). A contradiction is portrayed between, on the one hand, children's success in negotiations for family 'goodies' (such as parental time or consumer goods) and on the other adults' desire to produce children. Ultimately children's power will always be limited by adult choices. Others, like Hood–Williams (2001), argue that relations between children and parents remain remarkably traditional, within a 'patriarchal authority'. Children remain subjected to an 'age patriarchy', but one in which children 'are to be treated as if they were independent, as if they were individuals, and to be given choice and autonomy' (Hood–Williams 2001: 103). Over the past decades greater power over parents has been extended to children; this, however, does not upset the conventional power relations in which children are fundamentally under the parents' authority. Children's power may be exercised in areas of daily struggle, typically household chores or consumerism, and be experienced as the deprival of adult privileges, as Caldwell suggests. At the same time, age patriarchy remains of vital importance to adults in family matters, such as divorce or employment.

In the best interests?

Prior to the 1970s couples were commonly said to be staying together, even in an unhappy marriage, 'for the children's sake'. In the 1990s children are no longer given as a reason to stay. Studies have found that a majority of parents underline positive, rather than negative, impacts of divorce on children (Moxnes *et al.* 2001). The public discourse has shifted from the lasting marriage 'for the children's sake', to parental breakup 'in the best interests of children'. How can we deal with this development from the point of view of children and childhood?

At the personal level the effect of divorce on children's well-being is a matter of dispute. Is a good split better than a bad nucleus – even for children? Most people will agree that a bad marriage can damage a child's well-being more than a good divorce. Studies comparing the effects of divorce on the well-being of children reach mixed conclusions (see this volume) and renowned studies in the field are flawed with strong ideological positions (as demonstrated by Cherlin 1999). Do children have an agency and how does it interact with structure? What are the issues in which children have a say and in what ways are children's lives transformed beyond their negotiating power? To the individual child, a split between the parents may represent an improvement in their lives. The interests of parents and children may accord, but not always.

On the one hand, a split may be felt as a relief from daily struggles in the home, but to many children the parental breakup is just one in a chain of changes often leading to a deterioration in living conditions. The Norwegian CFS reveals higher incidences of geographical mobility among such children, often implying a change in day-care or school and a new neighbourhood and friends. There are increased risks of economic deterioration and social mobility is likely to be downward. Daily life has to find new forms and may involve considerable tensions. The child will have a visiting relationship with the father, which may or may not function well. The visiting relationship implies that the child will relate individually to the mother and father. Instead of having one home, they may (in the lucky cases) have two homes. These two homes may be in the vicinity of each other, but may also be some distance apart, implying a divide in playgrounds and friends. The 'insulated childhood' (Zeiher 2001) in which children's daily life is spread across 'isles' in a geographic area, includes not only leisure activities but also the home itself. This may function in the child's best interests, but it may also be the opposite. As described by Beck and Beck-Gernsheim, 'The children then have to live with divided loyalties' (Beck and Beck-Gernsheim 2002: 95). Several chapters of this volume (Robinson *et al.*, Moxnes, Wade and Smart, Berg) illustrate how children will have to negotiate in order not to increase distrust and battles between parents who argue their case 'in the best interests of the child'.

There is not one answer to the question of children's gain or loss in divorce cases. Seen from a child perspective, the risk of parental divorce is probably a part of most children's fears and anxieties. Children, even those living in stable families, start recognizing signs of parental conflict, aware that divorce is a common experience among their friends. The risk of family dissolution has entered the structure of childhood. Seen from this perspective, the individual parental choice may have resulted in enhanced insecurity among children as a group.

Conclusion

The conclusion is not obvious at the individual level. I have argued that children are no longer a justification for getting married, nor are parents expected to continue a bad relationship 'for the children's sake'. The essence of family change to children is the enhanced probability that they will not live their daily life with the father. Children's families are largely transformed outside their negotiating power. Is the choice of freedom for adults enhanced at the expense of safety and security of children? At this level an answer is: 'It depends.' Children may not be better off in a malfunctioning family than a divided, broken or reconfigured family. At the same time, this may have been replaced by an omnipotent divorce anxiety among all children. At the societal level, individualization and the personal choice of adults leave children at the margins. Demographic changes such as postponing – or avoiding – children, extramarital births, consensual unions and divorce suggest a generational conflict in which childhood may be sacrificed to other priorities in adult life.

Is there a generational conflict between adults' life aspirations and children's well-being in our societies? Several sources support such a conclusion, but the conflict is easier to trace at a general level (adult versus children) than at the individual level (parents versus children). The capitalist network society needs flexible individuals with flexible families. The conflict between the demands of the labour market and the demand to have children is solved through postponing or rejecting entrance into parenthood, having fewer children and substituting stable marriages with fragile consensual unions. These are the long-term family transformations, where adults are in charge of agency and where children's symbolic power is lost. However, most people want children and do not plan for a family dissolution. The fundamental conflict is probably not between adults and children, but between our possibilities to have and rear children on the one hand and, on the other, the social space and status afforded children in our society.

References

Beck, U. and Beck-Gernsheim, E. (2002) *Individualization*, London: Sage.

Becker, G.S. (1993) *A Treatise on the Family* (enlarged edn), Cambridge, Mass.: Harvard University Press.

Bourdieu, P. (1999) *Language and Symbolic Power*, Cambridge: Polity Press.

Caldwell, J.C. (1982) *Theory of Fertility Decline*, London: Academic Press.

Cherlin, A.J. (1999) 'Going to extremes: family structure, children's well-being, and social science', *Demography*, 36, 4: 421–8.

Clarke, L. and Jensen, A.M. (2001) *Cohabitation in Britain and Norway: A childhood perspective*, paper presented at International Conference Comparing Childhoods, Espoo, Finland, August 23–6.

Dyrvik, S. (1976) *Ekteskap og barnetall – Ei gransking av fertilitetsutviklinga i Norge 1920–1970 (Marriages and Number of Children – An Analysis of Fertility Trends in Norway 1920–1970)*, Artikler 89, Oslo: Statistics Norway.

Foucault, M. (1984) *The Use of Pleasure (vol II), The Care of Self (vol III), The History of Sexuality*, London: Penguin Books.

Giddens, A. (1992) *The Transformation of Intimacy. Sexuality, Love and Eroticism in Modern Societies*, Cambridge: Polity Press.

Gillis, J.R. (1998) *Marginalization of Fatherhood in Western Countries*, paper presented at the conference 'Children and fathers: togetherness, separateness and provision', Research Council of Norway, Oslo, October.

Goody, J. (1976) *Production and Reproduction. A Comparative Study of the Domestic Domain*, Cambridge: Cambridge University Press.

Goody, J. (1994) *The Development of the Family and Marriage in Europe*, Cambridge: Cambridge University Press.

Gould, J. and Kolb, W.L. (eds) (1965) *A Dictionary of the Social Sciences*, New York: The Free Press.

Haskey, J.C. (1993) 'Formation and dissolution in the different countries of europe', in A. Blum and J.-L. Rallu (eds) *European Population*, vol. 2 Demographic Dynamics, Paris: Éditions John Libbey Eurotext.

Hendrick, H. (1997) *Children, Childhood and English Society 1880–1990*, Cambridge: Cambridge University Press.

Hobcraft, J. and Kiernan, K. (1995) *Becoming a Parent in Europe*, discussion paper Welfare State Programme/116, London: London School of Economics.

Hood-Williams, J. (2001) 'Power-relations in children's lives', in M. du Bois-Reymond, H. Sünker and H.-H. Krüger (eds) *Childhood in Europe. Approaches–Trends–Findings*, 91: 116, New York: Peter Lang Publishing.

Jensen, A.M. (1999) 'Partners and parents in Europe: a gender divide', *Comparative Social Research*, vol. 18: 1–29.

Jensen, A.-M. (2001) 'Property, power and prestige. The feminization of childhood', in M. du Bois-Reymond, H. Sünker and H.-H. Krüger (eds) *Childhood in Europe. Approaches–Trends–Findings*, 185–214, New York: Peter Lang Publishing.

Jensen, A.-M. and Clausen, S.-E. (1999) '*Samboerskap som foreldreskap*', in Samboerne og samfunnet, Norwegian Public Reports, no. 5: 286–304, Oslo: Ministry of Children and the Family.

Jensen, A.-M. and Clausen, S.-E. (2002, forthcoming) 'Children and family dissolution in Norway: the impact of consensual unions', *Childhood*.

Lesthaeghe, R. and Moors, G. (1996) 'Living arrangements, socio-economic position, and values among young adults: a pattern description for France, West Germany, Belgium, and the Netherlands, 1990', in D. Coleman (ed.) *Europe's Population in the 1990s*: 163–221, Oxford: Oxford University Press.

McRae, S. (1997) 'Cohabitation: a trial run for marriage?', *Sexual and Marital Therapy*, 12, 3: 259–73.

McRae, S. (2000) 'Cohabitation or marriage? – Cohabitation', in G. Allan (ed.) *The Sociology of the Family. A Reader:* 169–90, Oxford: Blackwell.

Moxnes, K., Kvaran, I., Kaul, H. and Levin, I. (2001) *Skilsmissens mange ansikter. Om barns og foreldres erfaringer med skilsmisse*, Kristiansand: HøyskoleForlaget.

O'Brien, M. (1981) *The Politics of Reproduction*, London: Routledge and Kegan Paul.

Stone, L. (1990) *Road to Divorce. England 1530–1987*, Oxford: Oxford University Press.

Toulemon, L. (1995) 'The Place of Children in the history of couples', *Population: An English Selection*, 21, 4: 303–16.

Trost, J. (1978) 'A renewed social institution: non-marital cohabitation', *Acta Sociologica*, 21, 4: 303–16.

Zeiher, H. (2001) 'Children's islands in space and time: the impact of spatial differentiation on children's ways of shaping social life', in M. du Bois-Reymond, H. Sünker and H.-H. Krüger (eds) *Childhood in Europe. Approaches–Trends–Findings*: 139–60, New York: Peter Lang Publishing.

10 Childhood and family time

A changing historical relationship

John R. Gillis

> All adults ... transport their childhood from action to action like a previous incarnation.
>
> (James, Jenks, and Prout 1998: 20)

We understand family to be something that develops in time, that it begins with the arrival of children and ends with their departure. Marriage by itself is not sufficient to constitute family, for only children can make a family. When children leave home we say that the family has left. Yet children remain a symbolic presence even in their physical absence. Their birthdays and anniversaries are remembered and celebrated. Their rooms are kept as they were, the refrigerator remains stocked with their favorite foods, attics are crammed with their toys and schoolbooks and albums full of their pictures. The memory of children haunts the modern home, but it would seem that the earliest memories are the most appealing. Now that foetal images of the 'unborn child' are available, they have become the most precious of all.

Modern family time is organized to a very large extent around children. In households with children daily rhythms are synchronized with their comings and goings. The family dinner assumes their presence, while the family week is divided into schooldays and weekends, Saturday and Sunday are devoted largely to being with children and the annual calendar has become a series of children's festivals. Children's birthdays have acquired enormous significance in all Western countries, displacing the traditional saints' days as sacred moments. The old Jewish and Christian calendars have become a series of children's festivals. The most important of these, Christmas, is now the hinge on which the year turns, though summer, another season associated with children, has taken on growing importance. Family holiday times are largely set by school schedules, reinforcing the connection between family and children's time. Even after children leave home, family times require their presence. Christmas and, in the US, Thanksgiving are times to get together with children and grandchildren. Family reunions are organized for the same purpose. In both the US and Europe many people maintain second homes as meeting places for the generations.

It is not at all obvious why modern Western family time should be organized around children. It has few parallels in other world cultures and, as we will see, the very notion of family time emerged in Europe and North America only in the nineteenth century, and its focus on children was initially specific to Victorian bourgeois culture. Any explanation must therefore take into account not only class, but also gender and generational relations. For the peculiar notion of family time we are concerned with here was the product of a very specific set of historical circumstances that altered temporal and spatial sensibilities, ultimately reconfiguring the life course in such a way as to give new meaning to childhood. The reverberations of this radical transformation are still felt even now, as we grapple with the cultural practices bequeathed to us by the Victorians.

In the United States and the Western world more generally, the percentage of households with a single occupant has risen to over 30 per cent and households consisting of married adults with children at home are down from 40 per cent in 1970 to 26 per cent in 1997 (Putnam 2000: 277). But while rates of childless marriages are increasing, adults remain extraordinarily child-centred. It would seem that, although we no longer live *with* children, we insist on living *through* them. Children have become so central to adult identity that the loss of a child is now considered the worst thing that can possibly happen. Even the strongest marriages break under such circumstances (May 1995 and Finkbeiner 1996). As Paula Fass describes it, our need 'to live once more through our children, has made them dearer to us, while their loss has become all the more unbearable, to outlive them, a modern curse' (Fass 1999: 255).

In a secular age which has ceased to believe in eternity, children have become the guarantee of immortality. In other cultures adults live on through reincarnation in children, but we have reversed that process, preferring to view adults as reincarnations of children. There was a time, and not so very long ago, when children were regarded as miniature adults and encouraged to grow up as quickly as possible. Prior to the nineteenth century the wise child was honoured as being something special. The notion of the prodigy still remains, but now it is the adult who can manage to stay forever young who gets the most favourable attention. We fear rather than embrace the ageing process; modern family time has become one of the chief means by which adults connect not just with children, but with childhood itself, now commonly thought of as a principal source of regeneration.

There are far more times organized around children now than a hundred years ago, but the transformation in question is not just a quantitative one. It is also the quality of time spent with children that has changed dramatically. Time spent with children today is far more organized, far more ritualized. What is now defined as 'family time' has become a distinctive kind of time, time out of time, different from the other times of our lives. Not only do we spend more time with co-resident children, but certain moments are framed in such a way as to make them stand out from the flow of ordinary time.

Modern family time is above all memorial time, a time for reaching back into an imagined past for the mental and emotional resources that are thought to be in short supply in the present. It is not just the time adults spend *with* children physically, but the time they experience *through* them mentally, a kind of time no less real for existing in the realm of the imagination. In family time, children come to symbolize childhood, a vaguely defined, largely empty icon onto which we are able to project a host of fears as well as hopes.

While these times are child-centred, they are adult-created. They are also experienced differently by adults and children (Csikszentmihalyi 1997: 43, 88). We need to keep in mind that, 'the time of childhood – the ways in which childhood, as a discrete period of the life course ...', is different from, 'time for children – children's experience of and participation in the temporal rhythms of childhood through which their lives unfold' (James, Jenks and Prout 1998: 61). The time of childhood is an adult creation, representing that which adults yearn for but cannot have, namely their own lost childhood (Steedman 1995: 10, 95).

> The modern child is always a sign of a bygone era, of a past which is necessarily the past of adults, yet which, being so distinct, so sheltered, so innocent, is also inevitably a lost past, and therefore understood through a kind of memory we call nostalgia.
>
> (Higonnet 1998: 27)

But it is precisely this that adults now depend on for their sense of selfhood, causing them to construct a *time of childhood* which is often in conflict with *time for children*.

Born of adult needs, child-centred family time does not necessarily meet the needs of children. Like school time, it shapes the lives of children in ways over which they have little control. Time made for children is often contested by them, forcing adults into negotiations that, when they do not go well, can result in anger and even violence (Sirota 2001: 117–35). Clashes of opposing temporalities have become a permanent feature of modern life, the source of many sitcoms, something we laugh about, not because they are trivial but because they are so serious. It is these tensions that create a certain dynamism in family time itself, producing changes that constitute its history. In what follows, I will be concerned with the historical transformations that brought family time into being and gave it the fraught, contradictory shape that it has today.

The equation of family with children is a relatively recent development. Prior to the nineteenth century, family meant household. All the members of a household, related or not, were thought of as constituting family. It was space, not time, which defined familial relationships. The heads of household were the socially defined fathers and mothers to those 'children' consigned to their care regardless of age or parentage. Childhood was socially constructed in a similar way, depending more on whose household you belonged to than who you were born to. Generational relations were a function not of time but of one's place within the hierarchy of the household. Masters and mistresses of whatever age were adults, while servants, slaves and live-in workers were 'boys' and 'girls' regardless of how old they were. To be sure, there existed some general notion of the stages of life – infancy, childhood, youth, prime of life and old age – but our current understanding of the life course as a precisely age-graded sequence of human development was unknown before the nineteenth century. It was only then that life came to be seen as *development in time* and everyone was expected to have a childhood, an adolescence and an adulthood in a precisely ordered sequence (Lowe 1982).

When family was household, there was no notion of family time as we know it. The images of the pre-industrial family gathered at the hearth after long days of working together in the fields or the family business may satisfy our modern yearnings for togetherness, but they are wholly unfaithful to historical reality. High fertility and mortality rates prior to the nineteenth century guaranteed that a large percentage of parents would never see their children reach maturity. Grandparenthood was exceptional and orphans contributed to the massive circulation of children that distinguished the pre-industrial period from our own. The separation of children from their natal families was also a function of poverty. For the poor, sending children away to better-off households was a survival strategy. The rich and the powerful also encouraged their children to leave home, but for pedagogical rather than economic reasons.

It is clearly not the case that parents and children spent more time together in pre-industrial Europe and America than they do today (Gillis 2001: 19–36). But, even in those cases where parents and children were co-resident, there is no evidence of the family times that we now take for granted. In ordinary families meals were taken when and wherever available. There was no regular dining schedule and sitting down together was more likely to be a communal rather than a familial occasion. Waking and bed times were equally irregular, with none of the ritual qualities we associate with them. Schedules were set not by the clock but by the task at hand. The space of the household was not divided by age and, because most children did not attend school, there were no times special to them. Nor was church attendance a family affair. Congregations were more likely to be seated by household, with the children of the family occupying the same pews as the resident labourers and servants (Gillis 1996).

Weddings and funerals were similarly communal. Often separated from their older children by death or distance, parents had no formal role in the marriage ceremony (Gillis 1985). It was equally difficult for families to gather at the bedside of the dying and funerals were a communal rather than a familial responsibility. The practice of burying in family plots was reserved for the rich and powerful. Most people found their final resting place among their neighbours in graveyards without individual or family headstones. Remembering the dead was also a communal responsibility, keyed to certain fixed moments, like All Souls, rather than to the individual dates of demise. Indeed, the very idea of individualized anniversaries – of marriage, birth and death – were unthinkable at a time when most people did not keep personal calendars, but instead marked time according to local religious and communal practices (Gillis 1997).

Until well into the nineteenth century most people did not know the exact date of their birth, much less the birth or death data of other family members. In Catholic countries saints' days served as memory markers for all those sharing the saint's name. When Protestantism swept the calendar clear of saints' days the way was open for individualized birthdays, but it would be a very long time before these became the child-centred rites they are today. Until the nineteenth century birthdays were celebrated toward the end rather than at the beginning of life. A long life was taken as a sign of God's grace and thus an occasion for rejoicing. Among devout Protestants this was not a time of looking back but looking forward, a moment to dwell on that reunion with the family of God that was the goal of the good Christian's life journey (Gillis 1996).

In an age of very high child mortality rates, every stage of life was equidistant from death. No effort was made to hide death from children. In fact, their expo-sure to it was regarded as necessary to their salvation. In this, as in all other dimensions of life, children were treated as little adults, less capable cognitively and physically, but not qualitatively different. Children were neither sacralized nor demonized. While there were plenty of images of holy babes available in religious art of the period, no one confused these with real children, who were born with the burden of original sin. But even those adults who felt the need for stern physical as well as spiritual discipline of the young did not treat them as little devils. The degree of child abuse in earlier periods has been vastly exagger-ated, and if children often suffered levels of corporal punishment that we would regard as unacceptable, so too did adults, especially the poor, slaves and women.

Today's children are insulated from the adult world. Their spaces are increas-ingly 'islanded', separated from one another and from the adult world at large. The school, playground and summer camp constitute a kind of archipelago that had no counterpart in the pre-industrial world, where children and adults occupied the same mainlands (Zeiher and Zeiher 1994). Children's time today is equally segmented, ever more minutely divided by age. Our temporal land-scape is filled with special children's times that had no precedent before the nineteenth century. Prior to then children worked and played in the same places and on the same schedules as adults (Aries 1965). Their holidays and games were inseparable from those of their elders.

The holidays of pre-industrial Europe and North America represented the mixed legacy of Christian and pagan practices, many of which are still cele-brated today. But what was noticeably missing before the nineteenth century were the kinds of child-centred holidays that are the pivots of our weekly and annual calendars. All Souls' Eve had not yet morphed into Halloween, Easter was not yet associated with eggs and bunnies, and Christmas was far from the festival of childhood that it became in the nineteenth and twentieth centuries. In many parts of Europe, Yule remained associated with a robust traditional sat-urnalia, belonging more to the street than to the home. St Nicholas was still a saint whose visits to children, naughty and nice, had nothing to do with Christmas as such. At Yule, gifts were exchanged among adults, between rather than within households, with no particular attention paid to children.

It was not until the mid-nineteenth century that the child-centred Christmas, complete with the tree, crib and Santa Claus, emerged to become what is regarded today as the *traditional* Christmas. It appeared first in Protestant northwestern Europe and North America, taking hold somewhat later in Catholic regions. In the nineteenth century it was largely a middle-class practice, which gradually became a mass phenomenon, spreading beyond the Western world and even beyond Christian cultures to become the first global children's festival. In response to the popularity of Christmas, Jews have turned Hannukah, an almost forgotten minor holy day, into a major family occasion focused on children, while Afro-centrists have assembled a bricolage of African customs into a wholly invented holiday called Kwanza, also heavily focused on children (Gillis 1996: 98–104).

Most of what we call family times can be traced back to an extraordinary moment of social and cultural creativity in the mid-nineteenth century Victorian era. The Victorians were principally middle-class Protestants engaged in fashioning for themselves a new relationship to time and space during the initial stages of the capitalist industrial revolution. They were the first to experience what David Harvey has called modernity's 'time–space compression', an acceleration of time and corresponding conquest of distance that made the old temporal and spatial certainties 'melt into air' (Harvey 1989; Berman 1988; Lowe 1982). Highly mobile and uprooted, the new middle classes were faced with the additional problem of living with a specious present consisting of fleeting moments no longer firmly anchored in an accessible past or pointing toward a certain future. In response to a growing sense of the vanishing past and receding future, Victorians began to experiment with new kinds of cyclical time that provided them with the sense of continuity and certainty they found missing in everyday life.

One fruit of this remarkable effort was family time itself, a novel notion that allowed middle-class families, whose members' temporal rhythms were increasingly out of synch with one another, to gain some sense of togetherness and continuity. In a period when women's domesticated time was increasingly at odds with men's work time and when children's schedules were diverging from those of adults, an entirely new set of highly ritualized daily, weekly and annual occasions came to serve the purpose not only of synchronizing the presence of family members but, even more important, of providing a common sense of family past and family future. Family time ceased to be merely time spent with kin and became time spent anticipating and remembering family, often in idealized ways that did not necessarily correspond to existing realities.

The family day came to revolve around father's evening homecoming, the formal 'family dinner' and the bedtimes of children. The family week solidified around Sunday church attendance, gradually expanding to include Saturdays to become the modern weekend. The family year pivoted around Christmas, but also hinged on other seasons – Easter, summer holidays, All Souls' and Halloween – all of which had similar memorial and anticipatory dimensions. In the process, family time came to colonize the religious and communal holidays that had been the temporal markers in the pre-industrial era. To remain viable, religious institutions had to 'familize' their ceremonies. In a similar fashion, American public holidays such as the Fourth of July and Thanksgiving became family reunions. Today the economy has come to depend on the surge of consumption that is tied to Christmas. Tourism, now the world's largest single industry, is equally attuned to family time. Resorts such as Club Med and destinations such as Las Vegas, once known for their adult activities, are increasingly child-centred (Gillis 1996).

But it was not just the amount of family time that expanded. While it is true that lower mortality and fertility rates, together with the amelioration of poverty in developed countries, allowed parents and children a longer period of co-residency, modern family time is radically different in quality as well as quantity. Since the mid-nineteenth century, family time has come to be a repetitive series of occasions that, individually and collectively, create an experience of cyclical time unavailable in the linear temporal structures of work, school and everyday existence. Family time is defined as 'quality time', meant to represent that which is enduring in a world otherwise dominated by rapid change, in which nothing lasts for more than a moment. Family times, scheduled for certain fixed moments in the day, week and the year, present themselves as 'tradition', even when their elements are brand new and constantly changing. The function of these kinds of rituals is best described by Barbara Myerhoff:

> Ritual inevitably carries a basic message of order, continuity and predictability ... by stating enduring and underlying patterns, ritual connects past, present, and future, abrogating history and time. Ritual always links participants to one another and often beyond, to wider collectivities that may be absent, even to ancestors and those yet unborn.
>
> (Myerhoff 1984: 306)

Family time brings both past and future into the present. At such moments, we have the illusion of reliving the past, of bringing to life that which seems irretrievably lost in the time–space compression of the modern world. In a secular age which has banished older notions of eternity, immortality has become linked to posterity, 'the hope of living in the memory of future generations' (Becker 1932: 130). If we cannot be sure of the future, of an afterlife, then we still have our prior-life, immortalized in the memories of our significant others. Over the course of the nineteenth century, family occasions became increasingly devoted to creating lasting memories. The invention of photography provided a technological boost to this process. Captured on film or video, family times are now recorded for posterity.

> Photography becomes a rite of family life when, in the industrializing countries of Europe and America, the very institution of the family starts undergoing radical surgery ... photography comes along to memorialize,

to restate symbolically, the imperilled continuity and vanishing extended-ness of family life. Those ghostly traces, photographs, supply the token presence of the displaced relatives. A family's photograph album is gener-ally about extended family – and, often, is all that remains of it.

(Sontag 1973: 9)

The great majority of family photos are of children, of very young children, and now increasingly of the unborn child. 'We fend off death's terrors, snap-shot by snapshot', writes Anne Higonnet, 'pretending to save the moment, halt time, preserve childhood intact' (Higonnet 1998: 95). Children have become our favoured memorial object, our token of eternity, proof that something pre-exists this ephemeral lifetime. If we are no longer certain about the future, about the afterlife, we seek to reassure through representations of what might be called pre-life. Victorians such as James Anthony Froude taught us to think that, 'the wildest pleasures of after-life are nothing so sweet as the old game, the old dance, old Christmas' (Gillis 1996: 104). George Eliot added that, 'we would never have loved this earth so well if we had had no childhood in it' (Goodenough 2000: 191). We imagine the past to be a stable point of origins, a solid ground from which to contemplate the unsteady present and uncertain future. We use family times as a point of access to the supposed certainty of childhood. For us it is the guarantee that all has not melted into air.

'What the child *is* matters less than what we *think* it is' notes James Kincaid (Kincaid 1992: 62). The Victorians taught us not only what to think *about* the child but how to think *with* the concept of childhood. Childhood has become our source of selfhood, the thing we use to explain ourselves to ourselves and to others. As Marina Warner has observed, childhood provides us with our myth of origins but, 'origins are compounded of good and evil together bat-tling' (Warner 1995: 57, 60). We prefer notions of childhood innocence, but this 'image also has a dark side: a threat of loss, of change, and ultimately of death. Romantic images of childhood gain power not only from their charm, but also from their menace' (Higonnet 1998: 29). We find it easier to imagine children either as little angels or as little monsters than as just children (Warner 1995: 57, 60).

The Victorians supplied Western culture with a host of beloved child figures – innocent, adorable, timeless – but they also gave us a gallery of eroticized, seductive, even satanic children (Kincaid 1992: 12). It was during the nine-teenth century that, 'from being the smallest and least considered of human beings, the child had become endowed with qualities that made it Godlike, fit to be worshipped and the embodiment of hope' (Cunningham 1995: 78). But it was also then that the child became a symbol of what we find most disturb-ing – forbidden sexuality, primitivism, even savagery (Kincaid 1992, Cunningham 1991).

This preoccupation with good and evil was a legacy of the evangelical Protestantism that constituted the culture of Victorian middle classes in the early nineteenth century. The hallmark of this piety had been the obsessive search for signs of God's grace in every aspect of daily life. A crisis of faith at the middle of the century turned the Evangelicals away from institutional religion and introspective soul-searching, but left their obsession with good and evil intact. The 'Garden of Eden' and 'The Fall' remained for the middle classes a central myth, but one that was now told in personal rather than supernatural terms. Introspection was redirected into retrospection (Gillis forthcoming). The garden ceased to be a place and became a stage of life. Paradise lost became childhood lost. 'God has given us each our own Paradise, our own old childhood, over which old glories linger – to which our hearts cling, as all we have ever known of Heaven upon earth' proclaimed Froude (Gillis 1996: 5).

It was at this historic moment that middle-class family life began to turn in on itself. The capitalist industrial revolution was removing work from the household and, with it, unrelated persons. Domestic servants were to remain a part of bourgeois households well into the twentieth century, but strangers were no longer regarded as part of the family, now redefined as a biological unit. No longer the same as a household, family was now something that developed through time. As a temporal convoy of related persons, family ceased to be rooted in place and became subject to the vicissitudes of time, constructing the very sense of irreversible development through time that would induce such a powerful sense of loss at each stage of the ageing process.

It was during the Victorian era that children came to define family. The birth of a child, an event that had previously been surrounded by anxiety and taboo, became a kind of secular sacrament. It was no longer necessary to baptize the child and 'church' the mother to cleanse them of the polluting effects of parturition. Quite the contrary; among the middle classes the new mother was now a redeeming presence and for the first time men (at first only middle-class men) fought for entry into the birthing room. While it would take another century before fathers' presence at birth became almost universal, fatherhood took on a whole new meaning in the Victorian period (Gillis 1996). As a consequence, the new family rite of christening replaced the older communal ceremonies of baptism.

Birth and death had changed places. It was now the newborn rather than the dying person who provided the window on eternity. Infants were, wrote Wordsworth, 'fresh from the land of God, living blessings which have drifted down to us from the imperial palace of the love of God' (Cunningham 1995: 74). Having become the sign of family, the child became the focus of its ritual life. Children's birthdays were among the first of the newly invented Victorian family times (Gillis 1996: 165–71). The stages of childhood and adolescence set the pace of family life and parents began to gauge their own ageing by their children. The arrival and departure of children, which went largely unmarked in the pre-industrial era, now came to be seen as definitive moments in the adult life course. As adult identities became increasingly dependent on the relationship with their children, the death of a child became the greatest imaginable blow to a marriage or family. But just growing up also became a series of little losses that that led inevitably to the 'empty nest'. As mortality rates fell in the course of the late nineteenth and early twentieth centuries, parents and children shared longer lifetimes, but because fertility rates were also falling families were smaller and adult co-residency with children took up a diminishing part of the lengthening life course. The time adults lived *with* children contracted, even as the imperative to live *through* them expanded. The result, observes Elizabeth Goodenough, has been the emergence of a childhood that is 'both a chronological stage and a mental construct, an existential fact and a locus of desire, a mythological country continuously mapped by grown-ups in search of their subjectivity in another time and place' (Goodenough 2000: 180).

The life course was now seen as linear development through time, a series of discontinuous stages of life – childhood, youth, adulthood, old age – each producing its own sense of loss. The masculine life course, which was more sharply segmented and discontinuous than its female counterpart, was particularly subject to this sense of loss. In the Victorian era little boys were dressed and treated like little girls in their infant years, but were then 'breeched', put into trousers, a rite of passage that not only marked their separation from the world of women but also symbolized the end of innocence. A girl's development was more continuous, leading toward the fulfilment of her femininity in marriage, but for boys maturity constituted loss, resulting in a longing for feminized innocence that found expression in Victorian literature and child photography. The image of the adorable little girl was juxtaposed with that of the repulsive bad boy, setting up the split image of childhood that persists in popular culture today (Robson 2001).

Adult males were the first to map the mythological country of childhood, first through poetry and prose about children and then through the newly discovered technology of photography. By the end of the nineteenth century the Western world had acquired a stock of children figures, naughty as well as nice, that it has been recycling ever since. But now that women have entered the world of higher education and work, they too experience a similar sense of dislocation. Nostalgia for childhood and the work that it does in recovering the adult sense of lost selfhood no longer knows class or gender boundaries. In consumer society the symbol of 'the family' has become 'an image that can arouse culturally constructed nostalgia and longings' and is used to sell goods and services (Lowe 1995: 103). Childhood functions in a similar way, becoming ever more central to advertising and marketing (Cross 1997).

Already at the end of the nineteenth century childhood had become the object of intense nostalgia, attracting to itself all those longings which had previously attached themselves to a certain place rather than a certain time (Degler 1980: 68–71, Pollock 1983: 108–10, Kincaid 1992: 228). By then the world had been scoured for the existence of a Garden of Eden populated by innocent people representing a better, purer form of humanity. The age of the New Imperialism also put to rest ancient notions of a Golden Age, forcing the Victorians, particularly Victorian males, to find a more accessible, domesticated past through which to recover their lost selves. Childhood provided a kind of blank screen onto which they could project their longings. They were able to find in their own memories not only the mythical country they were seeking but a repository of the earliest stages of mankind itself. With late nineteenth-century evolutionary theory came the notion that each individual life recapitulated the history of the human species. Thus the child was the closest thing to early man and childhood our access to the mystery of human origins (Cunningham 1991: 98–100).

By 1900 childhood had replaced old age as the most telling part of the life course. Autobiographies focused increasingly on early childhood experiences, while a new set of commemorative practices developed to allow adults access to mythic childhood itself. Contemporaries such as Clement Miles wrote of Christmas:

> At no time in the world's history has so much been made of children as today, and because Christmas is their feast its lustre continues unabated in an age when dogmatic Christianity has largely lost its hold … Christmas is the feast of beginnings, of instinctive, happy childhood.
>
> (Gillis 1996: 102–3)

Over the course of the late nineteenth and early twentieth centuries family space also took on ever greater significance. What had once been a place of work, a part of the world, became the dream house, a space so precious and protected that it became 'both phantasmic and unattainable' (Garber 2000: 207). At first only some parts of the house, such as the parlour, were sanctified, but in time the ideal of home as a place of undisturbed peace and harmony colonized the entire house, ultimately making it unliveable. At this point, the dream of perfection moved elsewhere, to the summer house, which could be more easily imagined as a place apart (Garber 2000).

Family time also became so idealized as to be unattainable. The ideal of the perfect family occasion reached a point where it too became problematic. Expectations have now been set so high that even the smallest failing is viewed as catastrophic. Anxieties built up in anticipation of major holidays have become so overwhelming that psychologists have invented a term 'holiday trauma' to describe the emotions. There is now a whole literature on how to cope with holidays and there are drugs designed to ward off associated anxiety attacks and depression ('Social anxiety and the holidays' 2001: 37). Some experts advocate truncating the rituals and lowering expectations, but it is not altogether clear whether their advice is being followed. Many families have tried to reduce stress by 'outsourcing' their family times, having them professionally catered or moving them to commercial venues which specialize in such occasions. Children's birthdays have migrated to McDonald's, to theme parks and game centres, but in the quest for perfect child–centred family time the goal remains elusive, generating ever more elaborate fantasies and greater tensions between adults and children.

Family time makes its own demands on our finite temporal resources, contributing to the very sense of 'time famine' that it is supposed to assuage.

Ironically, even as family times proliferate, the nostalgia for an era of more and better family times increases (Gillis 2001). In the same way that homelessness haunts the increasingly home-owning societies of Europe and America, so time famine increases even as people devote more time to family occasions. As long as family time, like family home, functions as a symbol, as an ideal, it remains elusive, always just beyond our grasp.

Turning children into symbols of what is lost in the process of becoming adults is also bound to fail us. The quest for the original state of being, that solid ground on which to anchor an adult identity tossed on the stormy seas of modern life obsessed with getting ahead, with perpetual becoming, depended on keeping childhood itself safe from change, on keeping the child in a state of perpetual otherness. By creating separate times and places for children, Victorians had managed to build a kind of wall between themselves and the secret garden of childhood but, in the twentieth century, the garden has contracted until it contains only infants and very young children. Today, it seems that even this boundary no longer defines the mythical land of childhood and in this age of the 'hurried child' even infants are not exempt from the imperative to prepare for the next stage of life. Parents are encouraged to buy the Baby Einstein Library of stimulating videos for their six-month-olds to supplement the Baby Mozart tapes and Baby Webster flash-cards. Their guilt is heightened by ads that tell them that 'Smart parents want to give their children the best possible start in learning' (Gopnik 2000: 6).

In the era of Gap Kids the quest for innocence has turned from early life to pre-life. The condition of otherness, of pure being, is no longer associated with infants but is now projected onto the foetus, the so-called 'unborn child'. Exempt from the imperfections that entry into the world inevitably brings, the foetal image has come to function symbolically as reassurance of immortality (Holland 1992: 27). To some the womb has become the new garden of innocence, the residence of our newest little angels and, as such, requiring legal protection, even against the mothers themselves (Rothman 1999; Ludin and Akesson 1996: 44–6). Yet the foetus is not exempt from the processes which have turned childhood from a state of being into one of becoming. Notions of early childhood education have recently colonized prenatal care. There are many who recommend that physical and mental fitness begin in the womb (Gopnik 2000), and while this appeals to parents and others concerned with raising healthier, smarter adults, it threatens the very notion of origins, the base of our human beingness. In turning children from something pure into pure potential, this tendency threatens to obliterate not only childhood, but the adulthood which is so dependent on a certain version of it.

The blurring of the boundaries between age groups is evident in all Western societies and helps account for the changes in family time that we are now witnessing. While the cycle of daily, weekly and annual holidays remains largely intact, some previously child-centred festivities, most notably Halloween, have been appropriated by adults for their own purposes. In college towns and in some cities with large homosexual populations, Halloween has become a major holiday. Birthday celebrations, once confined to young children, are also popular among young adults and Christmas has migrated from the home to the office and the dorm. While it may be too early to call these a historical shift, these moments of childishness suggest that adults are trying to find in themselves the mythical country that they previously projected onto children. Even as fewer adults live with children, interest in what is called the 'inner child' has grown quietly but rapidly. Today this is sustained by a multitude of therapeutic theories and organizations that hold in common the idea that the recovery of one's childhood is the key to overcoming life's problems (Ivy 1995: 79–104). No longer dependent on children or family time to connect with childhood, these movements have created their own elaborate rituals that allow their members to connect to their own childhoods, becoming their earlier selves – children reincarnate.

Interest in reincarnation has spread in the West, but it takes its own form, at odds in so many ways with eastern forms of reincarnation. In Tibetan Buddhism deceased adults are believed to be reborn in very young children. In a culture where time is considered continuous and life and death inseparable, ageing is seen as gain and death is a new beginning (Gupta 2001). In the Western view, time is discontinuous, ageing means loss and death marks an ending. Where each new life is original and there is no afterlife in this world, the only hope of immortality is memory. Committed to the notion of development through time, we can only see a series of little endings, each prefiguring death and reminding us of it. We believe we can stave off death only by remaining young or by incarnating childhood (Lowenthal 1985: 8, 24).

In the underdeveloped world children are still everywhere, but in Western societies it is possible for an adult to go through a day without encountering them. Children live islanded lives, stranded far from the main lands of adult activity. They are on different schedules and travel in different circuits. The emergence of 'adult communities' precludes everyday contact, as does the fact that so many adults live alone. Families are smaller and single parenthood common, age of marriage has been rising and childrearing postponed, and lifetime childlessness has risen to unprecedented levels.

Yet contemporary society remains obsessed with childhood, even as it neglects and abuses real children. Images of 'lost' children appear in posters and on milk cartons, and there is now a large literature on the disappearance of childhood suggesting a more generalized sense of loss (Postman 1992, Sommerville 1982, Winn 1984, Kotlowitz 1991). Children have become more symbolically precious, even as they have lost real economic value (Zelizer 1985). But maintaining children as icons has been costly, particularly to children themselves. They live more scripted, cloistered lives and when they do not conform to adult idealizations, they are perceived as fallen angels, or worse, as little monsters. We are prone to treating as delinquent an ever wider range of behaviours and in the United States children are being incarcerated at every younger ages. We treat children with unprecedented solicitude and indulgence, yet at the same time impose on them a kind of generational apartheid. As John Demos has argued, where child and adult identities are so interdependent, childish misbehaviour is especially threatening to parents, producing anger and even violence directed against otherwise beloved children (Demos 1985).

Our unprecedented attempt to live through our children makes it all the more difficult to live with them. The problem is compounded when so many adults have no immediate experience of children and project onto them an otherness that prevents the adults from seeing how much like themselves children really are. Perhaps earlier periods were not so misguided in thinking of children as miniature adults, for it is by no means clear (if we disregard higher poverty and mortality rates in the past) that children are so much better off today. We could do worse than to divest childhood of some of the symbolic burden of purity and innocence it has borne for more than a century and a half. We need to stop living through children and begin living with them on a more equitable, reciprocal basis (Jackson 1970). But we will not be able to do that before we examine the source of the adult longings that sustain the mythical country of childhood. As Marina Warner has warned us: 'without paying attention to adults and their circumstances, children cannot begin to meet the hopes and expectations of our torn dreams about what a child and childhood should be' (Warner 1995: 62, see also Holland 1992).

References

Aries, P. (1965) *Centuries of Childhood*, New York: Viking.

Becker, C. (1932) *The Heavenly City of the Eighteenth Century Philosophers*, New Haven: Yale University Press.

Berman, M. (1988) *All That Is Solid Melts Into Air: The Experience of Modernity*, Harmondsworth: Penguin.

Cross, G. (1997) *Kids' Stuff: Toys and the Changing World of American Childhood*, Cambridge, Mass.: Harvard University Press.

Csikszentmihalyi, M. (1997) *Finding Flow: The Psychology of Engagement with Everyday Life*, New York: Basic Books.

Cunningham, H. (1991) *The Children of the Poor: Representations of Childhood Since the Seventeenth Century*, Oxford: Blackwell.

Cunningham, H. (1995) *Children and Childhood in Western Society since 1500*, London: Longman.

Degler, C. (1980) *At Odds: Women and the Family in America from the Revolution to the Present*, New York: Oxford University Press.

Demos, J. (1985) *Past, Present, and Personal: The Family and the Life Course in America*, New York: Oxford University Press.

Fass, P. (1999) *Kidnapped: Child Abduction in America*, New York: Oxford University Press.

Finkbeiner, A.K. (1996) *After the Death of a Child: Living with Loss through the Years*, New York: Free Press.

Garber, M. (2000) *Sex and Real Estate: Why We Love Houses*, New York: Pantheon.

Gillis, J. (1985) *For Better, For Worse: British Marriages 1600 to the Present*, New York: Oxford University Press.

Gillis, J. (1996) *A World of Their Own Making: Myth, Ritual, and the Quest for Family Values*, New York: Basic Books.

Gillis, J. (1997) 'La famiglie vicerdamo: La practca della memoria nella cultura contemporanea', in L. Paggi (ed.) *La Memoria del Nazimo nell-Europa di oggi*, Firenze: Scandicci.

Gillis, J. (2001) 'Never enough time: some paradoxes of modern family time(s)', in K. Daly (ed.) *Minding the Time in Family Experience: Emerging Perspectives and Issues*, Amsterdam: Elsevier.

Gillis, J. (forthcoming) 'The birth of the virtual child: a Victorian progeny', in M. Zuckerman and W. Koops (eds) *Beyond the Century of the Child*, Philadephia: University of Pennsylvania Press.

Goodenough, E. (2000) 'Introduction', *Michigan Quarterly Review*, xxxix, nr. 2 (Spring).

Gopnik, A. (2000) 'Children need childhood, not vocational training', *The New York Times*, 28 October.

Gupta, A. (2001) 'Reincarnation and childhood', lecture given at Vegasymposium, Stockholm, Sweden, 17 April.

Harvey, D. (1989) *The Condition of Postmodernity*, Oxford: Basil Blackwell.

Higonnet, A. (1998) *Pictures of Innocence: The History and Crisis of Ideal Childhood*, London: Thames and Hudson.

Holland, P. (1992) *What is a Child?: Popular Images of Childhood*, London: Virago.

Ivy, M. (1995) 'Have you seen me? Recovering the Inner Child in late twentieth century America', in S. Stephen (ed.) *Children and the Politics of Culture*, Princeton: Princeton University Press.

Jackson, J.B. (1970) 'Life worship', in E.H. Zube (ed.) *Landscapes: Selected Writings of J.B. Jackson*, Amherst: University of Massachusetts Press.

James, A., Jenks, C. and Prout, A. (1998) *Theorizing Childhood*, Oxford: Polity Press.

Kincaid, J. (1992) *Child-Loving: The Erotic Child and Victorian Culture*, New York: Routledge.

Kotlowitz, A. (1991) *There Are No Children Here*, New York: Doubleday.

Lowe, D. (1982) *History of Bourgeois Perception*, Chicago: University of Chicago Press.

Lowe, D. (1995) *The Body in Late-Capitalist USA*, Durham: Duke University Press.

Lowenthal, D. (1985) *The Past is a Foreign Country*, Cambridge: Cambridge University Press.

Ludin, S. and Akesson, L. (1996) 'Creating life and explaining death', *Ethnologia Europea*, 26 (1996).

May, E. (1995) *Barren in the Promised Land*, New York: Basic Books.

Myerhoff, B. (1984) 'Rites and signs of ripening: the intertwining of ritual, time, and growing older', in D. Kertzer and J. Keith (eds) *Age and Anthropological Theory*, Ithaca: Cornell University Press.

Pollock, L. (1983) *Forgotten Children: Parent–Child Relations from 1500 to 1900*, Cambridge: Cambridge University Press.

Postman, N. (1992) *The Disappearance of Childhood* (2nd edn), New York: Vintage.

Putnam, R. (2000) *Bowling Alone: The Collapse and Revival of American Community*, New York: Simon and Schuster.

Robson, C. (2001) *Men in Wonderland: The Lost Girlhood of Victorian Gentlemen*, Princeton: Princeton University Press.

Rothman, B.K. (1999) *Recreating Motherhood: Ideology and Technology in Patriarchal Society*, New York: W.W. Norton.

Sirota, R. (2001) 'The birthday: a modern childhood socialization ritual', in M. du Bois-Remond, H. Suender and H.-H. Kreuger (eds) *Childhood in Europe: Approaches–Trends–Findings*, New York: Peter Lang.

'Social anxiety and the holidays' (2001) *New York Times Magazine*, 28 October.

Sommerville, J. (1982) *The Rise and Fall of Childhood*, Beverly Hills: Sage.

Sontag, S. (1973) *On Photography*, New York: Delta.

Steedman, C. (1995) *Strange Dislocations: Childhood and the Idea of Human Interiority*, London: Virago.

Warner, M. (1995) *Six Myths of Our Times: Little Angels, Little Monsters, Beautiful Beasts and More*, New York: Vintage.

Winn, M. (1984) *Children Without Childhood*, Harmondsworth: Penguin.

Zeiher, H. and Zeiher, H. (1994) *Orte und Zeiten der Kinder: Sozial Leben in Alltag von Grossstadtkindern*, Weinheim and Muenchen: Juventa.

Zelizer, V. (1985) *Pricing the Priceless Child: The Changing Social Value of Children*, New York: Basic Books.

Afterword

Changing childhoods: a case study

An-Magritt Jensen and Lorna McKee

In 1959 Wright Mills wrote *The Sociological Imagination* making a plea for understanding individual life within the historical period. The sociological imagination, 'enables us to grasp history and biography and the relations between the two within society' (Wright Mills 1959: 6). Human life is coloured by historical changes, which may be difficult to grasp when focusing on children's lives in a particular period. We have chosen 'transformation' and 'negotiation' as key concepts to describe children's family change. Change is taking place in the lives of the individual children, as well as over time. One family type is prevalent at one time in history, another when looking at another time. At the end of this book we want to illustrate the links between history and biography through a case story, illustrating how children's lives are influenced by family changes in history and in children's life course (biography).

How does the family life of children two generations ago compare with modern childhood? The family histories of Marton and his grandson Thomas (both Norwegians) provide a powerful window on social change. Marton was born at the beginning of the twentieth century. His childhood was full of siblings, since he was one out of ten children. He had only a faint memory of one surviving grandparent, distantly resting in a rocking chair, taking little interest in the children. All grandparents died while Marton was still a little child. By contrast, Thomas, born in the mid 1970s, has strikingly different family circumstances as an only child and an only grandchild of his grandparents. Thomas was born to unmarried, cohabiting parents. His parents subsequently married. However, when he was eight they divorced and Thomas remained co-resident with his mother. He kept his contact with his father, but no longer on a daily basis. After a while both of Thomas's parents had new partners and homes. In demographic terms, his childhood regarding both family composition and parental configuration was markedly different from that of his grandfather. Such contrasts were also true in terms of employment and care arrangements.

Exploring changing conditions of employment first, Marton's parents ran a small hotel. Children participated in the business and their tasks included keeping the building heated (by gathering fuel), serving guests, working in the kitchen and so on. There were high levels of economic interdependence between the generations. Adults and children alike were expected to secure the income of the family. Work and family life were conducted within the same physical space and boundaries between them and between adult and child spaces were poorly defined.

Two generations later, Thomas's childhood reveals many contrasts in terms of boundaries and expectations. From his infancy, both Thomas's parents were in full-time employment outside the home. Thomas spent his daily life in different formal daycare arrangements separated from both of his parents during daytime. There were no expectations – indeed few or no possibilities – for Thomas to contribute to the economic provisioning of the family. The family had been 'liberated' from the economic, as well as the practical interdependence between the generations. Thomas had become instead socially designated as a 'cost' to his parents' budget: no longer regarded as an economic but rather an emotional resource.

Thus Thomas's childhood bears the imprint of great transformations in family employment patterns. Turning now to family composition, one remarkable change across the generations is the declining number of siblings. Marton was in a family where children were in the majority (ten children and two significant adults). Thomas's childhood by contrast was peopled largely by adults only (one child to eight significant adults). Interestingly, both Marton and Thomas have experienced family disruption, Marton through his mother's death and his father's remarriage, and Thomas through divorce and his parents' remarriages. For both, step-parenting has been a part of their childhood, but the stable parent shifted from the father in Marton's case, to the mother in Thomas's case. Similarly, while Marton shared his household with a stepmother, Thomas has a stepfather. As we have seen profound changes have taken place in the work and family interface and in the daily proximity and shared use of adults' and children's spaces. Workplaces have been distanced from homes and children occupy many diverse places outside the home – for example, in Thomas's case, school, formal childcare and the home of his non-resident parent. Grandparents have also assumed a greater place in his life through longevity. Children's and parental time schedules have also diversified and have become demarcated and fragmented in response to structural change.

Only 60 years divide the childhoods of Marton and Thomas yet much has also shifted in relational and ideological terms concerning children's position in the family. It is argued that modern western society has created more egalitarian relationships between parents and children. Yet it is instructive to ask: 'Does Thomas have more negotiating power vis-a-vis his parents than Marton had?' While this is complex and difficult to answer there are some senses in which we can say, yes, Thomas may have a greater 'voice' than Marton had. For example, we understand that Marton's childhood had the imprints of distant emotional ties between the generations. His father – being the stable parent throughout Marton's childhood – was remembered as an authoritarian, emotionally remote, traditional, hardworking man, struggling to feed his family and demanding discipline among his children. By contrast, Thomas's childhood is characterized as one demonstrating close emotional ties between adult and child. He grew up with a close-knit group of adult relatives, all of them adoring the only child in the family, not knowing how to do the best for him. Thomas was and is listened to. By and large he continues to have most of his demands satisfied. The emotional ties are close and the emotional investment is deep. Thomas's father is perceived as a modern father who has spent considerable time with his son during his childhood, even though – from the age of eight - they have lived in separate households. The modern parent–child contract involves putting children first.

Yet there are constraints. This case study reveals that in terms of the 'big' issues of Thomas's life, his power may be muted. It is not Thomas who is setting the rules. On issues such as the marital status of his parents when he was born, their decision to have only one child, parental employment, marital separation and moving apart and re-partnering, Thomas has had little influence. At an emotional level his parents, and maybe Thomas himself, are convinced that Thomas is the centre of their life and they feel he is given choices unavailable to themselves as younger children. They feel that their decisions have centred on what is best for Thomas. They do whatever they can to satisfy his needs, but always within the context of their family composition and employment patterns. However, our ideologies of personal choices and the primacy of children may conceal how families carry out their lives within designated social structures, which predetermine or impose some choices rather than others. It is questionable whether Marton's or Thomas's childhood was more circumscribed by parental circumstances or who has more agency. It could be that, because we feel that children are listened to within the space available, we have problems in seeing a persistent power structure of adults over children, as argued by Hood–Williams (1990).

These two linked biographies reinforce the need to appreciate both context and agency in making sense of childhood. While modern childhood has undoubtedly been transformed and there have been gains, there may also have been losses. The case story compels us to recognize that, 'no child can evade the impact of economic and spatial forces, nor ideologies about children and the family' (Qvortrup 2000: 79). Embedded in the concept of historical transformation are aspects which, in each particular time, are taken for granted and yet have great impact on childhood.

Within a market society themes of self-actualization, individualism and the ideology of personal choice may be masking persistent inequalities between children and adults, and children and parents. Marton's childhood had the imprints of destiny, death and a common struggle for survival. Thomas's parents 'chose' their family composition and employment patterns yet Thomas in many profound areas of his upbringing has had no more control over his life circumstances than Marton.

References

Hood-Williams, J. (1990) 'Patriarchy for children: on the stability of power relations in children's lives', in L. Chrisholm, P. Büchner, H.-H. Krüger and P. Brown (eds) *Childhood, Youth and Social Change. A Comparative Perspective*: 155–71, London: Falmer Press.

Wright Mills, C. (1959): *The Sociological Imagination*, New York: Oxford University Press.

Qvortrup, J. (2000) 'Macroanalysis of childhood', in P. Christensen and A. James (eds) *Research with Children. Perspectives and Practices*: 77–97, London: Falmer Press.

Notes

1 Children's changing families and family resources

1 Almost as many (35 per cent) were living in two-parent families – probably mostly step-families (we do not actually know how many of the men concerned were the child's natural father who may have joined the mother after registration). Many of the remaining solely registered children seem to have been adopted.
2 Although we cannot be sure that no episodes with two parents intervened.
3 A problem with missing data on birth registration (23 per cent of black children and 30 per cent of Asian children), mainly due to immigration after birth, means we do not know how many of these children are born inside marriage. However, even without classifying the unclassified information, it is obvious that more black children are born outside marriage than both children from Asian or white ethnic groups.
4 The remaining 5 per cent enumerated in privately rented accommodation are likely to be in heterogeneous circumstances upon which we do not focus here. Also we have ignored the 0.3 per cent enumerated in a communal establishment such as a hospital.

2 Children's perspectives on middle-class work–family arrangements

1 The core sample of families was accessed through children aged 8–12 in primary schools within three target communities. This strategy allows informed consent (or 'dissent') to be sought directly from the children, and places children firmly at centre-stage of the research. The parents reported that the children's enthusiasm and excitement about the research, and school-based activities encouraged them to participate in the study. (Brannen and O'Brien 1996).
2 Fieldwork in Kingscraig was conducted between August and December 1999, and separate interviews were conducted with each member (target-aged children and older siblings, mother and father) of 17 families. Eight focus groups were also carried out with 36 children aged between 8 and 12 (who came from a total of 34 families) who attended the town's primary school. One member of the research team worked as a teaching assistant in the school for four weeks, which allowed us direct access to families involved in the oil and gas industry.
3 According to the ONS 1997/98 Family Expenditure Survey, yearly gross average household income was £21,840.
4 Typifying the highly cosmopolitan character of these childrens' lives, one family had moved from Syria to Australia, then to Holland and finally to Scotland. Another family had moved from England to Holland, then to Norway and finally to Scotland.
5 For example, in the other two communities, 74 per cent of mothers were in some form of paid work. In contrast just 35 per cent of mothers in Kingscraig were involved in paid work.
6 The 17 fathers in Kingscraig worked on average 50 hours each week (from data collected from the family questionnaire).

3 Employed or unemployed parents: A child perspective

1 The Work Environment Fund funded 'Work-life and Children'. The Swedish Council for Research in Humanities and Social Sciences funded 'Unemployment and Children'.
2 Childhood is sometimes seen as a 'generation' (Alanen and Mayall 2001; James *et al.* 2001). The concept is unclear except in the case of family generations. I prefer the concept 'life phase' (Hareven 1995).
3 Of 23 groups, in one group in three, children played unemployment.

5 Children's experience of their parents' divorce

1 Some of the findings reported here were previously published in Butler, I., Scanlan. L., Robinson, M., Douglas, G. and Murch, M. (2002) 'Children's involvement in their parents' divorce: implications for practice' *Children and Society*, April.

7 As fair as it can be? Childhood after divorce

1 We draw our data from two studies. The first study we refer to was funded by the Joseph Rowntree Foundation (Wade and Smart 2002), the second study was funded by the ESRC, 'New Childhoods? Children and Co-Parenting after Divorce', L129251049.
2 The tender years doctrine assumed that children under seven years of age were best placed with their mothers, who could provide the kind of nurture that young children need.
3 Ten children 'solved' the dilemma posed in the vignette by suggesting that the parents should not, after all, split up, and eight thought it might be best if Lee lived with someone neutral like a foster parent or grandparent.
4 All of the children we interviewed were between five and 16 except for one 19-year-old who was interviewed with her younger brother, one young woman who had just turned 17, and a four-year-old boy.
5 For example, Families Need Fathers, the Association for Shared Parenting, the Equal Parenting Council, who campaign for fathers' entitlement to a 'share' in their children after separation or divorce.
6 The recent textbook *The Sociology of the Family* edited by Graham Allan (1999) is an example of how mainstream family sociology has still not recognised the place of children in the family – except in as much as they appear as appendages of parents.
7 See Jagger and Wright 1999, Stacey 1996 and Gillis 1996 for critiques of this depiction of contemporary family life.

8 Children's stories of parental breakup

1 Thirty fathers, chosen from the social authorities' list of fathers paying alimony, were interviewed twice with one year's interval, their children only on the second occasion. Almost half of the children could not be interviewed, but some of the fathers had two or more children. Twenty-four children were interviewed in all. The study was made when legislation for shared custody was carried through. In most of the cases the mother had custody, although many of the fathers lived with their children for more than two days a fortnight. The sampling loss was high, and our sample probably features the most engaged fathers. Few children under six years were interviewed, and the majority of these were regularly in the presence of their fathers. Some interviews with children between six and eight gave good material. By far the richest narratives came from a number of 10–15-year-olds and young adults (18–21), who were interviewed alone. All this gives us methodological problems, but while we have no ambition to generalize statistically, the types of problems and attitudes found can be generalized. The project was conducted by

the author and Thomas Johansson. It is reported in the book *Den andre föräldern* (*The Second Parent*) (1999). This article takes up aspects not focused upon earlier.

2 These have a generalist approach. More specific information is found in Wallerstein and Kelly (1980), McLanahan and Sandefur (1994), Elkind (1994) and Fürstenberg and Cherlin (1991), the latter of which deals mostly with socio-economic problems of divorce in the USA.

3 All interviews were narrative. Children, for example, were asked to tell us about patterns of living with fathers, what they do and want to do with fathers, real and ideal differences between mothers and fathers, what they think of living in two places, and bad and good aspects of the divorce.

4 Briefly, the argument is that the child feels aggression when the feeding breast is taken away. This feeling of aggression against the loving mother is repressed and transformed into a sense of guilt in an abstract way, but can be activated in concrete situations, e.g. divorce.

5 The Freudian 'omnipotent' child is, in a way, the emotional side of the Piagetian 'egocentric' child. The omnipotency has negative and positive dimensions. The negative one is relevant here: 'If anything in this family is wrong, it is likely to be my fault, because I am the supreme actor of the family.'

6 The implication is not, of course, that parents should divorce in order to improve their children's Self and intelligence development. Rather, when such processes take place, the child's capacity to cope with them can be much improved by not mystifying reality through silence, and by giving the young Self the democratic right to participate in the argument. Deliberate role-taking and conditions for empathy improve through this.

9 For the children's sake: symbolic power lost?

1 The surveys from countries included in this study were performed during 1988–95.

2 Sweden had a slight climb to a maximum of 16 per cent in 1926–30.

3 The degree to which extra-marital births are absorbed into consensual unions differs between European countries. In England/Wales there has also been an increase in the proportion of children born to lone mothers.

4 The Norwegian Crown Prince Haakon Magnus, who cohabited with lone mother Mette Marit before the royal wedding in 2001, illustrates the level of acceptance.

5 In 1996 in Norway 43 per cent of children were born outside of marriage, according to public statistics. In the CFS, we found that 34 per cent were born in a consensual union and 4 per cent were born to a lone mother, amounting to 38 per cent born outside marriage. The difference may indicate that the CFS has a slight undercount of births outside marriage (to five percentage points), or that public statistics overestimate the proportion. This may be true due to, for example, delay in the public registration of changing address. Since 1992 the rate of extramarital births has continued to increase.

6 Until recently an unmarried mother had sole legal parental rights to a child, while a cohabiting father might notify the authorities of joint rights if the mother agreed. Few fathers, however, used this opportunity. The process of achieving joint legal rights to children born in consensual unions was simplified in 1998 and may in the future change the strong position of mothers when such unions break up.

Index